# OPEN SPACES

## JIM DALE
## VICKERY

### NorthWord
PRESS, INC

BOX 1360, MINOCQUA, WI 54548

Library of Congress Cataloging-in-Publication Data

Vickery, Jim dale.
   Open spaces / Jim dale Vickery
      p.  cm.
   ISBN 1-55971-109-4: $19.95 -- ISBN 1-55971-096-9 (pbk.): $11.95
   1. North America--Description and travel--1981- 2. Wilderness
areas--North America. 3. Natural history--North America. 4. Vickery,
Jim dale--Journeys--North America. 5. Park rangers--United States.
I. Title.
E41.V53  1991
917--dc20                                              91-17763
                                                          CIP

Published by NorthWord Press, Inc.
Box 1360
Minocqua, WI 54548

Designed and illustrated by Mary A. Shafer
Typography by Copysetters, Milwaukee, Wisconsin
ISBN 1-55971-109-4 Hardcover
ISBN 1-55971-096-9 Softcover

For a free catalog describing NorthWord's line of nature books and gifts,
call 1-800-336-5666.

Printed in USA

# Dedication

*For my mother, Ella Mae Huot-Vickery (1928-1990), who knew the soft breezes and strong winds of Minnesota's Red River Valley*

OPEN SPACES

> *Hold your hands out over the earth as over a flame...Touch the earth, love the earth, honour the earth, her plains, her valleys, her hills, and her seas; rest your spirit in her solitary places. For the gifts of life are the earth's and they are given to all...*

*Henry Beston*
*The Outermost House*

# ACKNOWLEDGMENTS

Appreciation is given to the following publications (and editors) in which parts of these essays, in various forms and lengths, first appeared:

*Audubon* (Gary Soucie), *Backpacker* (Dave Getchell) *Backpacking Journal* (Lee Schreiber), *Canadian Geographic* (Ross Smith), *Canoe* (John Viehman and Virginia Hostetter followed by Judy and Dave Harrison & staff), *Cross Country Skier* (again Virginia Hostetter), *The Ely Echo* (Anne Wognum and Bob Cary), *Minnesota Out-of-Doors* (Dennis Johnson and Don Dinndorf), *Minnesota Times* (John Gaterud), *The New York Times* (several op-ed editors), *The Northern Review* (Richard Behm), and *Outsport* (David Thompson).

Tom Klein of NorthWord Press inspired new material, cracked the whip, and brought *Open Spaces* to fruition.

Bill Sutherland generously provided historical information about the Kaministikwia River-Dog River voyageur route.

Closer to home, Virginia See and Kathy Erickson of the Lazear Agency lent support at a needy hour. Judith Hadel read several of the essays and provided helpful comments. Angela Campbell shared office space while Dirk Hanson, a veteran of literary terrain, was at the right place at the right time with friendship: knowing the work, knowing the grind against deadline. Other people deserve thanks—Chris Trost, Ray Niedzielski, Dan Metz, Bob Madison, et al—but they live in these pages: outdoors, on the water, in the mountains, often under difficult conditions, and their contributions, enriching the way, are both implied and explicit.

# CONTENTS

# OPEN SPACES

My hand runs down the shaft of a canoe paddle in my cabin at Hocoka as my trails of power come to mind. It is late winter, after a long freeze-up, and my hopes are strong to visit once again North America's outback: its natural and wild areas, its national parks, lakeshores, wildlife refuges and other open spaces.

Near my paddle are maps. There are maps of the Quetico-Superior canoe country in northeastern Minnesota and adjacent Ontario where I've lived 11 years. There are maps of Ontario's Wabakimi-Kopka country, the Albany River and waterways further north. There are maps of New England's Thoreau country, the Pacific Northwest, and Alaska. Some are new. Others are worn and taped together. All are visual guides and food for dreams.

There is also, of course, one's internal mapless country — what John Muir biographer Michael Cohen calls the *pathless way*. Toward this I navigate. It cannot be helped. It is the way of mind and spirit leading to the most intriguing, most powerful landscape of all.

Still, I remain in love with real landscapes, open spaces and the flow of wild rivers. I've hungered for and found the fluidity of life among wild shores in regions little-known and relatively untrammeled.

Perhaps my fascination with landscapes and their effect on personal vision began when I was a boy. It was a subtle feeling coming with the turf and rivers of northwestern Minnesota. There at 48 degrees latitude, 300 miles west of where I now sit, was the Red River Valley, the bottom of ancient glacial Lake Agassiz, larger in its prime than today's five Great Lakes combined. Boyhood pals and I roamed the Valley's level plains. Although we knew dirt fields, we always ended up along rivers. There we found ourselves shuffling through cottonwood leaves along clay riverbanks, listening to brown water gurgle through weed-draped sweepers, and watching thrown sticks — *splash* — and float downstream.

# OPEN SPACES

They floated downstream to the Red River of the North, Lake Winnipeg in Manitoba, then to the mighty Nelson River and Hudson Bay of the Arctic Ocean. Although we were at the center of the North American continent, we were connected to the sea.

As boys we bonded ourselves to the Clearwater River. We played cowboys and Indians on its banks, our knees scraping soil that had known white boys less than a hundred years. We'd get shot, each in our own turn, shot in the heart. I'd roll downhill toward the river, ending up limp but alive in the musty smell of crushed leaves and dry riverside grass.

We fished along the Clearwater, once seeing a snapping turtle large enough to bring tears of fear to a barefooted boy's eyes. We caught catfish ("Who'd ever eat 'em?" we chided each other), northern pike, bullheads, rock bass and suckers. We brought some fish proudly home to the dinner table. Others we desecrated with jackknives as thoughtless boys do.

We sledded along the Clearwater, sliding down trails through woods on steep hills toward riverbanks. We skated on the Clearwater, sometimes racing cracking ice behind us or breaking through to a second layer of ice. Sometimes after heavy snows we would cross the river: skip the bridge, take the shortcut. We were leery of the slushy brown spots and the lively riffles of rapids that never knew ice. Although snow covered most of the Clearwater, it was always alive to us. ("People fall through," adults told us. "They get carried downstream under the ice by the current." Food for snapping turtles, we boys thought.) The river was always there: dark, sometimes frightening, yet always compelling with the wet spell of unseen events. Mystery.

Naturally it was in the Clearwater that I, at age nine, almost died.

I was standing in the river at a public swimming beach ("Don't you *dare* go swimming!" mother had said.) and, upon turning, was astonished at how far I was from shore. Then I went under for no recallable reason. I just went under. Everything looked yellow, the color of urine or beer. I felt like I was floating in space...weightlessly spinning downstream under the Highway 32 bridge. I didn't need to breathe. It didn't matter.

2

Nor did it matter that I was drifting under the bridge toward rapids of a rock dam.

I was reborn on the beach.

A lifeguard had dragged me from the river. I was coughing. Choking. Soon crying. I stood up fuzzy-headed and turned toward a friend's riverside home where I was spending the weekend. I bumped into a tree and scraped sunburnt arms against roadside bushes. Then, there was a gravel road beneath my feet.

Good old gravel, I thought.

I revisited the Clearwater 15 years later. Ken MacDonald and I were canoeing down the Red Lake River, having begun in my birthplace of Thief River Falls. We intended to paddle 50 miles in three days. As we passed Red Lake Falls we reached a shallow but swift bend where the Clearwater flowed lickety split into the Red Lake River on the left. I was reminded of how close I had come to death years earlier, of how life sometimes curls up like a frothing boil of whitewater in a constricted canyon.

From nature, by a heartbeat, comes flesh. From flesh and mind: awareness. From awareness: the sense, sometimes, of life as gift from mystery. But how is it, I asked myself (and still do), that rivers like the Clearwater flow through a person's life, like arteries, wearing grooves into the granite of boyhood-turned-manhood? Why does someone develop a thirst for *more* rivers? Why do people canoe, kayak, and raft down rivers like other people climb mountains? And how is it a person might grow up to seek a holy land, a special place *to* which and *through* which rivers flow?

Perhaps the answer is rooted in my appreciation of open space. I grew up relatively poor, and after 40 years I see how being short on cash teaches something about public land and free-flowing rivers not learned otherwise.

I'm talking about the wealth of having places to roam and walk, to sit and dream, and to explore and harvest visions without trespassing. I'm talking about the sense of belonging, of being at home, of freedom and of self-realization. I'm talking, inevitably, about growth and happiness: the meat of fulfillment.

When my parents separated, my mother took custody of me and my three sisters. We never had enough money to buy land or a house, so we rented. We moved from one apartment house to another. There was scant feeling of home, of permanent shelter from rain and winter's subzero cold, a constant refuge, a place to draw the line and not be violated. *Our* place. No. If mom's rent check wasn't good we knew we could be out on the street.

This possibility of revocable tenancy bred in me a fondness for city, county, state and federal public domains: the turf of "we the people." Open space. There I could explore riverbanks, cast my eye at the orange breasts of robins, listen to mourning doves sing above dawn dew, whittle sticks and whistle a happy boy's songs.

Only in open space, I felt, was I free.

I thought of the public domain and the dynamics of trespassing one day, decades later, while canoeing in northern Minnesota's Voyageurs National Park. MacDonald and I, back in the canoe saddle together, faced large whitecapped waves and were forced ashore near a private cabin. No one was home. We checked. We didn't intend to trespass. We just wanted to get off the water during gale-force winds.

Suddenly, as we sat on shore, a large motorboat roared across a narrows of Sand Point Lake. The driver stood up as he neared us.

"Get the hell out of here!" he yelled, no questions asked. "Get out!"

Although he was guarding a friend's property, playing policeman, his words struck home. We were reluctant to leave but got back in our canoe and pushed off into dangerous waters.

Eviction.

Private versus public.

Later I was on a four-mile walk near Blackduck in north central Minnesota. It had been a long drive from Ely, Minnesota, through a tunnel of fog and bog to visit my mother over Christmas. I needed to stretch my legs. When I reached the local golf course I headed across open terrain. I stopped at a green and scraped its snow-dusted surface with the toe of my boot.

"Get off the green!" a man yelled from the driveway of a nearby house. He had gotten out of an El Camino with a realty name emblazoned on its doors. "Go away! Get off the green!"

I headed across the golf course. I seethed. Again I was a trespasser. Again I felt the noose tighten around my need to roam.

Unable then to own land or a home, I wanted — at least — a place to walk, camp, watch wildlife, to be at peace and not feel alien in my own country. This was, as for every American, my alleged birthright. In time I judged my standard of living not by what I had but by the quality and size of open space around me.

When we whites, after all, swept across the North American continent we took possession of the land. We fenced it off as though barbed wire came with the Bible. We devised property lines, made and mounted No Trespassing signs, and herded the continent's natives, the resistance, onto boundaried reservations. Altogether we laid an abstract Anglo-Saxon grid of land ownership over the water, forest and wind-rippled grass. For those who couldn't adjust to that grid: tough. When it came to land, if you didn't own it, if you hadn't put your John Hancock on the right papers, you didn't belong on it.

Damn the free spirit.

*"Get the hell out of here,"* the man had said.

Against this backdrop it was difficult for me to empathize with people screaming about federal land grabs involving national parks, wildlife refuges and wilderness areas. Those who complained most about government protection or expansion of the federal domain were usually landowners who had a piece of the rock. Or they were people who might benefit financially by selling to individuals, thus commercially exploiting what could belong to everyone. It was my freedom from *No Trespassing* signs some of the landed gentry threatened. It was the need of people like myself to saunter unmolested that they couldn't, or wouldn't comprehend.

So how could I oppose public ownership of land?

As long as people were not locked out of open spaces, those spaces were gifts to the spirit. Not luxuries, but necessities. Not mere superfluous playgrounds, but commonly held homes for the needy freedoms of man.

I am not a man who gladly stands with his face or back to walls. This I understood as I gravitated over the years to the open spaces of North America. I wanted to know their freedoms and the texture of their landscape and watershed. There was the Basswood River, Maligne, Little Missouri, Little Fork, Kaministikwia, Big Fork, Kawishiwi, Kopka, Greyson, Horse, Dog, and other rivers. They formed for me, and still do, a metaphorical web of rivers flowing to and from a common center like liquid spokes of a wheel undulating in space: the space of my dreams, the hub of my hopes. The rivers radiate light, and the light bathes my eyes in silver water.

I call it my river mandala.

This mandala is not merely a literary doily. It is as real for me as a guiding vision, and it's just as powerful. It evokes change and growth. I scan the stars for it on clear nights. I sniff it out among pistils of pollinating wildflowers on hot midsummer noons. At dusk, when I close my eyes in the cabin loft, my feet toward the east as Sioux once lay, I sense the mandala's vibrant presence. It is around me and in me.

I'm at peace with it, and in the best of times it leads me to joy.

As fanciful as my river mandala appears, however, it is rooted in real landscapes with innate power. Landscapes affect people. They enlarge vision. They build strength. They expand the limits of geographical awareness. When, as adventurers, we pass through landscapes, we move through color, sound, smells, light, shade, taste and vegetative texture; our bodies swim through a cacophony of sensations. There is sometimes risk and danger as flesh dances with ecosystems and climate. There are encounters with people who live so closely to landscapes that they seem one with them, and, truly, they are. If fortunate, the adventurer returns home a different person, subtly better, forever branded, having been worked upon. Impressed. Whether we are alert adventurers, or people who awaken to and dwell in one landscape, we enter a chrysalis and emerge, like Thoreau from Walden Pond, a more perfect creature.

Do we not become in part manifestations of where we've been and lived our days? Do we not respond physically and psychologically, if not spiritually, to our environments? Will not March's hoarfrosted trees I see out my cabin window, or the snow-covered lake's brilliant whiteness affect my outlook tonight and tomorrow? Does a person ever lose the trees, animals, skies and sunrises of his or her outdoor hours? Or do these things forever provide us with a living mosaic of natural beauty which nourishes awe, if not hope, during mankind's sometimes grim search for meaning?

I think they do.

This, then, is my bias: We can nurture contact with nature in the hope of attuning ourselves to an ever-evolving wholeness and discovery, or we can risk death by alienation.

Collectively, the choice is ours.

In making my choice I've been fortunate in moving freely through the open spaces about which the following pages are written. For almost a quarter century, perhaps more, I've sought to imbue myself with the significance of North America's public domain. As an adventurer, woodsman, writer, Quetico-Superior canoe trip guide, National Park Service ranger, and in other capacities, I wanted to assess the value of these places in the context of the life I know best.

My open spaces range from Alaska's Wrangell-St. Elias Mountains before the area was made into one of the nation's most spectacular national parks, to New England's Concord and Merrimack rivers. There, with an unusual group of paddlers including Walter Harding, Thoreau's definitive biographer, and Anne LaBastille of *Woodswoman* fame, I retraced Thoreau's 1839 boat trip. There was a long trip down the Little Missouri River in North Dakota's Badlands, and a 23-day sojourn into Ontario's Wabakimi-Kopka country where a provincial park protecting woodland caribou was being contested. I canoed the Kam-Dog and retraced the longest and hardest voyageur route connecting Lake Superior with the Quetico-Superior. Plus other journeys. Inevitably I became a park ranger among the tallest trees in the world at California's Redwood National Park before working as a ranger in Apostle Islands National Lakeshore off Wisconsin's Lake Superior coast.

In 1988, the year of wildfires (including Yellowstone's) throughout North America, I ended up on Montana's Red Bench Fire where I was left with an abiding sense of one of nature's greatest powers.

OPEN SPACES, however, is centered at Hocoka, my cabin and land on the edge of northeastern Minnesota's Boundary Waters Canoe Area Wilderness of the Quetico-Superior, a region, as Gary Soucie, executive editor of *Audubon*, once wrote, that not only looms large in the American imagination but also has played a seminal role in the shaping of modern thought about American wilderness. Here in the Quetico-Superior I wanted to encounter and explore the enigma of timber wolves, little knowing I would do so through the death of my dog, Bojo. I wanted to study the area's Ojibway pictographs and, if possible, learn what it means to live close to the land, in one place, for a long time. Hocoka, without road access, became the center of my river mandala and the hub, for me, of open spaces everywhere. Today it is a departure point and a destination. From it I leave. To it I've always returned. It is at Hocoka that OPEN SPACES begins and ends.

Here, at this hour, I make my stand. "There will always be one more river," Edward Abbey says in *Down the River*, "not to cross but to follow. The journey goes on forever, and we are fellow voyagers on our little living ship of stone and soil and water and vapor, this delicate planet circling round the sun, which humankind call Earth."

What river is next?

As my hand once again touches the shaft of my canoe paddle, its wood worn smooth over the years, I'm left with the compelling notion my quest has just begun. There's the internal, mapless country, of course, which knows no bounds as long as the imagination and inquisitive spirit remain alive. But there is also the hard rock and flowing waters of place: lands with space. I think of Ontario's Albany River, Saskatchewan's Fond du Lac, and Ontario's Winisk River flowing through polar bear country 800 miles north of Hocoka. There's Arkansas's Buffalo River, Wisconsin's Namekagon and Alaska's wild Noatak. Most alluring, perhaps, are the Rainy River, Winnipeg River, Lake Winnipeg and Nelson River connecting the Quetico-Superior with Hudson Bay's wide open sea.

I imagine and anticipate the spattering of sunlight on rapids, of ospreys — wings wet — rising sunlit on updrafts, and of rivers flowing through darkness below waterfalls glistening with moonlight.

In the beginning I called my relationship with North America's open spaces and free-flowing rivers one of *love*. I'm not sure this is the right word. While canoeing a wild river through the heart of the country, however, or while standing next to my cabin to watch northern lights or listen to wolves howl, the word will likely dissolve into a lively, altogether recognizable, sensation.

For this I now know:

Only by awakening to the feeling I speak of — as thousands have — does one know it. It is organic. It is free. It is the grace of open space and it's shaped like a circle.

Jim dale Vickery
——Hocoka——
1991

# GEOGRAPHICAL AREAS EMPHASIZED IN OPEN SPACES

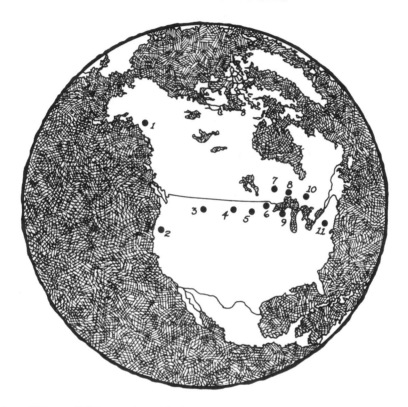

1.   Wrangell Mountains, Alaska
2.   Redwood National Park, California
3.   Glacier National Park, Red Bench Fire, Montana
4.   Theodore Roosevelt National Park, Badlands, North Dakota
5.   Mississippi River Headwaters, Minnesota
6.   Quetico-Superior/BWCA, Minnesota
7.   Wabakimi-Kopka Country, Ontario
8.   Kam-Dog Country, Ontario
9.   Apostle Islands National Lakeshore, Wisconsin
10.  Kanawsa Canoe Museum, Ontario
11.  Concord and Merrimack Rivers, New Hampshire

# PART I
# COMING INTO
# THE COUNTRY

# OPEN SPACES

*There are always two places, dream and actual life. When the two are brought together by an act of imagination there occur those sometimes brief moments of compelling clarity and completeness. And those moments are, or ought to be, part of the real life of humankind: place and image, reality and dream made one.*

*John Haines*

# CHAPTER ONE
# THE LAND IS ALIVE
# WITH WOLVES

*The land is alive with wolves...*

This truth stuck to my mind like a wet tongue on cold steel as I crouched down to feel fresh timber wolf tracks with my bare fingers. It was a winter afternoon and I had just finished working in my writing cabin on one of Hocoka's granite ridges. I was in the heart of Superior National Forest's wolf country. But the tracks, made beneath blue skies, nevertheless came as a surprise. Suddenly my sluggishness was gone and I was electrified as if plugged into the sunshine itself.

I glanced around, found fresh deer tracks among the wolf tracks, then noticed a snow-covered bush stained yellow with wolf urine near the cutoff to the main cabin where Chris Trost was waiting for me.

We were not alone.

The main cabin across the cove would have to wait.

Soon I was backtracking the wolves. I was a tall, relatively gangly creature shuffling through ash and birch swamp down a trail up which wolves had come. Later, on the lake at sunset, I would see that four wolves had been my way. No matter the number. For the moment I was obsessed with the snowy, five-inch-long tracks. Tracks led off the trail into brush. Other tracks came through alders to join the main path. The wolves had been sniffing things out, I supposed. Taut for the flush. Hoping to feed themselves, according to an old Russian proverb, by their feet. Maybe on snowshoe hare. Maybe on beaver or grouse. But most likely on white-tailed deer here in northeastern Minnesota.

With, I had to add, an occasional dog.

OPEN SPACES

Like Bojo.

Just when I was ready to end my wolf-tracking for the day I found greenish
wolf scat — embedded with bone chips and hair — on the trail in front of
me. The connection between wolf scat and my husky lunged up at me like
a shadow on a moonlit night. I was hit in the chest. I was trapped in the steel
jaws of a time I couldn't shake: the time Bojo was killed, when my
encounters with timber wolves made a quantum leap forward and changed
me forever.

I suppose my run-in with wolves began when I moved to the North Arm
of Burntside Lake near Ely in May 1979. What I wanted, like many
newcomers to the area, was to live near the Boundary Waters Canoe Area
Wilderness (BWCAW) in Superior National Forest, locus of three million
acres of trees, lakes, rivers, streams, bear, deer, moose and wolves. Across
the border in Ontario was Quetico Provincial Park, another million acres
of wild terrain. The entire Quetico-Superior area was underlaid with
Precambrian, Canadian Shield rock — a vast plateau of billion-year-old
granite extending southwest of Hudson Bay. Bordering this arena of rock
and water, watching over it from the north, was the Ontario town of
Atikokan ("caribou bones") beyond which stretched incomprehensible
wilderness, boreal and subarctic, panning out into the great Arctic itself.

There are only three east-west roads between the Arctic and the Quetico-
Superior.

Lindskogs Resort was the name of the place, a pine ponderosa of a couple
hundred acres sandwiched between Burntside Lake on the east and the
BWCAW's Cummings Lake country on the west. Ely, then a mining and
tourist town of 5,000 people, lay nine miles southeast as the raven flies and
ski glides, twice that distance by road. Although the resort was a bustling
place of rented cabins and second homes in summer, in winter the wildness
came home.

The change came around November when gray skies and freezing temperatures brought ice to coves and shoreline rocks. Most canoeists were
gone by then, as were swimmers, fishermen and hikers. Only orange-

jacketed deer hunters remained. After deer season the country was left to those who wanted it.

Like me.

My first two winters were spent alone at Lindskogs, my nearest neighbor a toss-up between Thor Nordwall, a silver-haired Swede in a log cabin on a ridgetop, and the Colloseys, a radiologist and his wife, a mile up the North Arm Road. I lived in a one-room log cabin the first winter, in a two-room frame cabin the next. The trick was to stay away from rubber rent checks.

"Your checks bounce," Marshall Lindskog — landlord, caretaker and surrogate father — would say nursing a whiskey-and-water, "and you bounce-ah. Life's as simple as that."

Words said, Marshall's blue eyes would break into a playful-but-don't-test-me smile. Then he would start talking lake trout or wolf.

"Are you a friend of the wolf?" he asked me once after he saw me wearing a t-shirt with Save the Wolf printed on the front. "I'm no friend of the wolf. The wolf no likee me."

Perhaps Marshall, who died three years later of lung cancer, liked the animosity he entertained for wolves, a hostility elevating his relationship with wolves to an assumed mutual respect. Both were predators. When it came to white-tailed deer, they were competitors. Marshall used the best part of his salary to hunt big game before retiring from the Minneapolis Park Board in 1973. Venison in the freezer was commonplace. A polar bear rug, big enough for him and his wife Bernie to lie on, once graced their Burntside cabin's floor. A Kodiak bear skin still hung on a wall. It was large enough to get a rise out of visitors and light up Marshall's memories, prompting him to tell stories — whiskey and Winston at hand — that darted in and out of fact and fiction like bass swimming shoreline shadows.

Stories like the tale of the Yukon wolf.

Marshall, hot-headed with freedom following a medical discharge from the

## OPEN SPACES

Naval Air Corps in the 1940s, decided to go wolf hunting. He headed into the Yukon bush with a bottle of Old Crow whiskey, his pet .30-06 rifle, a dozen rounds of ammunition, k-rations and a sleeping bag. No compass. Near Kluane Lake he started following wolf tracks which led him on a circuitous route. He became disoriented. No help from summer's lingering light on distant glacier-clad mountains. He stopped at dusk, made camp and listened to wolf sounds around him as night closed in. He dozed fitfully. His loaded rifle lay next to him in the sleeping bag. Marshall discovered in morning's light that the wolves had made a "cowpath" around him and his campfire.

Three days later, out of whiskey and cigarettes, and having been lost in wolf country, Marshall stumbled out onto the Alaska- Canada Highway. He had had enough. Seeing a truck coming towards him, he stood in the middle of the road with his rifle across his chest.

Stop or else.

Marshall's biggest need, he later told me, was for a drink and a cigarette. Yet I suspect Marshall needed something else. He had admittedly reached a point back in the Yukon bush when he had begun wondering if he would get out alive. The soul is uncannily sensitive at such times. Seeing those wolf tracks made a lasting impression. Perhaps for once he felt like prey. Like meat. And Marshall needed, when it came to predator-prey relationships, the illusion that he — master of his fate — was back on top.

&#10148; &#10148; &#10148;

Marshall's story fell on impressionable ears as I hunkered down on his land in 1979. Around me, Forest Service statisticians claimed, were approximately 1,200 wolves in a five million acre area. Here was the last viable population of timber wolves in the United States outside Alaska.

True, there were a few wolves in the Rockies of northwestern Montana, two or three dozen in northern Wisconsin, another two dozen on Isle Royale, Michigan, and rumors of a wolf comeback in the northernmost eastern states. Yet only in northeastern Minnesota between Lake of the Woods and

Lake Superior did wolves maintain a healthy foothold on American land and in the American mind. It was in the latter they had caused such a ruckus in the 1960s and 70s. As wolf populations fell to the American hunter and trapper, as they learned to fear people with rifles on snowmobiles and the sharp spark of rifles fired from low-flying airplanes, there arose an outcry by environmentalists which led to legislation designed to protect *Canis lupus* in the lower 48 states. Bounties on wolves, which had baited both casual and professional hunters for decades, were stopped in 1965. Then, in 1970, authorities closed the Superior National Forest to the killing of wolves.

The final blow, as some might look at it, came in 1974 — one year after passage of the Endangered Species Act — when the taking of all wolves in the 48 coterminous states was forbidden.

This, five years before I settled in at Lindskogs.

I had never seen a timber wolf before moving to Burntside Lake. Although I had grown up in Red Lake Falls and Crookston in northwestern Minnesota at a latitude the same as Ely's, you don't see wolves in Crookston country. You see farmers, sugar beets and red foxes.

Nor do you usually see wolves in White Earth State Forest and Indian Reservation in north central Minnesota. While living there for most of four years in the mid 1970s, in a primitive cabin a dozen miles southwest of the Mississippi River's Itasca headwaters, I never on my daily walks found wolf tracks or other sign of timber wolves. Brush wolf or coyote, yes. I found one that had been shot hanging by its neck in a tree along a logging road, and I sometimes heard them yipping and howling. But varmints didn't last here much past their first or second sighting.

Not until 1977 did my tracks finally come across those of timber wolves. While on a canoe trip through and beyond northern Minnesota's Voyageurs National Park, I found fresh wolf tracks trailing moose tracks on a sand beach of Lilac Lake. The next day, while photographing a stream falling down a rock ridge pocked with red maple leaves, Ken MacDonald and I heard a wolf howl from nearby ridges.

## OPEN SPACES

The following spring, during a snowshoe camping trip in the Boundary Waters with wildlife artist Dan Metz, we found signs of a wolf kill below Devil's Cascade: vertebrae, deer fur, and bloodstains on snow. There, at a small pool of open water, wolves had attacked a deer that had come down to drink. Parts of the same deer were found further down the Little Indian Sioux River where it widens into Loon Lake. Again the next day, near the end of a snowshoe hike to Lynx Lake, Metz and I found fresh wolf tracks cupping gold sunlight from a setting March sun.

The shadow of *Canis lupus*, however, like a raven's, had scarcely crossed my life.

This changed at Marshall Lindskog's ponderosa where there was a lot of wolf traffic. I often heard wolves howling at night as I walked down to a hole in the lake ice to get water, or when I stepped outside in subzero air to fetch armloads of firewood. I saw wolf tracks while cross-country skiing and snowshoeing, and found it curious when fresh wolf tracks followed mine back from my afternoon trips.

I tracked. I was tracked.

One morning I found wolf tracks circling the cabin and on the path to the outhouse. Alongside the path were depressions in the snow among alders. I hadn't slept alone during the night. Urine yellowed the snow beneath several white pines.

Was I being stalked? Watched? Played with like some wolf scientist in a Farley Mowat book? I never cried wolf. I kept the excitement to myself.

More soon came. On a blustery night in midwinter, while talking with a friend about shelters, I heard an odd noise outside the cabin window. I had left one of Marshall's burbot carcasses on a woodpile for the birds, and the strange sounds made me think a flying squirrel or pine marten was doing some nocturnal dining. When the subject of tipis came up with my friend, I mentioned a book I had. Soon I was breaking trail through the dark to my summer cabin where most of my books were cached until spring. Halfway to the cabin, as I sank knee-deep in blizzard-driven snow, I spotted canine tracks.

## Chapter One THE LAND IS ALIVE WITH WOLVES

My first reaction — rooted in a boyhood spent in towns — was dog. But it's hard to tell track size in deep snow. As soon as the paw is raised out of the snow, fresh powder slips into the track.

I entered the cabin, found the book and headed back to my winter log cabin on a different route.

The driveway had less snow, but here, too, were tracks, unmistakably wolf in size. They were going my way. My hackles rose as I stared at the tracks illumined by my flashlight, the child in me — or the wild in me — coming alive with ancient reactions. The tracks sometimes left the road to meander among brush, yet always returned. I wondered what scent, what hunger possessed this track-maker as I traced the tracks to the back of the cabin.

To the woodpile near the window.

To the burbot carcass now pulled to the ground.

A new hunger dogged me as I entered the cabin. I wanted to *see* a wolf. I was getting weary of reading signs and guessing scenes. Perhaps I should sit up some moonlit night awake to motion among trees and brush outside the window, awake to shadows alive and furtive. Bait wolves with burbot if I had to.

But, no, I told myself. That wouldn't work. It would be like sitting in wait for a bald eagle. It would be too much like holding one's breath in hopes of a vision.

 za za za

Bojo was the key to wolves for me. It was she, a purebred Siberian husky, that sharpened my senses and quickened my quest to get closer to the mystery which is *Canis lupus*.

I bought Bojo for $100 when she was six weeks old in April 1980, from friends at the *Ely Echo*, a weekly newspaper where I worked part-time for two years. I had always wanted a dog, and in northern Minnesota none is more at home in the south-sweeping Arctic cold than the husky. The Siberian's pelage, with its white eyebrows, cheeks and chest, with its other light markings and curved tail, gives it an added beauty — like the wolf's — that sparks the soul.

Huskies are rooted historically to the Quetico-Superior. During the French, British and Indian fur trade of the 1700s and 1800s, Indians and wintering voyageurs, or *hivernants*, used huskies to pull food and fur across the island-pocked snowy expanses of today's Minnesota-Ontario border. Huskies, descendants of Indian village dogs, were used as far south as the southern shore of Lake Superior. There Ojibway of the Apostle Islands, where I would one day work as a park ranger, greeted 18th century Frenchmen with "Bojo...Bojo" — a broken version of the salutary French *Bonjour*.

Bojo. The name not only appealed to my half-French heritage, it anchored time and husky to the land. I spoke the word countless times, rubbing it into my pup's mind like a salve.

The first thing Bojo did when I picked her up was piss down my leg. However, she soon had a rude awakening of her own. Burntside Lake's ice was going out. As the sun went down on our first day together, I led Bojo on a leash out to the end of a boathouse dock. Crumbling ice had washed up to the end of the dock forming a floe of ice chunks and chips rising and falling with wave swells. Although Bojo was nervous from being separated from her parents and fellow pups, she was frisky and playful. Without so much as a whimper of doubt she stepped out onto the ice. In she went, water closing over her head, then up she came with a cry of terror. I yanked her out by the leash, set her on the dock, then took her up to the cabin to be toweled off. We went for a warm-up run. But her baptism was over, and it had been bad. Never would she be a friend of water. She would tremble in canoes, whine and piss. A plunge of fate among shards of ice had her dead set against lakes.

These were the terms of her young life. And on these terms — my pants stained with urine, her mind stained with lake water shock — we became proverbial best friends.

Part of my attachment to Bojo was emotionally timed. Shortly before I bought Bojo I was divorced from my first wife. The sorrow and confusion were compounded by a later relationship in Ely which left me stressed, sleeping with a loaded rifle, and ripe for a much needed return to the simplicity and peace for which I had moved near the Boundary Waters in the first place. Bojo refocused my attention. We walked together daily. We played tag on old logging roads. We fished together, went berry picking together, and we sang.

Sometimes when I told Bojo she was the best dog in the world I ended the flattery by howling: first a little yip and a whine to get her attention, then a deep throaty howl coaxing her to join me.

Bojo had a mind of her own by the time the summer sun was hot, which didn't come as a surprise. Don Beland, one of Ely's top sled dog racers, had told me a Siberian husky will be obedient 75 percent of the time. The rest of the time it will do what it damn well pleases. Don's words. I sometimes saw such blatant rebelliousness in Bojo's eyes. I would call her, she would glance at me, size me up and...run. This couldn't be tolerated. Who, really, was master here? But when I ran after her she would slink under the cabin. If I was stupid enough to crawl after her she would dash out the other side. Here was no hug-me, pet-me dog, no poodle, tame dachsund or Irish setter. Here was an animal that as a species was only recently weaned from woods.

I cared not if she learned how to "speak," roll over or balance cookies on her nose. I certainly didn't care if she knew how to put out a tossed cigarette as a dog I once saw in Alaska did. Bojo simply learned to sing, come and stay, and sometimes, sit, and to run like lightning.

She did these things in husky glory. When she felt like it.

What Bojo never learned was to stand up for her rights. She kowtowed to every canine cantering down my cabin's path. Simply, sometimes, roll over, belly up: *lick me, don't hurt me*. She allowed city dogs let loose by vacationing tourists — the Fluffies and Fidos — to eat her food at my doorstep. Sometimes when strange dogs arrived she would scamper down the cabin path, circle around me, then watch the invasion through my legs, her head between my knees.

Bojo's cowardice, her apparent innate submissiveness, nevertheless had its limits.

The first time I heard her bark and growl with her lips curled back, hackles up, was when I found a large snapping turtle bobbing among leatherleaf bushes on the shore of Ole Lake, originally Horseshoe Lake, in the BWCAW. Green grass in the turtle's clamped jaws was still fresh. Bojo had followed me to the snapper. She crouched low, growled and snapped her teeth at the turtle: a primordial, dinosaurian invasion. I chased her back up the bank into Norway pines, back into patches of bunchberries and flowering wild lilies of the valley. We put the turtle behind us as we headed home.

I had a bucket of blueberries in one hand, a northern pike on a stringer in the other. Bojo kept sniffing both, heeling for the whiff.

&#10048; &#10048; &#10048;

We were headed for a rendezvous with a black bear. It wasn't Bojo's first time. We had once encountered a black bear when she was at that young, cocky age when she loved to jump up and snap at butterflies, or pounce with four paws on mice in tall grass like a fox. When I saw the bear beyond a rise on a logging road by Thor's cabin, Bojo, still a pup, couldn't see it above the rise. I simply grabbed Bojo and turned us around. The bear ambled away into brush.

Our hike's route? Changed.

When Bojo and I ran into our second bear, it was at Fenske Lake. It was in no mood to put up with a pint-sized pup. Lured by the smell of resort garbage, the bear walked down the driveway toward a resort cabin where I was visiting Liisa Tuomisto and her parents. Bojo immediately attacked the bear. She ran up to it, her hackles and tail raised, barking and snarling. The bear lunged at Bojo. Bojo charged again when the bear turned. I called

Bojo to come but I might as well have whistled for the bear. Bojo was steeped in something deep. I didn't exist. Suddenly the bear had enough. You could sense it coming like a black storm.

The bear turned with a ticked-off look in its eyes. It ran toward Bojo. Time to end the noisy nonsense. Time to end the bothersome bee at the banquet of life.

Bojo dropped her tail and ran toward me. She ran like a kid to papa after irking the neighborhood bully. This bully was black and 300 pounds. I was in the precarious position of having cocky Bojo run to me for protection from a mad beast who could bust skulls and cave in cabin walls.

*Thanks, Bojo.* I leapt to my feet toward the cabin door. *Cute.*

Liisa was standing in the cabin's doorway.

"Get outta the way!" I yelled, trying to escape the bear's rush.

Fortunately, bears sometimes have more sense than young dogs. The bear stopped, turned, and shuffled away. The Boss. It hadn't flinched as Bojo manifested new, reckless courage.

ò ò ò

I took Bojo for a walk on August 31, 1980, down a trail we had walked a dozen times. It was a private path known to few, a mile of forest and flowers leading to a small lake fringed with pines. There, on snowshoes, I had often checked esthetic traplines in search of winter's wonder. There, in summer, I had frequently fished.

It was a sunny Sunday afternoon as Bojo and I nosed through brush crowding the trail. I had no leash on Bojo. I didn't think twice as she broke off from a trot in front of me to hunt down a scent.

She had done this before. This was her wild haven, the nearest thing to paradise a husky could find.

OPEN SPACES

Bushes closed behind her. Without a glance backward she was gone.

I was putting a Lazy Ike on my fishing line a few minutes later when I heard Bojo yowl. It was an incredible cry: high, sharp, earnest, terrible. It wasn't the ferocious snarling and barking of a fight but a bawling howl of tearing pain. I ran down the lake's boulder shore with my fishing rod in my hand, then back up the path toward Bojo.

Her cries stopped. I whistled and called. Silence. Not even a rustle of wind in the dense leaves.

Hearing nothing more, and feeling helpless, I turned around toward the lake to resume fishing. It was broad daylight in late summer a mile from my cabin. Familiar ground. Yet I fought worry.

I didn't get 20 steps when Bojo started screaming again.

Again I ran down the trail calling for her. If only I could have heard a branch crack or seen something move. I was desperate. Anxious. *Where the hell is she? What's going on here?*

Bojo's howling, her yelping, stopped.

My pain began.

I looked for Bojo for the next five hours, then headed back to the cabin where I hoped she had returned. She hadn't. That night, for the first time since I had gotten Bojo, she wasn't at her food dish on the cabin steps. Her toys in the yard, even the old leather lineman's glove with which we had played tug-of-war, lay untouched. She was still in the woods. Lost. As I lay in bed, I recalled her bellowing cries. I had been her only friend. It was me she'd been calling for.

And I had been helpless. I threw back my blankets, got up, and looked out the door.

"Bojo?"

## Chapter One THE LAND IS ALIVE WITH WOLVES

Nothing but night.

I was back in the woods at dawn the next day. I searched through bogs, up ridges, through thick balsam fir windfalls, around and across swamps. I looked, called and listened, death drawing nearer one step at a time. On Tuesday, my friend Dan Kuhl and I scoured the woods with his dog, Babe, a yellow labrador retriever. Dan carried a 12 gage shotgun. I had a .22 rifle with scope. Near where I had last heard Bojo we found a pile of dark diarrheic scat.

I stirred it with a stick, found hair and, despite the smell, examined it closely. The hair was tan and white: Bojo's colors.

I was crushed. The mystery of her fate was solved.

But what, exactly, killed her?

Any noise on Bojo's fateful afternoon in those windless woods would have been heard. I ruled out a bear. Bears sometimes walk more like moose than deer through woods. Fearful of nothing, they muscle their way through obstructions oblivious to the noise. Besides, Bojo would have barked. A fisher might have killed Bojo, but she was already twice a fisher's adult size. Finally, Bojo could have fended for herself against pine marten, bobcat, or lynx. At least I would have heard both foes in the fight.

What killed Bojo moved silently through the woods, killed quickly, and ate dogs.

る。 る。 る。

Almost every woodsman I knew cried wolf. Particularly Marshall who, he was quick to say, wasn't born yesterday. He had gotten to know the sight and smell of different kinds of scat while hunting the furbearer on his cabin wall and the Yukon wolves in memory. The dark cow-pie scat, he said, indicated much blood in the predator's digestive system, possibly gulped raw meat. It was an observation I confirmed reading L. David Mech's book, *The Wolf.*

Maybe Bojo had sniffed out a wolf, rolled over in customary submission, and the wolf had grabbed her. Then maybe Bojo screamed and went into shock, or became unconscious from a throathold. I approached. The wolf relaxed its grip, perhaps even backed away. I left. Bojo regained consciousness and tried to move. The wolf struck again. She howled.

It was guessing. All of this. But all I had to read was an inkblot of sounds, scat, Marshall's opinion and my memory's reconstruction of the death scene.

Two events seemed to close the case as far as I was concerned. Call it primary evidence. Notch it up as wolf sign.

About six weeks after Bojo was killed, I was hunting grouse in Ole Lake country near where Bojo and I hiked and occasionally camped. Beyond Ole Lake the trail led up to a high granite ridge skirting Silica Lake before dropping down to an old logging road connecting Coxey Pond and Burntside. As I walked east, homeward, with the setting sun at my back, my eye caught something moving in the roadside brush. The animals's large size, burnished brown fur and startling motion led to a knee-jerk conclusion: deer. But I instantly knew I was wrong. A wolf was passing in front of me on a game trail from right to left, about 30 feet away.

As soon as it reached the road its identity was certain.

The wolf trotted for one golden moment through the sunny spot of needle duff on the road. Its size, grace and silence, its utter smoothness and confidence of motion, stoned me in mid-stride. My .22 rifle lay on my shoulder. Never had I been more riveted to the immediate moment. I was locked in a wilderness saunterer's satori.

Yet my mind made the Bojo connection.

*This wolf could be her killer.*

We weren't more than five miles from where Bojo had been killed, a distance a healthy wolf can easily cover in an hour. This wolf, moreover, was coming from the general direction of Bojo's last stand. Perhaps it was making the ridgetop rounds of its territory, moving through the woods like a salmon in a stream of scents and false starts. Or perhaps it was just sniffing out deer yards in a buffer zone between wolf packs.

*Mah-een-gun,* as the region's Ojibway called the wolf, picked up its trot through a stand of jackpine until it was out of sight. I stood silent, listening to its fading steps patter like raindrops on dry leaves. A wolf. Not for a second had I thought of leveling my .22 and firing a shot. I felt sensually heightened and transformed: astonishingly alive in a land that gave as well as took away.

My encounters with timber wolves, and the enigma of Bojo's death, assumed a new dimension when Bud Lindskog shot a moose off the Echo Trail near the Little Indian Sioux River north of Ely. After butchering the moose, Bud ditched the large bull's head at an old dump along the gravel driveway into the resort. Soon there were large canine tracks at the dump. The nose, ears, skin and flesh of the moose's head went quickly. One day I found diarrheic scat among the tracks. By then the skull had been tugged apart, its 17-inch lower jaws — stained with dried blood — scattered on green club moss.

The scat was exactly like the dark, soft stuff in which I had found Bojo's hair. I stirred this new clue with a stick, wolf sign spinning kaleidoscopically in my mind on the cutting edge of fundamental *Canidae* knowledge.

The clincher came a day later when Chris Trost and I stood on the shore of Burntside Lake's North Arm. It was a cool, clear day at the tail end of the open water season. Distant islands, tinted pink by a setting sun, appeared to float in a breeze-scudded sea. Next to us, not more than 1,000 feet from what remained of the moose skull, was a neighbor's log cabin. Suddenly we heard a scratching, shuffling sound as if someone were crawling out from beneath the cabin. When it had cleared the last porch log the wolf stood, 20 feet away, looking straight at us, its reddish-brown coat mottled with black. Then it loped off into the woods.

Before the wolf disappeared it stopped to look at us over its right shoulder.

"Wolf," I muttered to Chris in the shock of recognition, trying to name this vision. But with the word said the wolf was gone.

ও ও ও

Wolves seemed to be crawling out of the woodwork in much of Superior National Forest in 1981-82. In a bizarre incident on January 2, 1982, Ronald Poyirer, 19, of Duluth, was attacked by a wolf near Brimson, Minnesota. The attack was surprising because in it was then standard knowledge among wolf biologists that there were no documented cases of non-rabid wolves attacking humans.

Poyirer was hunting rabbits in a dense spruce swamp, an area where there are usually many winter deer. His brown jacket, pants and boots were saturated with buck scent from the previous deer season, the scent supposedly masking human odor. Suddenly Poyirer saw something running through the trees. He walked toward it. At that moment a wolf knocked him down from behind and for a terrifying span of three seconds all the wolf biologists in North America were wrong.

Poyirer, beneath the wolf, rolled onto his back to grab the wolf by the neck. He reached for his .22 rifle and pulled the trigger. The shot frightened the wolf which ran off into the woods. Poyirer headed back to his cabin. His face had superficial scratches. His leg had a bad cut from a claw.

Local biologists found out.

"It does not appear to be an overt attack of a wolf on a human," biologist Steve Fritts of the U.S. Fish and Wildlife Service told the *Duluth News Tribune and Herald.* "I think the wolf made an honest mistake. The wolf was probably as surprised and embarrassed about this as the guy was."

Perhaps.

Fritts and Poyirer reconstructed the apparent fluke like this:
The wolf might have been chasing a deer — the "something" Poyirer saw running through the trees — but when nearing Poyirer the wolf mistook

him for the deer and hit him from behind. Wasn't Poyirer dressed the color of a deer? Didn't he smell like one? If the wolf, they said, wanted to kill Poyirer, certainly it could have. Wolves kill elk, moose, caribou, deer, even muskox.

A fallen man is nothing: in this case a footnote in the annals of wolf texts.

Around the same time as the Poyirer incident, several leashed dogs were killed near Babbitt, south of Ely. More were killed near Section 30, a hamlet of homes near White Iron Lake. Some dogs, left free to roam, simply disappeared. Their names were last seen in the want ads of local newspapers. I winced every time I heard of a killed dog, but still, I couldn't hold it against the wolf.

It came down to this: I couldn't begrudge wolves their desire for food. A wild wolf needs anywhere from four to ten pounds of meat a day and I couldn't find their procurement of this any more repulsive than a pine marten killing a squirrel, a gray owl killing a grouse, a grizzly bear killing a caribou calf or even Bojo killing mice. For me to teach Bojo not to kill mice would have been like trying to teach a smallmouth bass not to swim.

Clearly, there was a circle going on. Bojo had stumbled into it and I witnessed it. To draw near it, and to feel unto pain the life-death dance was one of the primary reasons I had chosen to live in the shadow of the wolf.

This cycle, moreover, is what I now suspect most great wildlife artists tap in their best paintings of wolves. Their wolves are always alert, often moving, on the run, one ear cocked for prey, the other swiveling for sign of man. The painted wolves of Manfred Schatz and Dan Metz, of Dan Smith and Robert Bateman, are hunting, feeding, thirsting for banquet. They hunger and seek. They are full of energy and strength. They move from darkness into light, from obscurity into clarity.

The beauty here lies in truth, and truth lies in beauty.

As for Bojo, would I have shot the wolf had I come upon the killing with a gun?

OPEN SPACES

Perhaps. Despite the threat of a $20,000 fine. Despite a possible jail sentence of five years. Despite even a strong fondness for the wolf and the wilderness it represents. Some protective instinct of my own might have pointed the gun at the wolf and pulled the trigger. My reaction might have been the same knee-jerk contortion with which a cattleman protects cows, farmers their chickens, parents their kids. Behold the shepherd instinct.

On the other hand, my armed presence would likely have spooked the wolf away, leaving Bojo with a damn good lesson. I'll never know.

It was something to think about, though.

When I heard of friends like Les Deppe and Erik Lindskog, Marshall's woodswise son, who in daylight watched a wolf at close range gorge itself on a white-tailed deer killed at water's edge, I wondered. And when I was told by summer tourists after their canoe trips of how they sat around campfires, as I've done, listening to wolves howl, I wondered again. When wolves speak, the land speaks. It is a language understood intuitively by all who hear it.

I heard that language once again one New Year's Eve. I had stepped outside shortly after nine o'clock to watch the moon rise orange and two-thirds full above a serrated forest horizon. *So* beautiful. Stars whitewashed the sky at ten below. A dull concave lens of northern lights hung over Pine Island similar to — but lighter than — the auroral glow the night before. For the joy of it I started to howl toward the moon, my cry carrying across the lake cove below. I howled again, then several times more. I expected nothing. Yet when I turned to go back into the cabin I heard a close reply. It came from the east out of the silence, a wild voice rending the night. A wolf was howling back to me. Then another. Suddenly there were wolves howling out on the lake past Cedar Point and to the right of me from the crags of Rainbow Ridge. A pack had split up and surrounded me.

The last howls rolled off Rainbow Ridge as the risen moon threw a dull yellow light into the night.

This, far from parties and crowds, on New Year's Eve.

30

Twice during the night as I waited for midnight to strike I stepped outside because I heard quick, excited howling and barking south of the cabin. In the morning, I found wolf tracks on our snowshoe trail. Another set of tracks — these by a loner — crossed the cove beneath the cabin. The wolf had been running, kicking up wads of snow crust. Although I hadn't actually seen it, I visualized moonlight glinting off guard hairs as the great wolf, driven curious by my wails, policed its range.

🐾 🐾 🐾

Despite five years in wolf country, I still hadn't seen a wolf-deer encounter by the time I moved to Hocoka. This wasn't surprising. Many people who have lived their entire lives in northern Minnesota have never seen a wolf. During a period of 20 years, wolf biologist Mech saw only about a dozen wolves that were not tracked down by radio collar or seen from a plane. What wolves remain in the contiguous United States — where they've been trapped, snared, chased to death and poisoned — are around today because they have made it their business to steer clear of man.

My own experiences with wolves were by happenstance. Only on such terms, if lucky, could I expect more.

It happened on a late winter day. I was snowshoeing home on a bright afternoon after escorting friends to their car a half mile from Hocoka. As I topped a small rise of the trail where the lake comes into view, I noticed something moving on the snow-covered ice near the point of an island. I stood still, breathing heavily, and reached for the binoculars slung around my neck. Too late. I cussed. At once it turned, trotted my way, and I was ready. There was no mistaking the wolf as it loped easily along.

The wolf held its head low, hunting scents and tracks. Then it raised its head to scope horizons. Behind it sloped a shore of boulders topped with deep green pines against the northeast sky's dark blue. The wolf's coat, more brown than the normal gray, looked brushed and full.

I ran toward the cabin as soon as the wolf was out of sight. I knew Chris was inside reading, no doubt sitting by one of the cabin's six lake-facing windows, but it wasn't likely she'd be looking outside. I ducked behind a rock ledge hoping the wolf wouldn't see or hear me. I was at the cabin door in a moment, out of breath, bending over, unstrapping the snowshoe bindings and trying to talk to Chris.

"Wolf!" I said between gasps. "Grab your parka and follow me to the top of the ridge behind the cabin. We'll have a view of the lake in three directions."

The ploy worked. We watched two wolves come together in narrows between the lake's two main islands. One wolf had cut across Pine Island hoping, perhaps, to flush a deer. The other had gone ahead to round the island's west point. They met in the narrows as we watched them with binoculars.

What the wolves hadn't seen yet was the deer across the lake to our left.

The deer was alone on the lake ice next to shore, its white tail flagged up, its gaze over the left shoulder toward the wolves. It raised each leg slowly as it stepped forward. Only anxiously did it look away from the wolves to see where it was going. We wondered — binoculars at eyes — if the wolves, now out of sight on an island, would pick up the deer's scent. We also wondered if we were about to view a wolf-deer chase complete with the tearing, choking kill, the ripping of meat and cartilage to bellowing white-tail cries: a fearsome eruption of violence, a clash of tooth and muscle on a clear, cold day.

It had been watched before, this killing. It had been seen by wolf biologists, woodsmen and the occasional canoeist like the late Quetico-Superior naturalist Sigurd F. Olson. Olson eddied into it by chance in the 1920s.

He had been paddling down the Basswood River in the Boundary Waters on the way to Crooked Lake during his guiding days. He saw a deer running leisurely along a barren rock slope parallel to the river. Thirty yards behind it was a wolf, moving slowly, keeping its distance, seeming to drift along like a shadow. Suddenly the wolf sprang forward, bounded a few times, and grabbed the deer by the nose. The deer somersaulted, hit the ledge and broke its neck.

## Chapter One THE LAND IS ALIVE WITH WOLVES

"Instantly," Olson wrote in *Open Horizons*, "the wolf was upon it and the struggle was over. Only then did it see the canoe; it stood motionless for an instant, threw up its head, and bounded back into the spruces."

Olson and friends turned their canoe to shore, jumped in the shallows, ran up to the dead deer, bled it and cut off a haunch of venison for supper. The rest of the deer went to the wolf circling warily in the brush.

Olson had witnessed the exceptional wolf sighting, the ultimate encounter — one which Chris and I were spared. For it is in the kill, that which most offends the human senses, that which most grates against the wolf's romantic image, that the wolf survives. Here, perhaps, is the necessary climax to what Barry Lopez in *Of Wolves and Men* calls the "conversation of death" between a wolf and its prey: the possible recognition by both at the start of a fatal encounter, sometimes for the wolf, that the circle which is integral to all life is inescapable.

The climax, unlike the kill Olson saw, is rarely clean.

There is blood and bawling and viscera. Killing to live is not by nature dainty. But it is the way things are.

I thought of this as I followed the fresh wolf tracks near the cabin at sunset, tracks I had found near my writing cabin and which now led me down to the lake's edge. My heart, in one sense, was heavy.

What would Bojo — had she lived — look like? Would she have come when called? Would she have been lead dog of a sled dog team? Would she have sung for me, howling, beneath stars? Would she still have been this man's best friend?

Painful questions, these. Impossible questions.

Certainly I was justified in dropping them as I headed out onto the lake. There, more wolf tracks meandered — almost undulated — from side to side through a narrows at the east end of Pine Island. Soon they grew faint beneath windblown snow and I was faced with an alternate vision.

## OPEN SPACES

Bojo had known the freedoms and joys, the open spaces and wild scents, of wolf country. Here she had known the pleasure of rolling on her back among June's white blueberry blossoms, of snapping playfully at butterflies, sometimes not so playfully, and of ogling bald eagles from the cabin yard as they circled overhead. Here she had never known a cage or fence, rarely a leash. And here — as she lived and died on wolf country's terms — she inadvertently led me closer to the mystery and power of *Canis lupus*.

It was against this backdrop, this land alive with wolves, that the beauty of Bojo, her alleged assassin, and the Quetico-Superior so readily stood out.

I turned, finally, toward home.

# CHAPTER TWO
# SPRING ALONG
# SOLID BOTTOM CREEK

Home — before Bojo's and Hocoka's time, before the Wrangells, canoe expeditions and rangering — was, as I've said, a primitive cabin at 1,500 feet of elevation on Big Elbow Lake in north central Minnesota's White Earth State Forest. The forest was surrounded by the White Earth Indian Reservation, Ojibway country, just southwest of the Mississippi River's headwaters in Itasca State Park. Toward January's sunset was Tamarack Wildlife Refuge, home of bear, deer and ducks, and lots of eagles.

Unlike the 2,552-mile Mississippi to the east, however, which drained parts of 31 states while flowing south down the spine of America to the gulf of Mexico, Big Elbow's water flowed south at first from one lake to another — Little Bemidji to Many Point to Round — but then veered northwest via Otter Tail River until its union with the Red River of the North near Breckenridge on the Minnesota-North Dakota border. From there the Red flowed straight north, like most of the waters in my life, into Canada, to 300-mile-long Lake Winnipeg, eventually following the flow of Manitoba's mighty Nelson River, debauching, by northeast meanderings, into Hudson Bay at York Factory.

I could at my Big Elbow Lake cabin pluck a cone from a nearby spruce, chuck it into the lake, and send it — bon voyage — to a saltwater sea.

At Big Elbow Lake my love of nature was at its most formative stage. I was fresh from Minnesota's St. John's University where I had studied comparative religions, Zen, Christian mysticism, and the lives of hermits, hoping someday to wed Thoreau's yen for nature with a contemplative lifestyle. I was starting to hear a different drum. I began to hunger for natural beauty back then, as I do now, and en route to satisfying that hunger, I had decided to live in the woods.

## OPEN SPACES

It was an impractical calling on the heels of 16 years of Catholicism. The nuns in high school and the professors at St. John's were not to blame for my bent; they had their own lives and concerns. But they did fuel zeal and encourage listening. They didn't deaden the beat, or stop the whisperings.

This for the record.

I ended up on Big Elbow upon invitation of Father Gerald Foley, a farmboy converted to priestly calling. He was a diocesan priest who loved to canoe, no doubt one of the reasons he became director of Camp Corbett, an old fishing resort dating to the 1920s on the north shore of Big Elbow. Corbett was acquired by the Crookston Diocese in 1973. When Foley phoned me a year later he said he wanted a camp co-director, on-site caretaker, and steward, really three people in one.

Within 24 hours I was sitting on the shore of Big Elbow, my back against an overturned canoe on a warm June night, fireflies in the woods, a bright moon throwing a silvery beam across the water to my feet, ripples chuckling among rocks. Beginning the next morning, and for four years afterwards, I tromped the backwoods and logging roads of Big Elbow Lake country and canoed adjacent waters. Sure, there were camp groups to attend to, swimmers to lifeguard, six cabins to paint, canoe lessons to give, a lodge to periodically clean, and frozen waterpipes to fix, but my real mission, my undercover role, was immersion. I dove into bird, plant and tree studies while hiking around with guidebooks and binoculars. I looked for animal tracks. I studied northern Minnesota geology. I opened myself to the slow swing of seasons.

One morning I sat drifting in my canoe in a narrow lead of open water between Goat Island's shore and gray, melting lake ice. Fog was thick. I couldn't see my cabin nearby nor any other shore but Goat's. I was, in effect, in a lake level cloud. The sun was a gold orb behind the fog, lookable, its gold light saturating the fog. Suddenly a few swallows flew past my canoe, then more, then many. Soon they were flying all around me, a hundred swallows if not more, circling, dipping, diving, a swarm of swallows with me at the center. Some of the swallows flew so close — darting away from me at the last moment — I felt breaths of air against my cheek. They flew in and out of sight, fading into fog only to reappear moments later, banking and sailing, the sheen of their blue backs and white throats touched by gold. I sat mesmerized, beholden, paddle across my lap, drifting in fog the color of sun, schooling with swallows, embraced by their life, admitted. A wild pulse like a feather was brushing my senses with indelible beauty. It was a burning bush in swallow guise and I'd be damned if I paddled away.

So I didn't. The swallows, born of fog, went first.

These were days when I ricocheted from impression to impression, drinking woods and sky like a man sipping from a fire hydrant, getting doused; my senses flooded, life riding a current, gaining speed.

Although I came to understand Big Elbow country as semi- wilderness, lacking the timber wolves, grizzlies, and vast spaces of wild land to the north, it was nevertheless rich with life. Coyotes, bobcats, black bears, and the occasional rumored cougar owned the nights. Loons called at dusk and dawn. Owls hooted through summer nights, their last low hoots fusing into the sounds of wind rippled aspen leaves. Mallards and wood ducks swam silently on calm waters, some days between shores and ice floes. The startled squawks of great blue herons sometimes ripped the silence. Winging free from reedy shallows, long necks outstretched, *squawk*, the gray-blue body would bank away. Pink roses, white Canadian anemones, yellow green-headed coneflowers and fragile ladyslippers bloomed along trails. In autumn, from my desk, I watched nuthatches, chickadees, bluejays and juncos vie for leftover popcorn beneath the drooping boughs of Big Elbow's tallest spruce. Some birds stayed for winter, filling icy silences with their twitterings, yanks and wing flutterings; others, like the robins that pecked worms in the grass after a rain in the cabin's east yard, flew south, responding to the same instincts as geese, ducks and monarch butterflies. Red squirrels seemed to have more oak than wind in their veins, sleeping their long nights within bark and trunk. With nature a drip above freezing, all life seemed to be going or staying, riding wind or extending roots.

Winter brought brief days, the sound of ravens *ka-duck, kaducking* during moon-slivered sunsets, and the great stillness of subzero nights. The flush of woodstove heat against my body became a friend. I made fires of maple, black ash and birch; wood hauled, sawed, chopped and hauled again with my callousing hands. Snows fell upon snows. Drifts crept toward cabin windows. And starry silences became stark, brittle, sometimes brutally cold forcing me inside myself, winter's way.

I read voraciously in winter while hunkered down in the cabin, thirsting for knowledge, sometimes reading and trying my hand at the pen a dozen hours a day pausing only for chores and jaunts. Books included Thoreau, of course, Bradford Angier who had carved a life in the wilds of British Columbia, Annie Dillard and the wilderness visions of John Muir, Sigurd F. Olson and Aldo Leopold plus countless philosophical and theological texts. There were Plato, St. Thomas Aquinas, Thomas Merton, R.H. Blyth, Alan Watts, and Meister Eckhart. Jack Kerouac chinked the library these books built, and when I wasn't with him on the road I dipped into Ken Kesey for a magical mystery tour. Reading, like wood-gathering, was a way of life, the wake, perhaps, of academic scholarship, a dive into minds where neighbors were few. Maybe reading was a hunt for answers. Answers were not easy to find in the wind of cold nights.

≈ ≈ ≈

The cabin wasn't built for a Minnesota winter. Designed and nailed together when I was born, its 15- by 30-foot uninsulated frame construction had a concrete floor which was cool in summer, the cabin's target time, but downright ridiculous when the thermometer plummeted.

On a subzero night I could sit anywhere in the cabin, raise an arm toward the plywood ceiling, hold a hand near the floor, and feel a 20 degree to 40 degree difference. If I returned to the cabin after having been away several days, when windchills had been, say, -90 degrees, I might end up sitting next to the stove for ten hours as the cabin warmed, frost thickening on windows. It could take a day for the cabin to become warm enough for me to move about comfortably without wearing a parka. During cold snaps I awoke every two hours at night to feed the stove. At first I used an alarm clock then, trained, awoke automatically.

## Chapter Two SPRING ALONG SOLID BOTTOM CREEK

Once, half asleep, I stumbled across the cold floor toward the light switch and swung my bare foot against the sharp edge of a double bladed axe.

Big Elbow had drawn first blood.

The cabin had no running water except in summer, and then cold water only. It had an outhouse, the voracious old parlor stove, eight small windows, a braided rug, one electric outlet, and three large bookshelves made of aspen logs and gray, weathered boards.

"This is a wooden tent," a friend's son once accurately said.

It was spartan, to be sure. Thoreau would have been pleased. But its simplicity gave me a base to hike and canoe, to feel time slip by on its eternal flow, to experience ice come and go, to hear the year's first geese, and to be on hand when spring's first loons slid onto a bay's open water.

I wanted contact and close encounters of a natural kind. I wasn't disappointed.

I lived in the cabin's screened porch my first summer, sometimes falling asleep in a down sleeping bag as moonlight reflected off lakewater to dance on the porch's ceiling. One midnight a hen and ducklings swam silently by in the moonlight, silhouetted, a duckling dipping its head under water, holding it there, its butt straight up, then bobbing upright before all ducks swam out of sight. This was visual contact. But even after I moved inside the cabin it's simple design didn't sever senses from environment. Within the walls I could still hear wind in spruce, the agitated chatter of squirrels, ducks quacking in the reeds of Goat Island, and the softer rhythmic slide of waves on sand.

The sounds of my habitat, the cabin, were the sounds of its habitat, the lakeshore and forest environment.

I dreamt of lakewater lapping against moss-covered logs, or of clear water through which I saw stones, shells, darting lake zooplankton, and gracile weeds undulating in currents. No people, no action, just this.

## OPEN SPACES

Another time I saw myself paddling a canoe along a rock lakeshore. Framed by branches of a shoreline jackpine, I was silhouetted in the stern as I raised and dipped a paddle, one slow stroke after another, the scene silent, free of wind, morning fog smoking off water, me carefree and curious, happy to cruise the shoreline, content — in the innocence of that dream's hour — to move forward among natural glories.

ﾞﾞ ﾞﾞ ﾞﾞ

I became a pilgrim. I learned to walk "a la Sainte-Terre," as Thoreau put it in *Walking*, the essay called by naturalist John Burroughs "Thoreau's gospel."

Thoreau claimed he had met only one or two people who understood the art of walking, who had a genius for sauntering, a word, he explained, beautifully derived from idle people who roved Europe in the Middle Ages asking charity under pretense of going a la Sainte Terre, to the Holy Land, till the children exclaimed, "There goes a Sainte-Terrer," — a Saunterer, A Holy-Lander.

I loved to walk at Big Elbow Lake, a day lost if I didn't, especially in spring when the ground was hard with frost, the brush thin. April was best. It tightroped two seasons: winter behind it, more spring ahead. As shafts of light broke through clouds to sweep across lake surfaces, one cloud could snow while another outlined blue skies. April was a time of transition, an in-between, and the best of months to hoard sensations.

With the sun out and temperatures above freezing, water trickled from exposed roots and roofs, dribbled down slopes, dripped down needles and slid down twigs. Scents oozed from damp dirt, slush, last year's wet leaves, moist moss and wet bark — things not smelled for half a year, almost forgotten. Strawcolored grass appeared in patches on south-facing slopes. Buds tipped trees as bushes quickened toward leaf. There was a burst of catkins here, the rare shoot of green grass there. Pussy willows sprouted on purple branches above marsh grass, their puffed fuzziness silhouetted against dusk skies. Ospreys flew north on air currents above thawing waterways. Song sparrows sang on elm branches. Water lilies pushed up from lake bottoms toward light. Black bears awakened hungry and deer fattened lean limbs.

40

## Chapter Two SPRING ALONG SOLID BOTTOM CREEK

Spring was the morning of the year. Its first signs possessed power no other season could claim.

Unlike November, when a person looks straight in the face of winter and its long, cold nights, in April—woodpile running low, skin paled—one squints in the looming glare of six months of sun. Long days promise climatological freedom as skin feels warm in sunlight. The door's open. Mating instincts stir, as does wanderlust. Wanderlust peels open as romantic seas beckon and hints of possibility begin to control the mind.

Canoe trips are planned, excursions sketched, packs cleaned, paddles sanded and varnished. What little ice there is gives way. Frozen hopes thaw. Perhaps, as I came to know along Big Elbow, there is no happier, more stimulating time than spring after a long winter. There is no season with such high hope and carefree Huck Finn whimsy, no period latent with equal promise. Even a simple spring walk can lead to discovery and transformation: the walker, footloose and fancy-free, sauntering into a Holy Land.

ّ ّ ّ

There came a day, an April 4th, when I learned there are moments that are more than the sum of their parts, more — when walking — than a mere matter of moving legs on an aerobic stroll. There are moments that are stillpoints: crystallizations on the road to a new language: subtle shiftings in sensual and spiritual nuance after which life is never the same. Direction's changed.

I didn't expect this, of course, when I pocketed an orange, donned a cap and parka, shouldered my camera and daypack, then headed down a trail to Ox Bow Bay. My ultimate destination was vague, more a yearning and opening than a beeline, as much a walking inward as outward, yet this day it was wrapped in the mystery of Big Elbow's origins.

I twisted and bulled through dense brush, reaching and passing a beaver hut, footloose on the south edge of Clearwater County, T143-R38, square 31 on a Minnesota Fire Plan map, South LaPrairie Township, home of Solid Bottom Creek.

## OPEN SPACES

For a long time I thought Big Elbow was the source of Otter Tail River, that all local water flowing south then north to Hudson Bay began near my door, cone-chucking close. I knew several creeks drained into the northeast end of Big Elbow, with Solid Bottom the largest, but I inexplicably insisted on anchoring knowledge at my doorstep, going no further, ceding no ground. I simply froze geographical awareness where it felt best. Maybe I wanted Big Elbow to have heightened significance like Walden Pond, Leopold's Sand County, or Sig Olson's Listening Point. Certainly I didn't want to deal with a creek.

Too small. Annie Dillard could have her Tinker.

As I found my April stride, however, and headed toward Solid Bottom down a faint path into a maze of alder, young aspen and swamp grass, I recalled how my foolish notions about small creeks were dispelled a month earlier. I had been wrong to belittle Solid Bottom. I had gone snowshoeing alone to Lower and Upper Camp lakes to explore the creek's headwaters, and I'd discovered how Solid Bottom, despite its misnomer, drained thousands of acres of forest, marsh, bogs and uninhabited lakes like Luethi, Little Bass, Shuckhart, Big Rock and many with no names. The creek was at least eight miles long. It began in Leaf Hills, the high morainic country around Strawberry Mountain, at a 2,000-foot elevation Minnesota's second highest point. From there it flowed south past beaver huts, through beaver dams, down the middle of meadows and under branches of pine, birch, aspen, maple and oak, quenching them.

Rivulets of water fed into Solid Bottom everywhere. As the creek flowed it became a vein, ever wider, carrying the blood of the land to Big Elbow. Certainly — I was reasonable now — there were creeks and streams of all sizes draining into Big Elbow, not only on ground where I stood but to the southeast and southwest of my explorations. Big Elbow wasn't Otter Tail's source. The landscape was. It was a sponge, yes, a watershed which periodically — depending on moisture — released itself down numerous and widespread waterways. Big Elbow's source was everywhere.

It might even be said Big Elbow began in the sky.

Wasn't rainfall and snowfall, as the atmosphere's condensed and crystallized moisture, absorbed into the earth by dirt, moss, needle and duff? And didn't it pass straight through during drenchings giving rise to freshets...the veins of the land, like Solid Bottom, swelling?

It was a simple realization, perhaps, basic limnology, but those were basic days and I was a simple man. The land came alive for me, its liquid cycles apparent. Big Elbow's source and, by extension, Otter Tail's, perhaps even my own, was everywhere I looked, snowshoed and walked. There was no point in thinking otherwise. I'd been blind.

As for Solid Bottom's size, so what, really, if a person could wade across it? Who cared if this foot-deep creek merely trickled, rippling, rather than rushed, roaring? It responded to gravity as faithfully as a small river gushing down Colorado's Pike's Peak. Looked at closely, its eddies and whirlpools were the same only less forceful. Less size. Solid Bottom was a Clearwater, Red or Mississippi River on a miniature scale.

Solid Bottom even knew flood.

In June 1975, the same year rains flooded the Red River Valley, my birth country, the creek rose 16 feet in an afternoon. A man from Minnesota's Department of Natural Resources dynamited a beaver dam upstream, allowing Solid Bottom's water to fill a pond downstream; this burst another beaver dam and, in turn, a third. Poor work on the DNR's part. A wall of water rose 16 feet deep in places and swept away everything unrooted in its path: eroding, sucking, slurping, drowning, reaching Highway 113 to rise still higher, spill over the road then wash the asphalt's shoulders away.

Amazed men, ready to do manly things, stood around scratching chins. The county had another road repair project.

Roots, branches, leaves and clumps of grass, all flashflood debris, drifted past my cabin for days.

I remembered this as I stood next to Solid Bottom on my April hike, my mouth five feet above ground level, a wall of alders around me. I was arrested by bottomlands. Running from a flashflood was impossible. The thought of someone playing God with dynamite upstream and the fear of another flood grew. But I smothered it. Impossible. Besides, I couldn't see clearly through a ridiculous filter of fear.

As for the creek's name, it didn't fit. A person could leap across Solid Bottom if given a running start, at least firm footing, but firm footing didn't exist near the creek most of the time. Not in summer following rain, not in winter when snowbanks caved in beneath snowshoes among marsh grass. Brush alone — hazel, willows, alder — made walking difficult, a truth I rediscovered as the path I was on disappeared, making forward movement impossible: fitting to rabbits and moles certainly, and perhaps to white-tailed deer, but not to a biped standing five feet tall when hunched over.

I turned around, headed back toward the highway I'd crossed, and then stopped by a bend in the creek. Snowbanks melted on both sides, the air alive with tinkling sounds as water swept over moss-coated rocks. A white pine towered overhead, shading the creek's bend with boughs, sheltering the spot from the full force of spring's clutch. Here winter hung on. Here the pine toed the line between two seasons. Yet even here, as in the meadows and shaded bends upstream, time would marshall marigolds into yellow blossoms as bloodroots bloomed nearby. White petals would peel open to light followed by iris, vetch and ivy. Trout, finned extensions of the season, would swim upstream, coming, coming, searching with indomitable urge for a sheltered place to spawn.

Change seemed inevitable as earth tilted toward the sun, the great planetary wobble predictable, still untouched by people, beyond our ken.

I hiked onward, for the afternoon was young and I still wanted to poke deeper into spring's advances. I sensed a different bottom than the creek's, a solid bottom of wet and expanding response. Creek was bound to hill, water to air and light, mind to matter. As I awakened to this bedrock of being, the landscape I trod, I felt that as my understanding of Solid Bottom grew so did my awareness of Big Elbow and my presence on its shore.

## Chapter Two SPRING ALONG SOLID BOTTOM CREEK

But there was another dimension, too, a shifting of focus. I couldn't think about it, couldn't put tongue or foot on it, but I could feel it coming. I could sense the promise of a stillpoint, an epiphany, in a fluid world. For such moments I had come into the country.

It happened like this.

I reached the highway, the asphalt tentacle leading 20 miles west to Waubun or east to Itasca. I could have followed that road to Park Rapids, Minneapolis-St. Paul and, by extension, everywhere roads lead. To your place, perhaps. But the needle of my compass swung away, veering back toward woods. I found another logging road leading through scattered pines and rose bushes, and decided to hike it out. Take it back to Solid Bottom, to the end. My pace was strong now. I had foot traction, bipedal purchase. It was a free and basic pleasure after months of slipping on ice and slogging through snow.

I covered ground. Grouse caught my ear, their faint clucking and drumming intermingling with squeaky calls of red-winged blackbirds. I saw sunny spots where bedded deer had chewed cud. Hepaticas dotted slopes. A mallard exploded into flight as I neared the creek. Insects drifted like dust motes on the breeze.

A breeze which was growing. A wind which was brewing.

Clouds rolled in from the north, bunched, and grew dark. I moved through the woods hungry for wildness, as if the heat of my motion, spring-fueled, would hatch vision. I wanted life and I wanted it now.

I reached the top of a hill between small bogs where russet-colored grass nickered in wind. Dead trees — splintered at the top and leaning at odd angles, gray bones of the forest — framed distant hills. The wind grew stronger, gusting, and living trees, many budding, swayed like giant grass. It was then the wind caught my wings, lifted me up and reminded me of Washington's Pacific Coast where two winters earlier I backpacked for days along the windy edge of seastacks and foaming waves. Under great gray skies, through rain, I watched for whales offshore. I saw Nova Scotia's

45

northeast tip as I had in 1977 when a June storm beat waves against the Atlantic Coast. I could see Lake Superior's gales, feel again spray off granite slapping me in the face. There was the thrill of a river's May rapids, wind lost in the roar of whitewater, and the commingling of fear and excitement as I surfed my canoe, porpoising, on a large lake's whitecaps. Then I saw Solid Bottom, memory now a bald eagle circling back and around, lower and lower, wings outstretched, gold eye in white head cocked for view, the eagle inevitably alighting on a white pine shading Solid Bottom at the center of North America.

I had returned home, truly, this time to a room with a wide view. I could see that earth, this third stone from the sun, this livable planet among inhospitable others, was infinitely textured: furred by forest, veined with water, ribbed by mountain and ridge.

This, thanks to Solid Bottom and the forest's spring song.

What do you hear, really, when you listen to the wind? Just wind, isolated and local? Or the breath of the earth, freshened by rain forest, cooled by polar ice?

The wind sounded like the Zen smack of one hand clapping to me. Nature's voice of all time.

&#10;&#10;&#10;

Such jolts of natural beauty were quickenings of encouragement for me, and were central to what lured me to Big Elbow Lake, Solid Bottom Creek and beyond. Intellectually they were associated with the Zen and Taoism I had studied at St. John's. Zen sages had often turned to nature for spiritual solace. Unlike Christianity which is redemption oriented, locked in human history and traditionally antagonistic toward nature, Zen and Taoism were creation oriented. They found the natural world beautiful, prompting wonder. The resulting esthetic and spiritual appreciation of nature, solitude and poverty permeated Zen poetry, and in the simplicity of Zen masters I saw a way to relate, in part, to cabin living and the natural world.

Chapter Two SPRING ALONG SOLID BOTTOM CREEK

*Yield to the willow,* Basho admonished in a poem,

*All the loathing*

*All the desire of your heart.*

I was especially attracted to the Zen concepts of *fuga, sabi* and *wabi* as outlined in the work of D. T. Suzuki. *Fuga,* the spirit of eternal aloneness, literally meant "refinement of life," the chaste enjoyment of life in nature. *Fuga* originated when a person identified with the creative, artistic spirit of nature. Basho, the founder of Japanese haiku, said that whoever cherishes this identification accepts nature and becomes a friend of the four seasons.

The essence of *fuga* as I aspired to it at Big Elbow and, to some extent, afterwards, lay in the cultivation of *sabi* and *wabi,* two funny-sounding words with great spiritual importance. *Sabi* meant tranquility, inner peace, serenity and similar moods. It implied austerity and material simplicity. Beauty was seen in age, imperfection, and natural objects suggesting the paradox of eternity in the finite world. In a sense, *sabi,* like *fuga* referred to eternal aloneness: the smallness and mystery we feel in the great void of vast spaces, when looking up at stars, an awe rooted in impressions from objects like the meadow of dead trees I knew along Solid Bottom.

The meanings of *sabi* and *wabi* became clearer as I viewed them in light of their origins in the Japanese tea ceremony. The tea masters tried to avoid any stain of commercialism during their ceremonies by using lichens, stones, mosses, weathered wood and old tree stumps to decorate gardens surrounding their tea rooms or "sukiyas" — abodes of vacancy, essentially meditation huts. Even paths of flat stones leading to the tea rooms through gardens of ferns and flowers held spiritual significance as passages to self-illumination. They were portals between sacred chambers and the milieu of the "outside world," thus — like a church's vestibule — enhancing the atmosphere of contemplation within the tea room itself.

The tea rooms were often mere ten-foot square huts in the wilds of mountainsides or along rivers. They were built of tied-together grasses which in time, and as designed, would organically dissolve into the natural cycle of decay, bowing to entropy. What few things there were inside the huts suggested monastic simplicity. A three-foot high door was sometimes set into one wall which persons of all distinctions entered by stooping, thus manifesting a humble relationship to nature.

Rikyu, one of the greatest Zen masters, went so far as to design a hut and garden tricking visitors into spiritual response. As the story has been handed down, when Rikyu's guests arrived for the hut-warming, the tea room's first use, they were surprised to find large evergreens planted so as to obstruct the view of the sea.

They were puzzled.

Later, when the time came for the guests to enter the tea rooms, they walked single file to a stone water basin to rinse their mouths and wash their hands, symbolic physical and mental cleansing. Only as they stooped to scoop water were they able to see the shimmering sea in the distance through an opening in the trees. In an intuitive instant they realized the relationship between the dipperful of water in their hands and the ocean beyond them, between their individual self and the Great Spirit, the *Tao* they called it, permeating all things. Thus, through natural beauty, they found their place in the universe, their correct relationship with the infinite.

Once everyone was sitting quietly in the tea room, the ceremony's host usually prepared tea for his guests in silence. No one spoke. They listened to the simmering tea, the wind in trees outside, the flowing water of a nearby stream, or they simply sat — the gift of presence — in the soft hush, of windless moments. Senses arrived at a stillpoint in natural sounds. They were put to rest. Tea was served in a small bowl or handleless cup and drunk in one shot.

Afterwards everyone remained silent.

No ideas nagged the mind. No financial anxiety clouded the soul. Troubles were forgotten. There was, in theory at least, nothing but the Tao manifested in a jeweled string of natural changes. This quieting and shifting of the mind allowed for *sunyata*, an emptiness that, ironically, opened to fullness. As the normal dams of narrow awareness and petty concerns gave way, like the blasted and burst beaver dams of Solid Bottom, the droplet of self slid toward the sea.

Union was the goal. It could happen to anyone at any time. All it needed was the right stimulus and a crack in the mental wall.

In time, *sabi* — which arose from the quietude of the tea ceremony, and the esthetic impact of natural sensations — referred specifically to the objects and natural events evoking the inner equanimity: rocks, flowers, wind, sound of flowing water, and moonlight on lonely nights.

*I sat in the shadows,* Chiyo wrote,

*And bequeathed the chamber to the bright full moon.*

Another time:

*Behind me*

*I cast all my cares —*

*The summer moon!*

Even things savoring of rustic unpretentiousness, like old cabins tucked in woods, a hiking staff leaning against a tree, or a door made from recycled barn boards, could set off *sabi*. Whatever spurred the poetic sense. Whatever awoke appreciation of beauty.

I didn't, of course, exercise my sense of *sabi* at Big Elbow by walking around pig-tailed in a kimono while spouting Zen koans. But I recognized *sabi* in the simplicity of my cabin, which I fancied a northwoods *sukiya*, and in night winds dancing on star-studded water, in autumn aspens flaming gold beneath October suns, in old wagon wheels in rural gardens, in the glee of a child's eye while playing in a park, and in the glimmer of northern lights as coyotes howled from Leaf Hills headwatering Solid Bottom.

*Wabi*, in turn, was the contemplative lifestyle lived in touch with these things, which hungered for them, made room for them in the heart, longing. *Wabi* was living in accord with the flow, the *Te*, of nature. But there was an element of poverty in *wabi* that was foreign to western minds. It was a deliberate simplicity, a cultivation of material nakedness, an abandonment of possessions that separated — often in subtle ways — the mind from natural sensation.

There was a story in the annals of Zen, for example, of a hermit named Kyo-yu who owned nothing. He even drank water from his hand. Seeing this, someone gave him a bowl made of gourd. One day he hung it on the branch of a tree where wind made it bang about and rattle noisily, marring silence. Kyo-yu threw the gourd away and drank water with his hand as before.

Touching water. Wind silence.

I recalled Kyo-yu sometimes when I dipped my hands into Big Elbow for a drink, once reaching my fingers into the flashing silver shards of moonlight itself, my fingers silhouetted, disappearing into night light.

"Stated in terms of practical everyday life," Suzuki explained, *wabi* was "to be satisfied with a little hut, a room [with] two or three 'tatami' (mats), like the log [sic] cabin of Thoreau, and with a dish of vegetables picked in the neighboring fields, and perhaps to be listening to the pattering of a gentle spring rainfall."

Poverty in the Zen scheme of things meant closeness to nature. By not having running water I was forced to fetch it much of the time in the lake. My heat didn't come from adjusting a thermostat but, rather, by going into woods, choosing suitable trees and cutting them, splitting chunks, eventually bringing the heart of the forest into my home where it was consumed by fire so that I might live. Technological convenience, an armor bought with money, didn't — among Zen masters and on my most barebone days — insulate the mind's poetic sensibilities from the dynamics of nature.

Which, of course, in this early hour, is what I wanted most.

# Chapter Two SPRING ALONG SOLID BOTTOM CREEK

Poverty in *wabi* was never indigence, never true material insufficiency and wretchedness. It wasn't a lifestyle of someone beaten down by economic fate or bad luck. As Suzuki emphasized, there was always an active principle of esthetics in *wabi*, a sustaining by "the presence of something of the highest value, above time and social position." A focusing on the Great Spirit, perhaps? Settling for nothing less? Letting nothing get in the way? *Wabi* was an embrace of this aspiration and, at least for me in the wake of a religious education, a recognition — confirmed by comparing spiritual disciplines — that we seem to stand alone before God. It is an isolation counterpoising union. We're afraid sometimes, and we tremble, while at other times we are blessed with an awe that lifts us up, sparks wonder, and leaves us with deeper love and compassion for life.

It is a compassion not just for humankind but for all sentient life — the wolves, the bears, the bees — all of us caught up in the cosmic striving of evolution.

When I was a boy roaming the fields and water-filled ditches of the Red River Valley, I shot songbirds and knifed gophers like my playmates. I never felt good doing this but no one stood by to tell me killing harmless creatures, especially if I didn't eat them, was wrong. One day I shot a sparrow with my B-B gun, hitting it in the head, chipping its beak off. The sparrow fell from its perch. I picked it up. It was still alive, gasping for air, silent in its pain. In the clarity of that moment I felt the wrong I had done. For an instant I became that bird. I stopped casual hunting then and now can see that what I felt was compassion born of identification. It was a leap of awareness that went beyond my skin to encompass a sparrow, harmless and free, that met its end as the targeted plaything of a boy's ignorance.

This sense of identification came back to me in full force one night at Big Elbow. I was sitting alone in the cabin, writing in a journal, and listening to *In Search of the Lost Chord* by the Moody Blues. At one point in the music I put my pen down to let myself float with the music, really *listen* to the orchestral notes as they swelled in the cabin's silence. Inexplicably, I felt a shiver rush up my spine to the back of my head and then spread throughout my body. It was a wave of feeling that took possession of me, and as I sat there living my little life, meager in a material world, the boundaries circumscribing my sense of self seemed to melt away and I felt part of everything — the music, the cabin, the energy of night. I began to drift in a sensual sea. Everything seemed simultaneously circumference and center of everything. The walls of division between things were down. A single energy, more feeling than thought, flowed through the superficial diversity of life while the diversity — the fish, birds, deer, moon, water, sun, myself — were manifestations of the single energy.

And I felt love. God, I felt love.

Compassion was a part of it. Outside was inside. Inside: outside. There was one unifying nature with no true separation.

This was one of the strongest, most real, most joyous moments of my life.

The feeling stayed with me for several days. Whatever I did, wherever I went, the sensation of unity was constant.

Certainly my understanding of these things was colored by the language of theological academia and the spiritual metaphysics I had studied. It was a language, back then fresh on my tongue. In time my language would change, alter shape and take on new dimensions as age and experience came to bear. But on Big Elbow I used what tools I had to read what signs I saw.

As for *wabi*, rooted in *fuga's* sense of eternal aloneness found in wind and the lonely places of the natural world, wrapped in nature's intricacies, I related to it as best I could. I was an American, not an Oriental, but the concept was nevertheless cross-culturally intriguing. If it meant, as it did, to be fully awake, to be unencumbered by materialism in order to be sensually impressionable, so be it. Foolish or not, I was game. *Wabi* wasn't a running from life and nature but a turning toward it.

It was finding and cherishing the lost chord.

❧ ❧ ❧

This, then, was part of the ideology, part of a young man's peculiar musings and gropings, I brought back with me to my Big Elbow Lake cabin after exploring Solid Bottom. Ironies were everywhere. There was nothing solid about Zen. If the Zen way, I figured, incorporated such amorphous concepts as *sabi* and *wabi* with simplicity and wisdom as backup, then they were two sides of a coin which, flipped, fell through fingers into the waters of the world.

I was bushed when I reached the cabin: tired but elated, hungry but satisfied. It had been a good day, this April 4th, the ground hard with frost, the brush thin.

The afternoon's clouds were gone, the sun setting. I chiseled through lake ice to fetch fresh water, split kindling for a new fire in the woodstove, and brewed hot coffee. *"What is the secret of spiritual awakening?"* a Zen monk once asked his master. *"Hauling water, chopping wood"* came the reply. Yes, forget the metaphysics. Directness is all. Raven calls flecked silence in the cold air as the sun's last rays brushed the highest branches of Goat Island's trees with shell pink. I felt good, and in the gathering twilight — after reading a letter from Dan Metz suggesting we go to Alaska, to true wilderness — I sat next to the woodstove to rest my legs and absorb the stove's radiant warmth.

And I listened.

To the song.

To the silence, my aloneness and my restless heart.

To the hope of joyful days.

To the promise of more adventures.

To the whispers I'd first heard along the rivers of boyhood, in the woods of St. John's, and that still called to me now as I sailed night winds.

For good reason I'd grown fascinated with Solid Bottom. It was the song's latest note, a bridge between past and future. Listen to me, it urged. I didn't know where the song led. I didn't have a clue to what cabins I might someday call home, what trails I'd trek, rivers I'd run, or what wilderness I'd open my heart open to. But when it came to the song, when it came to the uncanny call I now recognize as my own, I hadn't — on Big Elbow Lake near Solid Bottom Creek in White Earth State Forest — failed, inevitably, to listen.

# WRESTLING WITH
# THE WRANGELLS

I felt like I needed a Colt .45 for the first time in my life when I saw the fresh eight-inch-wide grizzly track in mud along McCarthy Creek in south central Alaska's Wrangell Mountains. The claw marks of the grizzly track were an inch or two in front of the bear's front paw print. I hadn't hiked in grizzly country before where people are not at the top of the food chain, yet I knew for a fact from readings and talks that grizzlies occasionally kill and eat people, gobble them down and scat 'em out.

They've done it to hunters who had the misfortune of shooting a grizzly, wounding it, then going into the brush to look for it, the last looking they ever did, the grizz waiting with a bad temper. They've killed women who were menstruating while camping, the smell luring the bear, as happened a while back in Glacier National Park. And they've killed and eaten at least one photographer who sneaked too close for a shot of ma and cubs, his film later telling the story up to impact.

So I had reason to feel caution along McCarthy Creek in 1978. There was ground for fear. To get a sense of scale, I put my hand crossways in the paw print: eight inches from fingertips to upper wrist.

I stood up and adjusted my backpack. I looked around me in the bushes. I adjusted my cap and wiped sweat from my forehead. Hmmm. There was a large grizzly in the neighborhood. Perfect, I thought to myself, a little sarcastically. Just perfect. It was the first evening of a climb up Nikolai Peak and a local had been around to leave sign. The bear and its brethren would be with us now, every hour, and although we might not hear grizz (the rushing waters of McCarthy Creek took care of that), and although we might not see the lords of the Wrangell Mountains, they would be on our minds and in our hearts if not — God forbid — charging right at us.

# OPEN SPACES

With me was Dan Metz, the wildlife illustrator from Delano, Minnesota, whose letter I had read on Big Elbow Lake and with whom I had tracked wolves near Devil's Cascade in the Boundary Waters. With us was Karl Ludescher, also of Minnesota. While driving my new Ford F-150 pickup on the infamous McCarthy Road to begin our hike, Dan and I had caught up to Karl, a friend of Dan's, by accident. Karl, unrecognized, was driving a jeep in front of us and going too slow for Dan's eager taste.

"Get off the road, you old lady!" Dan, driving, had said. "Git." Dan finally passed the jeep, recognized Karl, then almost ruined the pickup's transmission by braking in second gear, forgetting about, oh yeah, the clutch.

We told Karl we were going to climb Nikolai, Would he like to come, and he did.

As I thought about the bear track, perhaps a half-day old, Dan and Karl debated the merits of bear bells. Theoretically, the tinkling of bells warn bears that people are approaching, hence they're not caught off-guard and startled into attack, sort of the way a person swings around instinctively to strike when spooked from behind.

Karl wanted to use the bells. Dan said no way. He had come to Alaska to photograph bears, not frighten them away.

I had to side with Dan. We had planned our two-month Alaskan trip together, shared expenses, and driven together from Minnesota to Seattle, Washington, where we boarded a ferry north up the wild coastline of British Columbia's Inside Passage. From the ferry's terminus at Haines, Alaska, we had driven across the northwestern hinterlands of Yukon Territory, re-entered Alaska, driven to Anchorage, east to the Wrangells, back to Anchorage, then back to the Wrangells. This was no time to abandon Dan, to disagree with his philosophy about bear bells. I knew Dan used photographs for the basis of his scratchboard artwork and oil paintings.

If Dan wasn't getting good photos, he wasn't happy.

"Do you think the bear might come by tonight?" I asked him. I knew he had studied animal tracks and habits more than I had. He was especially interested in large mammals, like grizz.

"If it does," he said, echoing my suspicions, "there's nothing we can do, so there's no sense in worrying."

It was impossible not to be a little worried later that night — it was dark — as we bivouacked in an old shack near the mouth of Nikolai Creek. A corner of the shack hung out over the creek, its bank washed away. The shack's plywood door was held shut by wrapping a wire around a nail. Tar paper on the inside walls was ripped and scattered. An old woodstove, no chimney, was sitting in an equally old washbasin half-filled with rainwater which had leaked through the roof. We would have put my dome tent up outside but couldn't find a clearing. We also would have hung our food packs in a tree except the trees were too small. Instead we brought our food inside the shack. Big mistake.

We feared a bear smelling our food and paying us a visit. Sure enough, sometime in the wee hours of that short August night an animal started moaning and clawing at the shack's corner.

It woke us up.

I'd been sleeping deeply, weary from the day's hike, and when I awoke I thought I was in Minnesota. Somebody was knocking at the door. No, something was moaning and clawing at the wall. My eyes strained to see in the darkness. When I realized where I was and what was happening I remembered the horror film *The Night of the Grizzly*. We had set the stage for a sequel. If that was a grizzly we heard, it would be able to rip off the door, amble in, freak out from the close proximity to people, and start slashing the three of us packed in the small shack.

I cursed Canadian Customs under my breath. At the border north of Haines, and adhering to government policy, they hadn't allowed handguns across the border. Because we had to cross Canada to get back in Alaska, Dan was forced to mail his Colt .45 back to Minnesota, no matter the bear horror stories the Haines gun dealer had told us...the bicyclist who was charged, knocked down, and mauled...the guy who, one night, fought off a grizzly with an axe. The gun had to go. Not only was it the law but Canadian officials had a pet peeve about Americans breaking it. They were liable to confiscate my pickup and all our camping gear, putting an up-front finale to our Alaska trip in the bargain.

So be it. I damned Canadian Customs anyhow.

Dan started shouting at the animal to go away.

"Get outta here! Vamoose! Get!"

Karl, sleeping next to me, sat up.

"Oh my God. A grizz. Holy shit." He was practically hyperventilating. "Oh my God."

Dan was lying on a rotting cot close to the door. I could hear him in the darkness on the other side of a flimsy partition. Someone lit a match for a light.

"Well," Dan said with a hint of final humor in his voice, "if we're going to bite the dust I may as well go down in style."

With that he put on his red Beechnut chewing tobacco cap, lay back on his cot, and crossed his arms on his chest.

The matchlight went out.

I smiled to myself as I lay helpless in my sleeping bag and thought, momentarily mind you, about Dan. He had cached a copy of Ernest Hemingway's *The Green Hills of Africa* beneath his makeshift pillow. He had read part of it during dinner, and I knew — from previous remarks — how much he admired Hemingway. He thought the great writer, who killed himself in the end, had guts. I figured Dan might even view himself as the Hemingway of the wildlife art world. If so, getting killed by a grizzly in some of Alaska's most spectacular mountains was a good way for Dan to go. As the final brush stroke on the painting of Dan's days, it had flair, color and class. Better, anyhow, than getting smacked by a pizza truck or choking on a fish bone in Delano. But did it have to happen now, with me, a footnote in Metz's brief biography, as second dish in the back room?

Adrenalin surged through my body as the clawing increased. We had to do something. Karl said he had firecrackers: "Sometimes they work to frighten bears.? I switched on my compact Mallory flashlight. Karl rummaged through the pockets of his pack until he found a Black Cat then handed it to Dan. What the hell. He lit the firecracker and tossed it toward the shack's corner, our only spark of defense arcing through the night. I hoped for an ear-hurting bang on the lines of an explosion. Instead — pop! The Cat's gunpowder cracked off with all the intensity of a kid's backyard cap gun.

Still, Lady Luck was with us. The animal stopped its clawing, walked around the back of the cabin, and shuffled away.

&ə &ə &ə

I took a good look at the outside of the shack the following morning. Although there were no fresh tracks or telltale claw marks at the corner where we had heard the prowler, the shack's opposite corner had claw marks as high as a tall man could reach.

In the past, a bear had used the shack as a scratching post, a place where it could stand up on its hind legs and do a little territorial stretching. Judging from the differently weathered claw marks, the bear had come around often. I didn't feel like a guest in its territory, and I knew there was a good chance we'd have the honor to meet as Dan, Karl and I — packs on back — headed up Nikolai Creek.

If we wanted wild country, and we did, we couldn't really do better. The Wrangell-St. Elias Mountains, then proposed as America's largest national park and preserve, had long been called the "Crown Jewels" of Alaska. Their 12 million acres stretch 170 miles north from Icy and Yakutat bays on the Gulf of Alaska to the southeast end of the Alaska Range near Nabesna (pop. 25), Nabesna River, the Tetlin Lowlands, and the village of Slana. The area is bound on the west by 235 miles of the Copper River (known as *Atna* to the natives) and 130 miles to the east by Canada's Kluane National Park and the eastern side of the St. Elias Mountains, Yukon Territory.

This is big mountain country: part of the western North America cordillera. Although most of the Wrangells are geologically young, uplifted in the last ten million years, they and the St. Elias Mountains have the greatest range of peaks over 14,000 feet in North America. Included are six of the continent's 10 highest summits. There is ice clad Mount Bona, Mount Blackburn and Mount Sanford, all over 16,000 feet. Mount St. Elias, at 18,008 feet, is the second highest peak in the United States. Even higher is Mount Logan: at 19,850 feet it's the second highest peak on the continent. Added to this mountain grandeur are the mile-high cliffs of Chitistone Canyon and Nizina River, larger than those in Yosemite and Zion national parks. Three mountain ranges actually come together here with the Chugach Mountains abutting the Wrangell and St. Elias ranges. For obvious reasons the park and preserve proposal — as submitted to Congress — described the region as having the greatest expanse of valleys, deep canyons and towering mountains in all of North America.

"It is my personal view," Earnest Gruening, the Alaska governor who first proposed the area for national park status, said, "that from the standpoint of scenic beauty, it is the finest region in Alaska."

This is especially true for anyone who likes ice. Some of the world's largest, longest and most active glaciers are found here. Malaspina Glacier is larger than Rhode Island. Nabesna Glacier, 75 miles long, begins on the slopes of volcanically active Mount Wrangell (14,163 feet), called *Kah-Una-Lita*, the Smoke Mountain, by the Copper River Indians because of the dusting of ash it periodically spread across the Copper River Valley. The Barnard Glacier, 30 miles long, begins in the snows of Mount Natazlat (13,440 feet) and ends in the Chitina Valley. In all, the Wrangell-St. Elias Mountains have 22 major glacial systems encompassing about 200 named and unnamed glaciers. It's a vast network of stationary or slowly moving icefields, looking from the air like smooth highways with white, gray and black parallel bands.

## Chapter Three WRESTLING WITH THE WRANGELLS

Close-up, it is a different story.

Almost surprisingly, given the area's wealth of inhospitable ice, the Wrangells teem with wildlife typical of Alaska: moose, bear (black and brown/grizzly), wolves, Dall sheep (about 10,000 in 1978), mountain goats, wolverines, red fox and coyotes. Caribou from three herds — the Chisana (1,000-2,000), Mentasta (2,000- 3,000) and Nelchina (a larger, fluctuating population) — roam slopes. There are even two herds of introduced bison (introduced in 1950 and 1963-64, totaling about 130 in 1978). Waterways and lakes have salmon, grayling, ling cod and trout. Down at Yakutat Bay, where mountains meet the sea, there are dolphins, killer whales, sea otter, sea lions and seals.

Nobody, in 1978, argued that the Wrangell-St. Elias Mountains were anything but a wild and healthy land.

Hunters loved it and took aim at it. Thirty percent of Alaska's sheep "harvest," for example, came from the Wrangells which was judged the best habitat for trophy sheep in the state. So when it came to the area being proposed as a national park and preserve, with the park portion of 8,147,000 acres being closed to sport hunting, well, as the 50 hunting guides that worked the area said, the feds had another thought coming.

It was wildlife, after all, that first lured Eyak Indians and Ugalakmiut and Tatitlek Eskimos to the Wrangells in the first place 8,000 to 10,000 years ago, their ancestors having crossed the Bering Strait. Other natives, the Tlingit Indians of coastal Yakutat Bay, and the Athabascan and Nabesna Indians of the interior and northern ranges of the Wrangells, also made the region their home. In their wake, when the Wrangells became part of Russia's Tsarist Empire, came Russian explorers like Vitus Bering, and hunters, hardy men who named the mountain range after fellow fron-tiersman-explorer Baron F. von Wrangell. In 1819 a Russian trader by the name of Klimowski built a trading post near Chitina on the Copper River, on the west side of the Wrangells, but he, too, like the rest of the Russians, knew he was a long way from home. He left the land to those who had the gall to come.

OPEN SPACES

Although hunting and exploration lured Indians, Eskimos and Russians to the Wrangells in the dawn of history, it was ore — silver, gold and especially, copper (*chiti*, the Indians called it) — that brought Americans, Canadians and Europeans prospecting for the economic light-of-day. The influx was spearheaded in 1885 by Lieutenant Henry T. Allen who ventured up the Copper River from the Gulf of Alaska and who, on his way to the Alaska Range, explored the Chitina River eastward clear to the camp of Nicolai, an Indian leader based near today's village of McCarthy and the Chitistone River, the latter named, Allen reported, "on account of the copper ore found by the Natives near it."

Allen went on to explore more of the Copper River basin and publish the region's first map, but his run-in with Nicolai near Chitistone turned out to be, for white people and business moguls down south, particularly productive.

As Gerald Wright, Gil Mull and George Herben explain it in Alaska Geographic's *Wrangell-St. Elias: International Mountain Wilderness,* mineral exploration of the Copper and Chitina rivers sprang forward shortly after nearby Yukon's Klondike gold rush of 1896. A stream of prospectors undauntedly and unabashedly crept throughout the land. Specks — to an eagle's eye — on rock. By 1901, Captain W.R. Abercrombie reported to Congress that the entire Copper River Valley was as well-known "as that of any mining district in Montana."

Abercrombie had reason to know. Three years earlier he had led the Copper River Exploring Expedition into the region, bearing with him two geologists working for the U.S. Geological Survey. While they mapped the Wrangells, an equally important map — from none other than Nicolai — pointed the way to an 1899 mine near Nizina River, not far from Chitistone.

Mining frenzy broke loose.

Bonanza Ridge was discovered within a year thanks to prospectors like Jack Smith and Clarence Warner. Soon, Jumbo Mine near McCarthy joined the growing network of ridges and mines, attracting thousands of men, a railroad, and a boom-then-bust prosperity. The $23 million railroad, financed by the Guggenheim-Morgan syndicate, was built by 1911, connecting what became the Kennecott Copper Company mines with coastal Cordova 196 miles southwest. The Kennecott mines, connected by tunnels, were extremely successful, yielding 10,000 to 20,000 tons of copper annually. From 1913 to 1938 the Bonanza Ridge alone produced over $300 million in copper and silver.

Total take: one billion pounds of copper, 9.7 million ounces of silver.

Inger Jensen Ricci, in *Childhood Memories of Kennecott*, recalls what it was like to live in the Kennecott Mine-McCarthy area during its heyday. Born in Kennecott in 1918, and living there 14 years, she says the mine's "camp" near the mill, almost five miles north of McCarthy, had a population of 300 people. There were houses, stores, offices, a school, hospital, community hall, machine shop, power plant, and a wooden tennis court built on the mountainside. There was Sunday school, ski trips, Saturday night dances, a masquerade ball on New Year's Eve, May Day dances, and Fourth of July celebrations. Tourist trains arrived in summer; the children made bouquets of wildflowers and collected copper nuggets to sell to the sightseers. Autumn was the season for picking berries: cranberries, currants and mossberries which Ricci's mother used for pies and jellies. Small black bears were seen often "but were more frightened than we. Now and then a brown bear appeared." In winter, avalanches blocked the train from Cordova. People guessed how long it would take to clear the tracks so the train could reach Kennecott.

One time: three months.

McCarthy, meanwhile, grew on the southern fringe of Kennecott. It had houses, stores, a school, two restaurants, several bars and a "red light district." Naughty ladies. Hungry miners.

"McCarthy," Ricci explains, "was off limits to us, as children, unless adults accompanied us there. At McCarthy the miners spent their hard earned wages in a very short time..."

Ricci remembered her girlhood days at Kennecott with great fondness, yet all wasn't well both above and below the ground. Labor disputes rippled through ranks of workers, there were a few natural disasters, and the normally fluctuating price of copper took a decisive plunge in the early 1930s. The mines finally closed in 1938 during a labor strike. Workers and managers left as fast as they could as McCarthy, where the population had approached 1,000 people, quickly became a ghost town.

Almost.

Fred G. Payton of Billings, Montana, lived in McCarthy throughout the summer of 1959 while helping map the McCarthy quadrangle for the U.S. Geological Survey. Payton roamed around the old houses during his free time and noticed how everyone had left rapidly. Some houses still contained personal belongings. Old letters dated back to the 1930s. Payton also looked over rock core sample records in the mine buildings and, a prospector at heart, searched nearby streams for gold and copper nuggets, eventually finding a 30 pound copper nugget in McCarthy Creek.

Years later, however, it was the ghostly atmosphere of McCarthy that Payton remembered most.

"Outside people hadn't discovered [McCarthy]," he wrote the editor of *Alaska* magazine, "and its location was far away from the military bases."

This changed as people trickled in: the hardcore homesteaders, the trappers, the back-to-the-landers of the late 1960s and early 1970s, the never surrender drifters and prospectors, and the hunters who came but stayed put, shot by Wrangells beauty. By the time Dan, Karl and I first set foot in McCarthy, however, it still remained a wilderness outpost in the truest sense of the word. Its stable population was 12, buildings were few and old, and its dirt streets led off into the Wrangell foothills.

But they didn't go far.

Electricity, where it existed, was self-generated. Water came from creeks. There was no television. The only radio station was broadcast from Glennallen a hundred miles west, its missionary programming — religious songs and fundamentalist Bible preaching — grating on more than a few McCarthyite nerves.

"How'd you get here?" we were asked when we entered McCarthy, and for good reason. It was hard to get there. You either flew in at considerable expense or, like us, drove the 63-mile McCarthy Road — mistakenly called a highway on maps — east from Chitina (pop. 50) on the Copper River. The road, paralleling the Chitina River Valley, began fine enough with a new multi-million dollar bridge more suited to Atlanta than Alaska, but a short way down the road a sign warned the rest of the road wasn't maintained by the state of Alaska. Travel was at one's own risk.

Worse, perhaps, when it came to remote road courage, were the road warrior horror stories of people paying hundreds of dollars to have their vehicle towed from some godforsaken shoulder of the McCarthy Road back to the "civilization" of Chitina or Glennallen for repairs.

Let's see now, a mechanic might say. That'll be $700 not counting the transmission. Depending, of course, on whether we can get the parts from Anchorage. If not, Juneau maybe. That could take a week.

The McCarthy Road was part of the original railroad bed connecting Kennecott Mine with Cordova. Rails and ties were simply removed, either salvaged as in the 1940s, or tossed in the ditch. (No, I argued with Dan, I will not haul a two hundred pound railroad tie back to Minnesota in the back of my pickup. He wanted it for a fireplace mantle. Good idea, but I was thinking of the many nights ahead we'd need to sleep in the back of the truck, dealing with a hewn piece of oil-preserved lumber heavier and less cuddly than a third person.) The McCarthy Road's bridges, like the single-lane bridge over the 200-foot Kuskulana River Gorge, were the old railroad trestles. There were no railings: nothing to bounce off before an accidental plunge. Planking was nailed down for tires, a precarious innovation for drivers not knowing exactly where their tires were. Overall, for visitors accustomed to smooth rides on two-lane asphalt roads, driving to McCarthy from Chitina was a jostled nightmare of wash-outs, chuckholes and at least one good highwire act.

OPEN SPACES

We averaged 15 miles per hour covering the road's 63 miles.

ða ða ða

The road was rough but the real surprise lay on the west bank of Kennicott
River where the road came to a dead end. The bridge that had led to
McCarthy on the other side of the river was gone. We looked at our maps;
the topographics showed a bridge. We looked at the river. We looked at the
cluster of buildings called McCarthy, at the old Kennecott Mine ruins
upriver, and at distant Regal Mountain.

Yep, we're in the right place.

Only later did we hear about the bridge fiasco.

Apparently in 1973 a local contractor was paid approximately $20,000 to
build a log bridge across the glacial Kennicott, replacing in effect the
bygone railroad trestle. Unknown to the 1973 contractor, however, or at
least unknown to the bridge's financiers, there was a lake by the fitting
name of Hidden eight miles up the Kennicott at the base of Kennicott
Glacier. Hidden was full to the brim. Known to scientists as a jokulhlaup
or self-dumping glacial lake, Hidden's normal drainage would periodically
be dammed by ice and gravel, the lake's level would rise, volume would
swell, and the lake, as in 1974, would suddenly drain, dump, down a 10-
mile long subglacial channel to create a flashflood downstream.

The 1974 flood took McCarthy's new bridge out in one fell swoop. Cars
and trucks trapped in McCarthy were suddenly up for sale at true bargain
prices. They weren't going anywhere.

The next year the bridge's contractor was paid another handsome sum to
remove most of the ruined bridge's remains.

McCarthy, we discovered, solved its access problem with a handtram: a
wooden seat suspended by pulley from an iron cable stretching across the
river. The seat's passenger, his feet dangling above the churning river,
pulled himself with nylon ropes from bank to bank, perhaps with help from

companions on shore. River water splashed on the seat when the Kennicott was high, like at mid day from sunshine-melted glacier runoff; otherwise one rolled dry across the river in full view of glaciers, moraines and snow-clad mountain peaks — the Rime-Atna-Parka Wall, with its Stairway Icefall — to the north.

The handtram, of course, weeded out the weak of heart and the Winnebago crowd which suited the most independent of local tastes just fine. McCarthy had no traffic problem. It's air was clear. Polyester folk didn't mill around snapping photos, asking stupid questions, or going ga-ga over store window gewgaws and gimcracks.

The prescription was simple. Visitors arrived at McCarthy by bush plane or handtram, having purpose, or they didn't arrive at all.

Although our hike from McCarthy to Nikolai began with the handtram, it was the last thing on our minds as we left the village and bushwhacked up the east bank of McCarthy Creek. All the mining road bridges, shown on our U.S. Geological Survey maps, were, like the Kennicott bridge, washed out. Hence we had to choose between fording swift McCarthy Creek four times or bushwhacking.

We chose the bush.

"Be sure to climb up over the shale bank on the east side of the creek," an old timer told us the night before in the dim kerosene light of the McCarthy Lodge. "There's a marked trail that goes on up over, then continue to a shack on Nikolai Creek."

It was apparent when we reached the cutbank that our advisor's idea of a marked trail was drastically different from ours. We felt our way up an animal trail through raspberry thickets and brush, then climbed on our hands and knees up a steep slope to the top of the cutbank. There thick spruce grew from patches of green-gold moss sprinkled with crowberries. Branches scratched my hands, drawing blood; they knocked my glasses from my face, my hat from my head, and managed to undo my daypack strapped to the top of my tourpack.

Sweat blurred our vision as McCarthy Creek growled in small but rocky gorges to our left.

We continued over the cutbank, then down through knee-deep moss and thick foliage to the creekbed and mining road. Again the road disappeared into the creek — no bridge — and we shouldered back into brush. We literally pushed on, whipped by branches as we twisted, cut by briars as we crouched, stopping once, frustrated, to try crossing the creek on a make-shift bridge of scrounged creekbank logs. No way. "Damn it!" Karl hollered when he slipped and scraped his elbow. Gnats buzzed my eyes and mouth, and bit at the nape of my neck.

The way was hard, emotions thin, as we pushed on through more miles of brush. Animal trails provided brief respite, better travel, before disappearing God knows where. It was then we saw the eight-inch-wide grizzly track, our senses suddenly keen. We had an easy hike down a long gravel bar — good grizz country, I thought — and a final stretch down an old ore-dreamer's road chest high with bushes. Finally, six hours from McCarthy, we reached Nikolai Creek, built a log-and-boulder footbridge across it, and stepped up to our grizzly-scratched shack.

ᘓ ᘓ ᘓ

The hike up Nikolai Creek to Nikolai Peak from the shack under sunny skies the next morning began on another abandoned mining road ending above the 2,500-foot timberline. Moose and bear tracks punctuated our route as rock slopes, grassy meadows, waterfalls, distant ravines and foothills came into view. Arctic ground squirrels squealed and fled from us before they dove into dens and crannies. Golden eagles rode silent air currents above cinnamon- brown ridges. We reached an abandoned mine shortly after noon, a reminder that the lure of wealth brought men and machines to the Wrangells long before us, and perhaps would again depending on the Alaska National Interest Lands legislation, being considered at that time in Congress.

We snacked and napped at the mine. Buffeted by wind yet warmed by sunshine, I lay on a foam pad on a south-facing slope, occasionally opening my eyes to reach for more dried apricots, prunes or a generous swig of Dan's lime-flavored Wyler's drink. Karl wanted to continue climbing. Dan didn't care. I was content to rest in the sun, ramble packless among foothills at twilight, or maybe join Karl, an amateur geologist, on a hunt for mine-discarded malachite.

When Karl acquiesced, the mine was home for the night.

Morning brought gray overcast and drizzling rain on the heels of a midnight drenching. By the time the clouds thinned we were setting up a base camp in a wide green valley below a black eastwest ridge leading to more ridges and our objective: 7,400-foot Nikolai Peak. A reconnaissance hike in the afternoon led to a 6,500-foot ridge, not high by mountaineering standards, but a fine perch from which to view the glaciated foothills of McCarthy Creek's watershed, the distant Root and Kennicott glaciers, and the wild Nizina River — Nicolai's old turf — a mile below to the east.

"Look at this!" Karl cried.

We were descending a sharp ridge pelted by slush and sleet.

"The hair on my hands is standing up!"

Mine was, too. I held my hands palms-forward and watched as atmospheric electricity, generated by passing clouds and air currents, made the hair on the back of my hands dance. My moustache twitched. My eyebrows tickled.

Karl, the scientist among us, was worried.

"We better get down from here," he said as he picked up his pace. "With this charged air we could get hit any second by lightning."

So down we went, electric currents weakening, to camp. We aired our sleeping bags, used gas stoves to fix a twilight supper of Mountain House freeze-dried spaghetti, then made plans to climb Nikolai in the morning. Push ourselves. Do it. I meandered away from camp before sleep. When I returned, Karl was pissing in a wide circle around our tents.

"What the hell are you doing?" I cried.

Karl finished and zipped.

"I heard one time," he said, "or read it, that if a bear smells urine he'll respect it as the scent of another animal's territory. He'll stay away."

It was news to me and I laughed.

&#10086; &#10086; &#10086;

Dall ewes and lambs nibbled alpine plants on distant talus slopes at dawn, no bear in sight, as we filled our daypacks with camera equipment, rain gear, water, jerky and dried fruit. Cloud whisps fingered ravines and ridges near Sourdough Mountain. We climbed the steep 1,000-foot black slope to the ridge we had electrically descended the day before, then kept going, clouds filling some valleys as other valleys flooded with sunshine.

Icefields on the flanks of Regal Mountain and Rime Peak appeared through shifting cloudbanks. Glacier-furrowed river valleys snaked into view. Gone were the managed wildernesses of America's national parks and forests. No trails, signposts or cairns here. We were hiking on a rock rim of one of the world's last mountain frontiers. Over five million acres of ice hunched on horizons around which rock, alpine plateaus and untouched, little- known valleys of vegetation — green against the tan and cinnamon of mountainsides — stretched in all directions.

It was the view, rather than our elevation, that made standing on Nikolai's summit so enchanting, so exhilarating for a young buck from the flatlands of Minnesota. Although Nikolai at 7,440 feet is a full thousand feet higher than any mountain in New England, including the infamous Mount Washington, Nikolai is dwarfed by the arena of summits surrounding it. Yet from its top we had a clear view of the Wrangells to the west, north and east where rivers drained from snouts of glaciers and distances were lost to the gods. To the south, across the broad Chitina River Valley, the eastern Chugach Mountains punctured the sky with snowcapped stabs of geological teeth. Everywhere, it seemed, was wilderness and space: the essence of Alaska. Nikolai shared this essence. It was a peak with a view. There we sensed what lay beyond without, for the time being, going a step further.

We couldn't have imagined the real climax of our hike in the Wrangells would come the following morning when we wanted one last look. Frost sparkled on alpine plants beneath a cloudless sky as we crawled out of our sleeping bags at 5:30 a.m. One thought was on our minds: climb back up the black ridge for a clear view of some of North America's highest mountains. We gaped awestruck an hour later. Mount Blackburn at 16,390 feet stood unsheathed against the northwest horizon, Kennecott-way. Layers of brilliant white ice folded down from its summit and shoulders. More ice and snow blanketed flanks of neighboring Rime Peak and Regal Mountain.

The silence was bottomless, the air still and crisp.

To the east was the incomparable University Range: Mount Sulzer (10,926 feet), Mount Churchill (15,638), Mount Bona (16,421) and University Peak (14,470). In the foreground below was the mouth of the Chitistone River Canyon with its whorled mile-high cliffs and series of waterfalls. Clouds shrouded smaller mountains in the southeast although their rugged rock summits jutted clear of the clouds like rock islands in a sea of swirling vapor. To the west and south were more peaks, endless peaks.

We stood in an Alaskan ocean of frozen waves whose rocky crests were whitecapped.

Our legs were strong, our hearts large, as we returned to base camp, packed gear, then hiked back down to the shack at the confluence of Nikolai and McCarthy creeks. If we had wanted to be baptized by Wrangell terrain, as we had; if we had wanted to see what the high summits of the Wrangells-St. Elias were like; and if we had wanted a glimpse into one of the world's last mountain wildernesses before it became a national park, before bureaucracy attached its regulatory tentacles, then we had stood on Nikolai's peak just in the nick of time.

This we knew. This counted. And we felt good.

The next day, no bear having visited the shack, Dan and I — full packs on backs — raced each other, sometimes running, back to McCarthy. We covered the last five miles in an hour and a half. Dan won, though barely, and it didn't make a wit of difference later that day when, in McCarthy Lodge, I cracked open a cold beer to toast the likes of Chief Nicolai.

His name was Tony and he, too, had retreated to the lodge's bar — a small south wing of the main part of the framed building's store and restaurant. Outside, moose antlers hung above windows painted with *Meals, Rooms, Showers, Cold Beer, Wine* and *Pool Table*, red letters on glass, while a single caribou rack was nailed at the peak of the roof. Inside past the patio's round tables and chairs, were wildflowers in vases, furs, stones, several davenports, an old *Shoe Repair* sign, old photos on the wall, and various momentos of the copper years.

A separate door led into the bar, and as the Alaskan day ebbed toward twilight it became clear the bar, albeit small, was the human hub around which the social life of the south central Wrangells revolved.

There was Tony who wasn't, at the moment, happy.

"I don't care what you think," he said, slapping his hand down on the wooden bar next to his dollar glass of Lambrusco wine, making sure everyone would hear him. "The radio station in Glennallen is awful! All they air is that religious crap. I don't need anyone to tell me I'm a no-good bastard. Just like everyone else, I look at myself in the mirror every morning.

"I can see exactly what I am."

## Chapter Three WRESTLING WITH THE WRANGELLS

Tony paused to glance behind the bar to study his five-foot-eight frame reflected in a mirror. An aging man, 50 or 60, looked back at him: graying hair, a chest-long wispy white beard, weathered wrinkles at the temples, a black and white checkered woolen shirt, and green army pants. He couldn't see his brown shoes but I could. His eyes, fixed on himself, shifted to nail me where I sat. Tony had a cabin up the road. McCarthy was his home. I was the outsider.

You want local color, his body language seemed to say. You're looking at it.

Jack Pasture came into the bar and sat next to Tony, an innocent—almost pained—expression on Jack's long tan face as if he had a long, unwanted journey to the south ahead of him which, it turned out, was true. Jack was originally from Belgium but spent most of his life in Whitehorse, Yukon Territory, before moving to San Francisco. He had been in McCarthy six weeks helping a developer subdivide land parcels of 2.8 acres, all sold for $10,000 apiece.

"The lots are misplaced," he said holding his reading glasses, his eyes smiling. "They're too close to the river. When Hidden Lake breaks open next time, it's going to cause problems."

Tony wasn't listening. His business was wine.

"I like you, Jack," he blurted out, wanting attention again. "You're a good guy. You can come to my house anytime. Even if you don't want any booze. There might not be any water at my place, which I get in the creek, but there's plenty of booze. Without booze I may as well be dead."

Jack reached into the pocket of his black and red checkered flannel shirt for a package of Pall Mall straights and a pencil. Kelly, in his late twenties with a sturdy build, black hair and beard, and hard, dark hands, had just parked his yellow motorbike in front of the bar and walked in the door. His face was tan above a khaki shirt, his pants smudged with dirt and grease. He wore heavy leather hiking boots and had a snuff box in his back pocket. Although he'd lived in a tent the previous winter, he was busy fixing a cabin and needed to talk business.

# OPEN SPACES

"And another thing," Tony cried, for he now had more ears, the stagelight a little brighter, "I hate milk."

Tony knew Jack liked milk. He also knew milk could never outwit wine.

"Animals and Europeans get weaned from milk when they're young. But, oh no, not we Americans. We're all supposed to drink milk until we're 80! I drank two glasses of milk two weeks ago, and I'm still sick!"

Tony went outside, disappeared around the corner of the building, then came back.

"That milk made me puke again," he said laughing as he closed the bar's door. "In the morning there'll be a bunch of dead pollywogs floating on the pond."

I glanced at the door, a sucker to Tony, unable to tell if he was joking, telling the truth, or upchucking wine. Dan, sitting near me, was laughing. Mr. Hemingway himself in the green hills of Alaska. Another $1.25 beer was placed in front of me, thanks to Jack. Rain began falling outside, snapping on August leaves and pelting a roof of plastic sheeting Jim Miller, the lodge's owner, had tacked on a wooden frame adjacent to the kitchen, outside, Wrangell way. Chilled by the rain, I missed my down vest and wool sweater left in the pickup on the other side of the river. But no way was I going to cross the river on the handtram. Not now with another full beer at my elbow while Jack and Kelly talked hardwood.

Lumber was an expensive subject in McCarthy, and the subject came up in a roundabout way. Jack, who had just bought a house in McCarthy, with a green four-wheel drive jeep thrown in for good measure, was flying to San Francisco in several days to get his belongings and wife, and was going to drive a truck back to McCarthy. He asked Kelly if he could pick up anything for him.

"You can't bring back what I want," Kelly said, giving Tony a wink.

"How about 50 gallons of red *vino?*" Tony piped up, swinging around on his stool to face me. "Don't they make great wine in California?"

Kelly gave Jack $300, forking over cash.

"I paid 111 bucks," he said, "for three hardwood boards in Fairbanks last spring, which is nuts. See if you can get me a mix of hardwoods."

Jack: "What are you going to use it for?"

"Work on my cabin," Kelly said while picking a stone from his vibram sole. "Maybe build a dogsled. By the way, you going to be here for Elevator's surprise birthday party?"

Elevator was a local bush pilot who, although only in his early twenties, had avoided killing himself flying too many hours, while bringing locals necessities like mail, food and beer. Plus Tony his wine.

"Sorry," Jack said, lighting another Pall Mall with a kitchen match. "I'll be gone."

᠅ ᠅ ᠅

I was interested in Elevator's party, and his circle of McCarthy friends, so I spoke with Jim Miller after I feasted on a $12 lodge meal of barbecue ribs, homegrown lettuce, cream corn, onion greens, fresh buns, baked potatoes, and a large slice of fresh blueberry pie. Jim was one of the lodge's owners, a native of Fairbanks, Alaska, and when I first saw him sitting shirtless at a kitchen table, his black hair below his ears, a moustache to his chin and a large tattoo on his right shoulder, I figured he had been around, seen the sights, and that as one of the chiefs of McCarthy and no dummy behind the bar, he probably had his finger on the pulse of local sentiment regarding the proposed Wrangell-St. Elias National Park and Preserve. He, his wife, and their children were getting ready to wind down summer, to cut wood, plan projects, dust off all the old books to read when winter temperatures and the long nights clamped down hard.

"People here have mixed feelings about the proposal," he said. "We could all make more money with a tourist boom, but everyone doesn't want that. Some of us, like Tony, came here because of its remoteness, its beauty, its freedoms and frontier flavor. Things would change if this place was made into a park."

I thought of small, glamorous towns that had mushroomed in size next to national parks — places like Estes Park in Colorado and Jackson Hole in Wyoming, villages that had quadrupled development, if not more, while catering to a park-hungry public. Already, on the other side of the Kennicott River, a red and white sign nailed to a tree showed how McCarthy was being subdivided and sold. Nonexistent streets were already named.

"If the Wrangells do become a park," I asked, "will the road be improved? Bridges rebuilt? Campgrounds developed?"

"What do you think?" Miller said. "Look at McKinley Park, any national park. People scream for access, access, access. There's already the new bridge over the Copper at Chitina. Sure, park people and the state will probably come in here building bridges, campgrounds and improving roads. This place might be crawling with Winnebagoes in a few years.

"But," and he added this with a smile, "if you ask me, some local longhair will probably sneak off some night and blow the bridges up."

❧ ❧ ❧

None of the local longhairs looked like bridge saboteurs when Dan and I showed up back at the bar for Elevator's party, McCarthy-style. A birthday cake shaped like an airplane was half eaten on the bar. Beer flowed, as did wine. Most everyone ignored the gray Siamese cat beneath a table. Near the door, a kerosene lantern — tinfoil on top to reflect light — lit the pool table where consecutive games kept the packed bar entertained.

Every time Tony missed a shot he'd blame it on being "too sober." So he gave it up, turned in his cue, then danced with Kelly's blonde girlfriend forty years his junior.

Chapter Three WRESTLING WITH THE WRANGELLS

It was a happy night there on the Kennicott. The men laughed and women clapped hands to music. Village dogs appeared in the lantern's light as the lodge's door opened and closed, people going, perhaps, to the outhouse with its sign: *Danger: Men Working Below.* It wasn't just the post-hike high and beer that made me feel good, although they helped. I was out on the edge 4,000 miles from Solid Bottom Creek and my cabin on Big Elbow Lake. And the people at McCarthy: how they could joke, sing and dance, how — despite controversy and perhaps even partly because of its uncertain outcome — they knew how to have a good time.

Dan and I, somewhere around midnight, stepped outside under a starry sky. It was time to move on. Two dogs, one a tan mutt, the other half husky and malamute with bushy white tail, followed us to the river, their tails wagging on the heels of strange folk. Although ahead of us was the handtram, a dark ride across the Kennicott, and a night in the back of my pickup, I couldn't help but think of the people we were leaving and the many millions more to the south. *Down below,* Alaskans called it. *Outside. The lower forty-eight.* From there people were coming. Some would be backpackers like Dan and I, hungry for wild country. Others would be rafters, mountain climbers, history buffs, amateur geologists like Karl, bird and wildlife watchers, and photographers: the living heart, the outside staff, of America's growing wilderness preservation movement.

I knew some of these people, had begun to rub campfire elbows with them, had read their environmental magazines and studied their history. Most meant well.

Some wanted to save Dall rams, caribou, and bears because they had an innate right to exist unmolested by human hunters, or they wanted to protect them for the enjoyment of future generations. Others wanted to preserve Alaska's most beautiful wild areas before more Kennecott mines and oil rigs altered landscapes. They knew, when it came to the wildest of country, Alaska was America's last stand. Still other people, men and women who would never make it to Alaska, nevertheless needed to know — for peace of mind and expansiveness of heart — there were places where mountain goats faced the wind on electrically charged ridges, where glaciers, remote and dangerous, snaked out of valleys, and where grizzlies lazed in creekside willows.

These were not mere daydreams and idle wishes.

And because they were shared by a democracy of millions, by people willing to flex political muscle — to vote, finance campaigns and lobby Congress — it was my bet as I clambered off the handtram for the last time that Alaskan prospectors, land developers and sporthunters, in the Wrangells and other parts of Alaska, were going to have to step aside. For better or worse, they were going to have to share the outback with fellow Americans of different persuasions.

≈ ≈ ≈

So it happened.

Later that fall, when the 95th Congress failed to resolve Alaska lands legislation in late October 1978, President Carter was flooded with requests to protect Alaska wilderness before the December 18th deadline when temporary protection was due to expire. Over 1,400 national, state and local citizens' groups from every state, representing combined memberships of over ten million people, signed a 28-foot mailgram urging the President to "take bold action for the immediate and permanent protection of our natural heritage on our federal lands in Alaska."

Simultaneously, 130 members of the House of Representatives and 19 senators sent President Carter twin letters asking him to invoke the Antiquities Act to protect the proposed conservation units.

Carter responded. On December 1st, through proclamation, he established 17 Alaskan national monuments. Thirteen, including the Wrangell-St. Elias Mountains, were assigned to the National Park System.

"Because of the risks of immediate damage to these magnificent areas," the President said, "I felt it was imperative to protect all of these lands. These areas contain resources of unequaled scientific, historic and cultural value, and include some of the most spectacular scenery and wildlife in the world."

The temptation was to say Amen, but protection was still only temporary. It gave Congress time to hammer out the details of what was likely the most important conservation bill of the century. It affected more than 100 million acres in Alaska, approximately a third of the state, in aggregate an area equal to more than 90 Boundary Water Canoe Area Wildernesses and larger than California. Debate continued throughout 1980 until December 2nd when President Carter signed the Alaska National Interest Lands Conservation Act.

The bill doubled the size of the National Park System and National Wildlife Refuge System. By protecting 25 Alaskan rivers it doubled the size of the nation's Wild and Scenic River System. And by classifying 56 million acres as wilderness, it tripled the size of the National Wilderness Preservation System.

Despite the outcry from sporthunters, over 12 million acres were included in the new Wrangell-St. Elias National Park and Preserve. Eight million acres were designated park, closed to hunting. The preserve of over four million acres was left open to the gun. Subsistence uses, where established, were allowed to continue.

As for the McCarthy Road, R. Gerald Wright of the National Park Service — who was chief planner for the Wrangells — felt that if the road needed improvement as the result of visitor demands and native interests, it should only be done 15 miles to Strelna. There a mining road gave access to the Kotsina and Kuskulana river drainages providing good hiking in alpine country. Richard Holden, however, as Deputy Commissioner of Planning and Research for Alaska's Department of Transportation, was really the man holding the ball on the road issue. While deflecting my question whether the McCarthy Road would be upgraded, he gave me the estimated cost of improving the road to a minimum standard: $40 million.

Despite considerable interest in improving the road, despite public hearings and workshops, nobody was holding their breath.

Thinking of Tony, Kelly, Elevator, Jim and Jack, I expressed concern about the effect of park designation on McCarthy to the Park Service's Wright. An ad by the Great Kennecott Glacier Land Company had appeared in *Alaska* magazine offering one-to-ten acre lots at the old Kennecott Copper Mine. Low down, easy terms, no property taxes. Surrounded by new national parkland, McCarthy and nearby Kennecott were in bits and parcels on the real estate auctioning block.

"It is likely," Wright wrote to me, "that development will proceed faster than our ability to control it, and at some point in the future the communities may become far more commercial than they are at present.

"Bear in mind, however, that McCarthy was originally developed as a commercially oriented community, servicing, in all meanings of the word, the needs of the mill site...The transition to a quiet, remote, residential area for people escaping the troubles of the world is of recent vintage."

&#x218; &#x218; &#x218;

Tragedy struck quiet, remote McCarthy several years later.

In early March 1983, 39-year-old Louis D. Hastings, an unemployed computer programmer from Anchorage, allegedly snowmobiled into McCarthy and killed six of its 22 residents. The shooting spree began when Christopher Richards, 29, invited Hastings into his cabin for coffee. As Richards reached for a cup he was shot near the right eye and in the neck.

"Look," Richards recalled Hastings saying, "you're already dead. If you'll just quit fighting I'll make it easy for you."

Richards grabbed a knife, slashed Hastings, then ran in stocking feet outside and fled to the McCarthy airstrip. It was midday and most of the area residents normally converged on the airstrip to get their mail when the plane arrived. The plane was already there. According to Associated Press reports and Lynnell Mickelsen of the *Duluth News-Tribune*, as Richards told the pilot what had happened, two other McCarthyites, Tim and Amy Nash, drove by on their snowmobile and stopped to listen. The pilot had seen Hastings go into the home of Florence and Lester Heglund, the postmasters. Tim Nash went to check and was shot in the leg when he entered the house.

Nash made it back to the airstrip. He told the pilot to take Richards to safety and to get help. Nash could have left. Instead he decided to stay to warn others away. His wife, Amy, stayed with him.

It was, for the Nashes, a mistake. By the time Alaska troopers arrived, capturing Hastings on the way, they found six people dead: the Heglunds, Harley King, 61, Maxine Edwards, 52, and the Nashes shot by high-powered rifle. Donna Byram, 32, was shot in the arm but survived.

For the Nashes, as reporter Mickelsen explained, the tragedy was particularly poignant. Tim, 39, was born in Duluth, grew up in Angora, Minnesota, received a football scholarship from the University of Minnesota, then spent two years in the Army overseas. Afterwards he studied Alaska and decided to homestead in McCarthy because it was remote and had mountains.

He moved there in 1972 where he hunted, fished and raised a garden.

"He was an outdoorsman, loved the woods," his mother, Lucille, said. "He wanted...to be away from all society. Knowing Tim, we never interfered, never worried. We knew he was strong."

His marriage to Amy Ashenden, six weeks before the shootings, seemed made in heaven. Amy, 25, was born in Massachusetts, graduated magna cum laude with a Bachelor of Arts degree in Comparative Religions from Harvard University in 1979, and had worked for the National Park Service at Sunset Crater and Yosemite. She moved to Alaska in 1981, *came into the country* as author John McPhee would say, and hoped — in the Great Land — to meditate and write.

Both she and Tim were loners until they met.

"Amy found it very difficult to know what she wanted," her father, David

Ashenden, explained. "She was never satisfied. Yet after she met Tim, something changed. When she came back from the wedding [at the St. Louis Catholic Church in Floodwood, Minnesota] we noticed she had never looked better, never seemed happier."

Apparently — wrote Mickelsen —Ashenden paused.

"They went up there hoping to live a very peaceful, tranquil life...They were just at the wrong place at the wrong time."

# CHAPTER FOUR
# STUDIES IN RED OCHRE

It is said it takes 30 minutes or more for a person's eyes to adjust to the dark: a half hour before he or she makes sense out of the blackness, finds shape and meaning — if not more courage — in the dim glow of what seemed to be a lightless world.

Yet what of those among us, the Leakeys, Eiseleys and those many of lesser fame, or no fame at all, who keep watch on the dark mystery of mortality, the great stream of the peopled past? How long does it take our eyes and hearts to see the fleeting nature of things, to observe and conclude evidence, to accept that at least our bodies are finite, that there were people before us who cast midday shadows on green moss and reflections on water, or who dipped fingers in red ochre to paint images on rock cliffs fronting waterways?

How long?

It was October 1979, precisely one year and a month since I left Alaska's Wrangell Mountains. With a clutch of magazine assignments from *Backpacking Journal, Camping Journal* and *Canoe*, I had moved from Big Elbow and Solid Bottom country to the cabin at Lindskog's on the North Arm of Burntside Lake — Bojo's eventual home — near Ely on the Minnesota side of the U.S.-Ontario border. At the moment I stood with Ray and Rich Niedzielski, brothers of close age, both Minnesotans, both Viet Nam veterans, on Warrior Hill of Lac la Croix in the heart of Ojibway pictograph country. This wasn't the heights of Nikolai, but from the top of Warrior's granite ridge we could see the expanse of Lac la Croix to the west, Boulder Bay to the south, and toward Bottle Portage in the southeast where, on the Kam-Dog trip, Chris Trost and I would need to tough it out.

Below us, beyond our canoe, rock islands — many with pines — sailed the gray, rippled waters.

OPEN SPACES

Two hundred Octobers earlier, Ojibway warriors had raced up Warrior Hill to prove fitness among themselves, their women, and the *manitos*, the spiritual guardians they believed ruled their destiny. It became an Ojibway tradition to leave tobacco or other gifts at such places: sites of extraordinary power. The offerings appeased the manitos, communicated good will, and served as prayer for passage.

We'd need the safe passage.

I reached into my jean pocket for my finest tobacco and thumbed a pinch of it into a crack in the ridge. Perhaps I should have spared the gesture.

The expedition was my idea. Having come into wolf country, I had developed a strong interest in three of the finest groups of Indian rock paintings in the Quetico-Superior, perhaps the world. I studied their locations on maps, plotted canoe routes connecting them, and asked the Niedzielskis to come along. We started on the Nina-Moose River off the Echo Trail northwest of Ely. We then paddled north to Agnes Lake and Boulder River beneath Indian Summer sun. T-shirt weather. This changed by evening when winds blew hard out of the northwest and we were forced to bivouac at a grateless site in a lee cove of Boulder Bay, Lac la Croix. We awoke to snow the next morning: large flakes swirling down from gray skies as we burned pancakes over a makeshift fire. We swabbed peanut butter on the pancakes anyhow, washed them down with coffee and hot chocolate, then broke camp, canoed north to the pictographs at Lac la Croix Narrows, and veered south to Warrior Hill.

From here we planned to continue south and establish a base camp on Iron Lake, make a long — perhaps illegal — daytrip across the international border to the pictographs of Quetico Provincial Park's Darky Lake, then a couple days later head east and south across Crooked Lake to pictographs near Lower Basswood Falls. We'd take notes and photos. With luck, and to paraphrase Thoreau, we would also work and wedge our understanding of pictographs downward through the silt of opinion, past prejudice and appearance, through poetry, philosophy and hearsay until we arrived at a solid bottom we could call reality.

Perhaps then, partly through pictographs, partly through their attendant cosmology, I'd begin to understand an early people of a land that had become my home.

I had done my homework. I knew that of the 15,000 pictograph and petroglyph sites in North America, there were approximately 300 documented sites in 1979 running in a northwesterly direction from the Great Lakes to Great Slave Lake in Canada's Northwest Territories. All lay within the paper birch's northern limits and the southern edge of Canada's Precambrian Shield woodlands, and extended east to a single site on Lac Wapizagonka, a source of Quebec's St. Maurice River.

The Quetico-Superior, on the southwest edge of the Shield woodlands, had at least 30 pictograph sites. Some paintings were on major fur trade canoe routes dating to the late 1600s. Others, like the paintings I'd seen on North Hegman Lake in the Boundary Waters Canoe Area Wilderness, were tucked away on remote lakes.

Paintings ranged from moose and elk to cranes, from tally marks, people in canoes, handprints and the rare fox or wolf to thunderbirds and *maymaygwayshis*: rock medicine men, supposedly mischievous fairylike spirits, imps standing two or three feet tall, no noses, who lived inside the cliffs on which their image was painted. Legend claimed *maymaygwayshis*, by nature tricksters, liked to steal fish from Indian nets. When the Indians tried to catch them, the *maymaygwayshis* — in canoes — hid their faces. An Indian from the Lake Nipigon area said *maymaygwayshis* had hair like a monkey. Another said Ojibway shamans could enter the rock of *maymaygwayshi* sites and exchange tobacco for potent "rock medicine."

Rock medicine? What's that?

What, really, did the pictographs mean? Unlike petroglyphs which were chipped or carved into stone, pictographs were painted on rock, but who painted them? When? Were they signposts or cosmic calling cards?

According to the late Selwyn Dewdney, who documented over 150 pictograph sites for his and Kenneth Kidd's book, *Indian Rock Paintings of the Great Lakes*, fully half of the drawings were indecipherable abstractions beyond contemporary Ojibway (Chippewa) understanding and the American-European mindset. Ten percent of the paintings represented man-made objects, ten percent were of other human subject matter, ten percent were mythological creatures, ten percent were animals and birds, and the last ten percent, like most of the images and smearings at Lac la Croix Narrows, were handprints.

The handprints were intriguing. A kind of signature, they date back 30,000 years in other parts of the world. When grouped together they might represent identification with a tribal unit, or they meant "have done" and "death."

In the area Dewdney studied, handprints doubled in frequency as one moved northwest toward and into Manitoba. There were none in the southeast range of the region where abstractions were more commonplace. Like the handprints, thunderbirds and snakes increased in proportion as one moved southeast to northwest. Bison appeared in paintings near the prairies.

Most Quetico-Superior pictographs have two things in common. With variations in hue, all but one of the drawings are red, a sacred color of aboriginal rock art worldwide (whether in France where it's known as *art rupestre*, in Russia as *naskalnye izobrazheniva* or in Germany as *felszeichnungen*). Paint was made from red ochre, an iron oxide hematite pulverized into clay, sometimes heated to deepen the red, or molded into cakes for storage. The binder, or glue, mixed into the ochre, which made it adhere well to rock, probably ranged from fish oil from the swim bladder of sturgeon to bear grease or glue made from boiled moose and caribou hooves. In some cases the binder might have been spit and water. Whatever it was, it worked well. When a vandal used house paint to mar the Agawa pictographs on the east shore of Lake Superior, the house paint faded away relatively quickly while the red ochre remained as vivid as before.

Besides color, the other commonality of Quetico-Superior pictographs is that the vast majority are near water. Generally they're two to five feet above water level, suggesting they were painted by someone sitting or standing in a canoe.

"We are dealing with a 'canoe culture'," Dewdney emphasized after a 1957 pictograph expedition into Quetico, "as devoted to its water craft as we of the 'automobile culture' are to our land craft."

Canoes, hence, were the medium between vision and art, and, in reverse, between art and vision. I hoped as much for ourselves.

እ እ እ

Ray, Rich and I visited Quetico's Rebecca Falls on the north side of Iron Lake but settled for a campsite below the rapids of Curtain Falls, the largest waterfalls on the border. Although years later I would come upon Curtain's rapids just as a man had drowned and was still somewhere in the water, the first night on Iron with the Niedzielskis was a peaceful one lit with sky beauty. We set up camp. After canoeing up the first rapids we beached the canoe and hiked along the waterfalls.

We took the Canadian side. Above us, appearing through thinning overcast, were northern lights, not what a northern Minnesotan would call *bright*, but casting enough light so we could see: go beyond being groping batmen in bushes to stand upright waterside in the dim glow of an auroral world.

Rich and I thought of attempting photographs but the logistics were formidable. It was cold. The clouds could thicken at any moment and we'd lose our light. Besides, there were riffles to run on the way back to camp. Skip the photos. Better go. And after looking at the falls for a few moments it was a good thing we left. It was pitch dark when we drifted through the riffles, navigating more by sound than light. The clouds were back. Night was back. The northern lights were gone.

እ እ እ

It looked like snow again the next morning beneath a cold, overcast sky. Gray was the color of the day. After packing day trip supplies and securing camp, we shoved off, portaged around Curtain Falls on the American side, and headed northeast into Canada on the other side of Crooked Lake. Mist, not snow, soaked us as we paddled two unnamed lakes north of Crooked, crossed Roland Lake and skirted clearwater Argo to portage north.

Darky Lake's sky gave us a bad welcome. As we quartered against whitecaps driven by a northwest wind, large cumulus clouds trailed rain showers our way. Time to seek shelter ashore. Without having seen a single pictograph we beached our canoe among boulders, scrambled out, and sat beneath dripping birch and aspen, their leaves gold or fallen among the rocks at our feet. We muttered about unappeased *manitos*, ate dried apricots, gulped down gorp, and taped a broken paddle.

Thunderheads passed. Rain stopped. Sunshine swept across Darky turning gray water blue.

"Look at that!" Ray or Rich said.

A faint rainbow was forming above a cliff. Beneath the rainbow but above the cliff, a hawk circled slowly. I swear it. Here, certainly, was an omen. Here was a clear and shining sign to continue on.

Moments later we drifted up against the rainbowed cliff beneath the hawk. As our cold hands clutched granite we looked at a covey of paintings on the cliff's face, some at eye level, others higher: a cow moose with an unpainted spot where its heart was supposed to be, a calf, dots possibly indicating moose tracks, and a large serpent curving around the bottom of a cluster of five canoes with two paddlers in each.

The serpent, I knew, was probably *Mishipizhiw* (pronounced mishi-pesh-you), the Great Lynx, Ojibway demi-god of water, sometimes called a "night panther" or "lion." Images of *Mishipizhiw* were scattered throughout Ojibway canoe country. Some versions had large ears, horns, a long tail or spines along the back. No matter the exact configuration, it was the feared *manito* of large lake bottoms: its tail could whip lakes into wild chops, capsizing canoes, killing. It was a mythological creature to take seriously. It didn't, legend went, abide scoff.

To the right of *Mishipizhiw*, aiming the opposite direction, was a drawing of a man with a rifle. Here among all Canadian Shield pictographs was one of the few clues as to how old the pictographs were. Time shot backwards. As I gripped rock in a blast of more rain it was easy to imagine the cliff — ebbing and fluxing with lichen and light — being brushed by a finger dipped in red ochre. Perhaps the drawing captured a moment of astonishment, a cry by a soul that had seen and heard, if not felt, the coming power of the gun.

≈ ≈ ≈

Historians are uncertain when Indians first lived in the Quetico-Superior. Robert Treuer, author of *Voyageur Country: A Park in the Wilderness,* thinks the clovis and stone spearheads found in northern Minnesota indicate Indian inhabitants around 7,000 B.C. or earlier. The Copper Culture of Lake Superior's Isle Royale, 50 miles east of the Quetico-Superior, mined copper to trade with other tribes as early as 8,000 B.C. A bison kill site at Itasca State Park's Nicollet Creek, in north central Minnesota, dates from 7,000 B.C.

More recent peoples — the Woodland Tradition and Blackduck Culture (Sioux ancestors) — lived from 1,000 B.C. to approximately 1,700 A.D. in an area bounded by Voyageurs National Park northwest of the Quetico-Superior, south to the Mississippi River's watershed in north central Minnesota, west to the Red River of the north along the northern half of the Minnesota-North Dakota border, and east to upper New York. The Ojibway, variously called Chippewa, thought of themselves as the "Original" or "Spontaneous" people. White men claim Ojibway drove the Sioux from Quetico-Superior to the Great Plains in the late 1700s. Born of the East Coast's Algonquin stock, the Ojibway lived a nomadic life hunting, making maple syrup, picking berries, fishing, harvesting wild rice, and warring. Their religion — the midewiwin or *mystical society* — encompassed myths, ancient traditions and hallowed visions brought on by fasting, sometimes ten days straight, and by sweat lodges.

Because the midewiwin was the Ojibway faith 100 to 400 years ago, when many of the pictographs were drawn, it's likely the roots of Quetico-Superior pictography are hidden in the religion's tenets.

"They saw all life as a personalized mystery," Landes wrote of Ojibway in *Ojibway Religion and the Midewiwin*, "voicing this in their tremendous esteem for visionary shamans who succeeded at life's risky activities. They pursued magical formulas, philosophies, and techniques we outsiders can separate from religion only by our civilization's alien opinions about magic's impersonality.

"Adept shamans were believed to manipulate the manito super- naturals as we do electricity...They strove to locate the founts of Mystery and contain them for survival, both on Earth, which they called an 'island,' and in the ghost-phase they conceptualized as following death. The preoccupation appears in all reports, from the first European records of missionary and trade encounters with the tribe until present ones."

Manitos governed reality and were the spiritual prototypes of plants, animals and seasons. As Dewdney noted in his essay, *Ecological Notes on the Ojibway Shaman-Artist*, beyond the world's evanescent phenomena the Ojibway knew of another "normally hidden from men's eyes but more real and substantial than the world around him. There, in that other world, were the presiding powers...whose whims determined the unpredictable twists and turns of a man's life and all else besides."

Manitos were approached through dreams, a quest begun in puberty when young men went alone into wilderness to fast and meditate until a guiding manito presented itself. What the young Ojibway dreamed of — a heron, for example, or a rock, otter or wolf — assured him during the dream that it would protect and guide him through life's trials. As an adult, a *mide* (midewiwin practitioner) continued pursuing manito power through the ritual of the sweat bath, fasting to the limits of endurance and, in some cases, abstaining from sex. Asceticism energized spirituality.

Sometimes a *mide* asked a shaman for help in warding off sickness, for good luck when hunting, to sweeten revenge or to increase sexual prowess. The shaman would dream a song and often write it in symbols on birchbark so his parishioner, so to speak, could recall the lyrics.

These birchbark scrolls were deliberately kept secret. Speaking of dreams, sharing them diminished their power.

"My interviews with the older people who have retained some knowledge of earlier ways," Dewdney concluded before his death in 1979, "have convinced me that most of the rock paintings were intended for supernatural rather than human eyes, as a sort of reminder of the dream content.

"Where a man included among his identity marks a pictograph that referred to the dream guardian of his puberty fast, this too must have been intended as a kind of communication with the manito. For he could only disclose the content of his boyhood dream to any other person at the peril of losing his guardian, and in the known instances where the dream symbol was used as an identity mark it was so disguised in one way or another as to offer no clue to its meaning."

There are two other reasons for believing there is a direct link between the midewiwin faith and the Quetico-Superior region's pictographs. There is a painting on the Bloodvein River northwest of Quetico showing what is likely a shaman holding an otterskin medicine bag of a kind found on midewiwin birchbark instruction scrolls, and most of the pictographs are in the same area as historic midewiwin centers.

The anthropological glove fits the pictographic hand.

The password was "trouble" when the Niedzielskis and I left Darky, crossed Argo Lake and portaged in chilly rain to the large west end of Crooked Lake en route back to our Iron Lake base camp. Maybe we should have left the manitos a pound of tobacco at the Darky Lake pictographs. Perhaps we should have left our canoe, our clothes, our souls.

Storm clouds veiled the sunset and smacked us with rain and whitecapping wind, head-on, as we began paddling Crooked's waters. It was Ray's turn to duff in the middle of the canoe, and he began to shiver, the first sign of hypothermia. Although we had taped our snapped spare paddle on Darky it wasn't strong enough to be used with the force required to make progress against the wind. Darkness. Head-on wind. Hypothermic waters. The odds were rising against us. The red warning lights were flashing. Where were the manitos when you needed them?

Or was this *Mishipizhiw's* response?

Had we doubted the underwater monster? Had we snickered at the serpent like good Christian men? Did we *know* what lurked at the bottom of Crooked Lake, thrashing its tail in muck and mire, sweeping mossy granite, churning up walleye bones?

Rapid-fire questions, one to each stroke of the paddle.

While resting behind the last island before open water, we realized our only chance to reach camp safely was to keep paddling into the wind. We had to hope another paddle wouldn't break and that waves wouldn't capsize us. We rounded the island to face swells in dusk's fading light. If the waves and swells were too large, if they licked over gunwales and our canoe began taking on water, we would be forced — at best — to turn around and spend the night on the island.

The dark, shadowed island.

Despite years of wilderness tripping, we had grown careless and were unprepared for emergency. We had no flashlight, no tent, no sleeping bags, no dry clothes or food. Perhaps no usable matches. Perhaps little hope to live the night.

If we were unable to find dry kindling and firewood while crawling around on the island's wet ground, would we survive a night as temperatures dropped to 35 degrees in pitch darkness? Would we shiver, grow comatose, speak to imaginary mothers? Would we cry for pity? Would we place a call on a pay phone attached to a pine as a hypothermia victim in the Boundary Waters once did? Would we feel our friend's tears with numb fingers?

 za za za

Apparently I had a thing for islands, Indians and possible fatal play in the fields of the lords.

There was a day, 20 springs before the threat of Crooked Lake's island, when friends and I heard through Mt. St. Benedict High School's nun grapevine that an island on the Red Lake River had Indian remains. There were bones, supposedly, plus arrowheads and pottery shards of the river's first people: men, women and children who had sniffed the morning air of spring days long before my coming; long, even, before trappers, traders, preachers, soldiers and plows. We weren't told where the island was, but I knew the river, and from a preponderance of Catholic verbal slips I knew the island's location.

We were told not to go there.

There were *laws* against collecting shards and bones. We were not archeologists with degrees, not government agents. The island, like all graveyards, was sacred.

I went anyway.

The river was my turf, there was a rumored trace of Indian blood in my family, and besides, I was curious.

Fortunately it was easy to get to the island. The river was low and all I had to do was tightrope a narrow neck of exposed stones and clay connecting island to riverbank. It was a bright, sunlit day and for this I was glad. I wasn't alone. I mean, no other living boys were with me in the woods. But there was a presence on the island I couldn't account for. It had to do with Indian warriors and smoky camps: land fought for, won, and lost, yes, inevitably lost to white men with guns. It had to do with the sweep of rivers over time, in this case the Red Lake River's silt settling down through the surface's opaque waters to bury what lay on the bottom.

There are times in a boy's life when he can't turn back, when he can't just keep running to indoor light when he hears strange sounds in the dark or senses uncanny feelings on banned islands. This was such a time.

OPEN SPACES

I slapped hard, killed a half-dozen mosquitos, and my hand was sprinkled with blood. I dodged poison ivy, walked hands-up through stinging nettle, burning weed, we called it, and let the gurgling river guide me along the island's banks. Noon sun waned toward the west as my body moved through light-dappled shadows. When I saw the depressions in the earth near my feet I knew I had found the spot I was looking for.

I knelt down, brushed the ground gently with my fingertips, and then began to dig. I looked for odd shapes of stone, pieces of pottery, charred wood, rocks resembling spearpoints, and axeheads.

Had women, I wondered, knelt here to make their meals? Had old men died here? Had boys like myself sat here listening to stories told by elders whose faces flickered in campfire light? Had men and women made love here? Did the lonely at heart sit in moonlight, or pray — with awakened imagination — to their Great Spirit?

Bloodroots, blooming on the island, were in the way. I broke the stems of several. As I watched their orange juice stain my hands I remembered something my grandfather, Joseph Huot, son of Eucharist, grandson of Regis, had said.

"When I was young, when I looked past the horse and plow, I saw sometimes off on the horizon, silhouetted against the orange sun, Indians on ponies. It was the last of 'em. Once they stopped, dismounted, seemed to blend with the earth, then mounted and moved on."

"Did you find any arrowheads?" I asked grandpa.

"Many of them. They were in the plowed soil."

"Where are they now?"

"The Indians?"

"Yes," I said. "I mean no. Where are the arrowheads?"

I wanted them.

"They are gone," he said. "I don't know what happened to them."

I didn't find any arrowheads or any other artifacts on the Red Lake River Island. Archeologists had beaten me to the graves. If I was to find something I would need better tools than an eight-year-old's fingers. Heck, bring in the dozer, move some stones and bones. I stood up. I had gone far enough. Machines shouldn't do what hands should do.

Maybe this was respect. Or maybe I'd dabbled enough in the long night, had played archeologist long enough with the fates of men, women and their children like myself.

My fingertips felt raw, chafed by dirt and darkness.

Part of me just wanted to back away and forget the island, to isolate and dispel the urge that had brought me there, but it was too late. Some innocence stayed behind. It wasn't necessary to have found something tangible. It was the looking that mattered most: the dawning gall to glance at mortality, to enter the haunted house in the chain of natural being. There was evidence of a crime, if crime it was. My hands were dirty. My shoes had left tracks. There was even the good old Catholic guilt for doing something I was told to forget. But the lasting mark of that early island hour was the draning sense of precious life being part of the passing shapes of things. It took eight years for my eyes to adjust to this light. Never again did I sleep with a child's comforting trust — like a thick quilt on a cold night — of unlimited life.

Except when I didn't think about it.

≈ ≈ ≈

The Niedzielskis and I weren't ready for death on the Crooked Lake island, not ready for a long grip of discomfort and terror, so we risked the whitecaps. We paddled hard despite sore muscles, tired backs, cold skin and fear scratching at the door. The canoe rose and fell between waves. It smacked down into troughs between swells. It took a little water, and then more. Less rise, more scratching.

Each paddle stroke brought us closer to the distant silhouetted shore and lee water, darkness deepening. Unable to accurately tell direction, or to pause from our frantic paddling to consult a map, we used the dull roar of Curtain Falls to guide us to its portage. Mist from the falls met us as we put boot to rock. Hustling, we portaged down the near half-mile trail, reloaded the canoe above small rapids, slipped through, then paddled silently to camp.

"It's not the Hilton," Ray said of our tent once we were zipped and drawstringed in our dry down sleeping bags, "but it beats the hell out of the island."

*Mishipizhiw* was alive that night.

ଶ ଶ ଶ

The great serpent had played with us. Others were less lucky. Unknown to us at the time, two of three campers from Ely drowned in Crooked Lake as we struggled across its west end. As two of the men left shore in a motorized canoe, they realized they had forgotten their lifejackets so they turned around. The canoe capsized in wave chop. They couldn't turn the canoe rightside up because of the weight of the motor, and they were too far from shore to swim back.

*Mishipizhiw* had struck.

ଶ ଶ ଶ

Our paddle to the famed "Picture Rocks" at the southeast end of Crooked Lake, a cliff immortalized by artist Francis Lee Jaques, was postponed the next morning by more bad weather. We were tired of it. Most of our clothes were wet. Our campfires were small, windswept and smoky. Skeins of geese flying south overhead, although beautiful, were harbingers of more cold weather. Just as Rich suggested we abort our trip to the other end of

Crooked, the west side of Iron Lake faded, disappeared and turned white.

Snow: blowing our way.

We stashed dry gear beneath the canoe then dashed to the tent as strong winds lashed snow around us in a brief but forceful blizzard. We crawled back into our sleeping bags, might as well be comfortable, and I read aloud from Landes' *Ojibway Religion and the Midewiwin*.

The snowstorm stilled, then started up again.

ॐ ॐ ॐ

From Landes, Dewdney and other scholars, it was obvious early on that dating pictographs was no easier than discerning their meaning. Besides the Darky Lake pictograph of a person shooting a rifle, there were only six other pictographs from the Great Lakes to Great Slave Lake that were obviously painted after contact with the western vanguard of Americans and Canadians. There was another painting of a human with a gun, a mounted horse, two boats (one with pennant, the other with rigging and mast), and a pictograph of a building resembling a stockaded fort replete with rectangular flag and ball-topped mast.

Dewdney found dating the other pictographs more complex.

Although he consulted with pictography experts in Russia, China and Europe, he realized establishing pictograph creation dates — in North America and abroad — was reducible to a combination of laboratory techniques, weathering and patination studies (water access, water retention, acidity factors, solar radiation, other atmospheric factors, and paint/substrate considerations), and also lichenometry, prehistoric clues, and ethno-historical investigations like those involving Ojibway birchbark scrolls.

Carbon-14 testing, so helpful in archeological dating, seemed hopeless with pictographs.

"Even to collect enough paint to ensure the inclusion of a thimbleful of binder," Dewdney wrote of carbon-14 testing in his *Dating Rock Art in the Canadian Shield Region* (1970), "it would be necessary to scrape off an indeterminate number of paintings, without any guarantee that most of the binding agent had not already been leached away by weathering. At best, it would be possible to establish a mean date for the destroyed paintings, some of which might be quite old, others very recent."

Dewdney, albeit cautious with carbon-14 testing, nevertheless hazarded a guess of pictograph age.

"All the evidence so far," he opined in the *Ontario Museum Bulletin* (No. 26, 1957), "points to [the red ochre] having endured from one century to four."

The meanings of pictographs remained a wilder guessing game.

There was the possibility, of course, that some — especially the handprints — were nothing but 1600- or 1700-style graffiti. Or maybe the animal images were dodaim (totem) symbols, signs of Ojibway clans whose collective manito was an animal — the eagle clan, for example, or the loon, bear, wolf or moose — as suggested to me by Paul Summer. Summer, a longtime resident and potter of the Ely-Winton area, once lived along Pipestone Falls inside the Boundary Waters Canoe Area Wilderness. There he entertained an avid interest in native history, eventually subscribing to the totem theory when it came to pictographs. Before his death he put images of totems on his pottery. He was quite sure of himself.

There have been other possible pictograph interpretations.

"If they were intended as messages," Kenneth Kidd of Ontario's Trent University wrote, "some were probably addressed to the attention of other Indians."

Some pictographs might be memorials, illustrations of myths, or markers of natural or other significance whose meaning we might never know because of our radically different mindset. Dewdney averred to the end they were basically communicative rather than decorative or aesthetic. He cited Franz Boas' *Primitive Art*, explaining that a drawing's form is simply its visual aspect while its content houses intended meaning.

"The aboriginal artist," Dewdney said, "was groping toward the expression of the magical aspect of his life...Origin and purpose remain mystery."

🐦 🐦 🐦

It was only right during the course of my pictograph studies that I took my questions of pictograph origin and purpose to two men I considered authorities by blood and experience. The first was Ely's Robert Gawboy, 80, the Ojibway grandson of Ne-Ganik-Abo, the great scout who lived to be 106 and taught the famous Grey Owl, a.k.a. Archibald Belaney, much of what he wrote in *The Adventures of Sajo* and *The Men of the Last Frontier*. My other contact was Shan Walshe, 46, head naturalist of Quetico Provincial Park.

Gawboy used his hands a lot when he spoke, and when I met with him in Ely's Pioneer Apartments, with his wife, Helmi Jarvinen, at his side, he had much to say. His Indian name, Aykenshigeshegoub, meant "Man from the North Star" and as a boy he had roamed the canoe country of the Minnesota-Ontario border with his family. His father, Jim Gawboy, or Teh, was known to fellow Indians as Pe-now-a-we-say: "Falling Snowflakes." His mother, Bessie, was part white, the daughter of a "chief white man." Many summers were spent near Kettle Falls and on the bank of Moose River opposite Blind Man's Channel on Kabetogama Lake, one of the largest lakes in today's Voyageurs National Park.

"Teh," Gawboy said of his father, "was a wolfer, a wolf trapper. He killed wolf. Every time there were too many wolves, no matter where it was, they'd call for him."

Gawboys eventually moved to Vermilion Indian Reservation near Tower-Soudan west of Ely. "The old man," Gawboy explained, "wanted to live near law and order...it was safer, according to him." Young Robert became known as a "learner." He was all ears. He listened to Bear Grease who taught him to hunt and trap; to Joe Big Nose the canoe maker, who taught him canoes should have "liveliness" because a canoe "has to be a part of you"; to George Marsh who slipped him camping tips; and to Ne-Ganik-Abo himself.

"I seen him," Gawboy said. "I heard him. But was always scared of him. I don't know. A man should adore his grandfather, shouldn't he? He was an old man already."

I understood.

It was on the reservation Gawboy heard about one of the tests to become a medicine man, a shaman: crawl through a tunnel of brush for a mile to stab a knife into the ground next to a dead man. "It was terrifying," he said, "due to superstitions." He learned young scouts studied under chief scouts three to four years: "Don't ever let them kid you that white men surprised the Indians. They never did." And he learned how young warriors were taught to fight, ways of breaking arms, backs and kicking groins that made jujitsu and martial arts look like "kindergarten."

Work status was simple for Ojibway men. They were scouts, warriors or medicine men. Three classes.

As for the women, they were traditionally treated well. They inherited at marriage everything belonging to their husband. Although women were avoided by warriors a week before, during, and after a war party, women nevertheless called the shots.

"When a woman got tired of a man," Gawboy said, "she put his things outside the door, usually his clothes and weapons, and he had to leave."

Helmi: "Go back to momma."

"What if he comes in?" I asked.

Helmi: "He don't come in."

"Why?"

"That isn't cricket. That is the way things are done. That's why a lot of the white prisoners who were women didn't want to go back."

Slowly, I turned the subject toward pictographs. Gawboy had spent 80 years in pictograph country, had canoed its waters, harvested its wild rice, and had sat at the feet of his forebears, listening. What did Man From the North Star think? What in his estimation did the Quetico-Superior pictographs mean?

Gawboy's answer, despite a glance out the sunlit window, came quickly.

"Everybody and their kids can read them."

Wait a minute.

I explained that Canadian scholars like Dewdney had conducted interviews with a wide range of elderly Ojibway and Cree, and that their answers were so widespread, so like a dance from myth to guess to pure bafflement, that the scholars concluded contemporary Indians didn't understand the pictographs. This was the ace up my sleeve, my last and best card to get Gawboy to talk. He simply sat back in his chair and swatted the air with a hand.

"That's all nonsense," he said. "Indians aren't going to tell authorities nothing. The pictographs were signs to passersby of the country which lies around. They were sort of a road map."

🐦 🐦 🐦

Which was probably news to Shan Walshe when I caught up with him in Fort Frances, Ontario, in a motel room after a Quetico Park management hearing. Walshe had taken seven or eight ten-day canoe trips a year, for eight years, into Quetico, partly to work on his book, *Plants of Quetico*, but also to research and photograph pictographs. He had several thick files on the subject. The spring prior to our visit, he had discovered a new pictograph on Quetico Lake.

"The outlet of Quetico Lake had been blocked for years by a logjam," he explained. "A few years ago, the logjam was removed and the water level in Quetico Lake began dropping. The image I found looked very much like the Darky Lake *Mishipizhiw*, the Great Lynx."

In 1971, a year after Walshe began working for Quetico Park, he joined Dewdney on a pictograph expedition to Mackenzie and Darky lakes. Apparently they used Dewdney's canoe which had a painting of *Mishipizhiw* on the bow. On the trip, Dewdney refined his method of tracing pictographs.

"He would hold a piece of very thin tracing paper over the pictograph," Walshe said. "Then he would run a wet paint roller over the tracing paper until it became absolutely transparent. He would then trace the pictograph's outline with a pen, and, when finished, remove the paper."

I asked Walshe, of course, for his understanding of pictographs.

"First I would look into the obvious meaning," he said. "On Puckamo Island there is a pictograph site with a canoe turned upside down and a man turned upside down. Now this might indicate a canoe had capsized. Right beside the canoe is a thunderbird, an Indian mythological spirit. Perhaps an evil thunderbird capsized his canoe. The Indians were just depicting the fact that the thunderbird caused the capsizing. In some respects I think the pictographs could be just a historical documentation. I'm sure that's it in some cases but definitely not all of them."

Walshe cited another interpretation:

"On Darky Lake there is a cow and a calf moose, and there's a hole in the heart of the cow moose. Now, some people believe this indicates a documented shooting. Or else perhaps the hunter wanted to shoot the moose and drew a picture of the hole in the moose's chest to bring him luck in the hunt.

"The Indians did this on purpose. They would draw a picture of some animal and draw an arrow sticking in that animal. They were of the opinion that drawing this picture with the arrow in the animal would bring them good luck in hunting. This has been documented."

Walshe, like Dewdney, recognized the possibility of some pictographs representing dreams. He knew about the medicine men and young braves, their solitudes and fasts, their deadly serious quests for spiritual guardians not to be spoken of lightly — the bear and eagle and moose guardians. Walshe knew about these things. But as the night interview in my motel room drew to an end, as the day's long hours of listening and talking took their toll, he confessed pictographs could mean different things to different people and, the assumption was, they likely always would.

"For instance," he said before I switched off the tape recorder, "if a small child looked at a pictograph he would see rather superficial things. He would get enjoyment just from looking at a picture of a moose or bear. Whereas an older person, with more sensitivity and spiritual development, might see some significant moral in the pictograph."

಄ ಄ ಄

Pictographs as moral inkblots.

Aspiring shamans dreaming guardians.

Warriors connecting with their totemic past through scattered images on rock cliffs.

Road maps. Graffiti.

All the explanations flowed together like orange sap from a bloodroot stem as the Niedzielskis and I paddled east from Iron Lake to the southeast end of Crooked Lake and our expedition's last group of paintings. It is normally a courtesy to leave firewood behind for future campers at a campsite, but on Iron we had truly gone the distance. When not reading Landes during our snowbound day, when not glancing at migrating geese or the search plane that flew by low looking for drowned men, we gathered, Sven-sawed and split dry driftwood, mostly black ash, ultimately stacking and leaving about a quarter-cord covered with rainproof birchbark. Someone in our wake, perhaps at a critical hour, was set up for good luck.

It was a nice gesture, like my offering of tobacco on Warrior Hill, but it didn't prevent the strong wind and whitecaps we battled on Crooked Lake's Thursday Bay. It didn't keep the second of our three paddles from breaking although we managed to splice it with duct tape and cedar splints. When it came to reading a fading language on rock shores, we were on our own.

The paintings at the southeast end of Crooked near Lower Basswood Falls were as mysterious as any. There was a pelican, a heron or crane, an elk, a boat filled with people, and a moose — what? — smoking a pipe. Nearby was a crude painting of a tree (the only pictograph of a plant on the Canadian Shield), a red orb (the sun?), and what looked like a large fish, an upside-down canoe, and a thunderbird.

Some paintings were partly covered by lichens, others faded, some mere smearings of red ochre (where the artist wiped his hand clean?). Most were beyond reach, apparently painted when Crooked Lake's water level was higher.

Oddly, the paintings were never mentioned in accounts by early white explorers passing by this precise spot, unlike the cliff on which they're painted.

David Thompson, for example, canoed by in 1730.

"In the crevices of a steep rock," he wrote later, "are a number of arrows which the Sioux shot from their bows; the arrows are small and short. The Chippeways, the natives, say: These arrows are the voice of the Sioux and tell us 'We have come to war on you, and not finding you, we leave these in the rocks in your country, with which we hoped to have pierced your bodies.'"

Granting that arrows probably had more impact, left more of an impression than pictographs on explorers in hostile country, the Niedzielskis and I kept going. We paddled to Lower Basswood Falls, portaged around it, then headed up Horse River. We had been canoeing almost a week, it was raining, and we were cold. Worst of all, we had run low on food and were hungry. Tempers were short, nerves harried.

When darkness caught up with us along a Horse River portage, a long way from a designated campsite, we were in no mood to argue the wisdom of pitching our tent illegally right where we were. So we did. No one came by portaging or writing tickets, and we were better for it by morning.

Ray shouldered the canoe shortly after dawn and headed up the portage. Rich and I broke camp. Moments later, canoeless, Ray was back.

"There's a moose in the river," he whispered. "C'mon."

We followed Ray, spotted the antlered bull standing belly- deep, and then, whenever the bull submerged its head to eat underwater stems, tubers and roots, we skipped across river stones to the other side and scrambled up a granite ridge overlooking the moose. We were hungry: I knew beyond doubt that 200 years earlier, at the time hunters raced up Warrior Hill, we — on empty stomachs, and thinking of our women, children and parents in camp — would have shot that moose as fast as we could unleash an arrow. Blood the color of wet red ochre would have spilled drop-by-spurt into the Horse River's brown current, flowed downstream into Basswood River, then followed gathering waters into the heart of the country.

The moose's death would have meant food and life for us, life flowing in and through us in a timeless, sacred circle. Perhaps only by taking the moose, relying on it, would Ray, Rich and I have realized at a gut level the true significance of the moose pictographs scattered throughout the Quetico-Superior.

Moose as meat. Moose as *manito*. Moose as sustainer of physical and spiritual life.

# PART II
# TRAILS OF POWER

*A sense of one's standing in the natural world is not instinctive, not automatic, and only in the most general way culturally transmitted. In any usable degree it is, like all learning, a personal acquisition, arrived at only by becoming acquainted with the basic texts, with wild places.*

*— Paul Gruchow*
*The Necessity of Empty Places*

# CHAPTER FIVE
# MEANING AND MISERY ON THE KAM-DOG

It's one thing to take a canoe trip in search of pictographs, to follow tracks of red ochre into the heart of moose and wolf country, risking one's life on darkening waters and aching for meaning from old paint. Poking around, really. Checking out sign. It's another gambit altogether to turn your back on *maymaygwayshis* and *Mishipizhiw*—assuming you dare—to tackle a 230-mile historic canoe route known infamously as the Kam-Dog.

That's what the few people who know the Kaministikwia River- Dog Lake- Lac des Mille Lacs-Sturgeon Lake-Maligne River voyageur route call it. The Kam-Dog. It connects Thunder Bay, Ontario, on the north shore of Lake Superior, with Lac la Croix, home of Warrior Hill, on the common border of Canada's Quetico Provincial Park and northeastern Minnesota's Boundary Waters Canoe Area Wilderness. En route it crosses a height-of-land between the St. Lawrence and Hudson Bay watersheds, thus once connecting Montreal with the fur-rich Athabascan country in the Northwest. It is arguably the oldest, longest and hardest canoe route used by the original voyageurs heading into the heartland of Canada's central wilderness.

I know the Kam-Dog. I speak from experience. Those who dream of relaxing outdoor vacations, a Northwoods canoe trip perhaps, should forget the Kam-Dog. It's rarely fun. It is closed to the weak. It is a place demanding determination or, like Alaska's McCarthy and Wrangells, purpose. Most people should—and will, if they go far enough—leave the Kam-Dog alone.

I nevertheless liked the route's name from the start. It was short, to the point, and clapped off the tongue like an axe chop with echo.

I had forgotten about the Kam-Dog, having read of it in passing years earlier, until April 1981, when Ray Niedzielski of the red ochre expedition, and his future wife, Ann Healy, invited me to supper. Ray, 31, was working as assistant director of Camp Easton for Boys on Little Long Lake north of Ely. I was dreaming at the time of spending an autumn month paddling the perimeter of Quetico Provincial Park, a contemplative voyage of personal and geographical discovery. Ray, however, had been reading J. Arnold Bolz's *Portage Into the Past*, a narrative of how Bolz retraced by canoe the Pigeon River voyageur route from Grand Portage on the north shore of Lake Superior to Fort Frances-International Falls on the Minnesota-Ontario border.

When, over dinner, I saw a sparkle in Ray's eyes, the same twinkle he seemed to get whenever he thought of canoeing, I knew we were going to be covering ground.

I wanted calm lake waters. Ray wanted rapids and swamps.

I wanted a mellow experience. Ray wanted challenge.

Ray grabbed Bolz's book as bait.

"Listen to this."

*"Seems to me,"* Ray read, *"I've heard of another route west of Lake Superior,"* *Harvi grinned* [when Bolz and Harvi were deciding whether to take the Kam-Dog or southerly Pigeon River route]. *"Wouldn't that be easier?"*

*"That must be the Kaministikwia route from Fort William..." I replied. "No, it's not easier. The voyageurs had to be coaxed into using it."*

*"Well, that's out," Harvi quickly replied.*

Ray clapped the book shut and eyed me daringly. I had known him about seven years, ever since he was discharged from the aircraft carrier *U.S.S. Oriskany,* and I was beginning to understand how he thinks. In this case what was out for Harvi and Bolz was going to be in for us. Bolz had publicized the Pigeon River route. The Kam-Dog was comparatively unknown. If the Kam-Dog, furthermore, was avoided by the voyageurs, it was 1) certainly difficult, 2) likely little-known by historians, 3) rarely paddled by today's canoeists, and 4) thus the truest of challenges, a severe test of skill, and a route demanding nothing less than two diamonds of determination.

"Well, Jacques?" Ray asked.

Jacques was my voyageur nickname.

"Yes, Pierre?" I said.

❧ ❧ ❧

Information about the Kam-Dog was scant and discouraging.

According to E.W. Morse, in his *Fur Trade Canoe Routes of Canada: Then and Now*, the Kam-Dog as of 1967 was impassable. Over five miles of portages across the height-of-land midway on the route were buried in windfalls and logging debris.

Bolz claimed the portages on the Kam-Dog were so long and swampy that the Northwest Company paid its voyageurs bonuses to canoe the route. Some still mutinied.

More promising, but still intimidating, was K. Denis's description of the Kam-Dog in *Canoe Trails Through Quetico:* "For experienced canoemen interested in travelling a historic route. Definitely not a pleasure cruise."

❧ ❧ ❧

If we were going to have history, not pleasure, on the Kam- Dog, and if history was going to be much of the expedition's meaning, then at least we were dealing with the oldest history in the Quetico-Superior.

By the time Chris Trost dropped Ray and me off at the mouth of the Kaministikwia River in Thunder Bay on September 9th, we knew use of the Kam-Dog by white people dated back to 1688, just 68 years after the Pilgrim Fathers founded the colony of Plymouth, Massachusetts. In 1688, Jacques de Noyon—a 20 year-old Frenchman from Trois Rivieres, Quebec—paddled up the Kam-Dog to Rainy Lake. Although Daniel Greysolon, Sieur Dulhut had built a fort at the mouth of the Kaministikwia River about ten years earlier, and although *coureurs de bois* who were allied with him probably canoed north up the Kam, it was de Noyon, young and feisty, who explored as far as Rainy Lake in today's Voyageurs National Park, and headed westward to Lake of the Woods.

The route was used sporadically for the next 40 years to transport furs and trade goods between Lake of the Woods and Montreal.

Around August 1731, however, Pierre Gaultier de Varennes, Sieur de la Verendrye arrived at Grand Portage on Lake Superior about 30 miles down shore from the Kaministikwia. With him were his four sons, a nephew, and 50 voyageurs. They were on the way, they hoped, to the fabled Western Sea via Pigeon River, Lake Saganaga, Knife Lake, Basswood Lake, Lac la Croix and beyond. Far beyond. They had a navigational ace up their sleeve. Several years earlier, while La Verendrye was head of a fur trade post on Lake Nipigon, he had been given a birchbark map by an Ojibway chief named Ochagach. It showed three rivers heading northwest: the Fond du Lac (now the St. Louis River at Duluth on the western tip of Lake Superior), the Nantouagan (Pigeon), and the Kaministikwia, variously spelled Kaministiquia. La Verendrye had chosen the Pigeon River route because it had fewer rapids than the Kam-Dog and reduced the distance from Lake Superior to Lac la Croix, where the Kam-Dog and Pigeon routes merged, from 230 miles to 150.

The Pigeon was the choice of a practical man wanting to minimize miles while hunting an ocean he'd never reach.

Despite the Pigeon River's eight-mile grande portage, the route quickly became the major fur trade highway between Lake Superior and the Canadian interior. The fort at Kaministikwia was abandoned for one at Grand Portage. By 1759 there were French trading posts on Saganaga and Basswood lakes. There was Fort St. Pierre on Rainy Lake, Fort St. Charles on Lake of the Woods, and Fort Bourbon at the mouth of the Saskatchewan River. River traffic changed dramatically in 1783, however, when the Treaty of Paris between Great Britain and the U.S. ended America's Revolution. It forced the Northwest Company to find an alternative to the Grand Portage-Pigeon River route. Grand Portage was in new American territory and the U.S. threatened to impose duty on all trade items.

Back to the Kam-Dog.

Roderick McKenzie re-explored it in 1798; a few years later the Northwest Company moved its Lake Superior headquarters to Fort Kaministikwia (renamed Fort William in 1807 in honor of William McGilivray, a leading partner and director of the company). Although the move was expensive, it paid off handsomely. In 1805, furs sent east by the Northwest Company included 77,500 beaver, 2,132 otter, 40,440 marten, 2,268 fisher and 4,328 mink. According to Bruce M. Littlejohn in *Quetico-Superior Country*, as many as 2,000 voyageurs traveled through the area every year.

There were other kinds of Kam-Dog travelers.

In June, 1843, Sir John Henry Lefroy journeyed on the Kam-Dog to make magnetic surveys in the north. A year later, four nuns traveled the Kam-Dog on the way to the Red River settlement, en route praying aloud and singing hymns to offset the foul language and songs of the stocky, no doubt sometimes exuberant, French-Canadian voyageurs paddling the nuns along. The artist Paul Kane travelled the Kam-Dog in 1846 followed by Sir John Richardson in 1848 on his way north in search of the Franklin expedition. In 1857, Toronto geologist Henry Youle Hind covered the Kam-Dog on his Canadian Red River Exploring Expedition. In 1870 Canadian voyageur artist Frances Ann Hopkins, together with her husband who was a chief factor for the Hudson Bay company, visited the Kaministikwia which inspired Hopkins' later paintings. That same year, the expedition of Colonel Garnet Wolseley—with 1,400 men and 150 boats—used part of the Kam-Dog, together with the makeshift Dawson Road, to reach and quell the Riel Rebellion at Red River near today's Winnipeg, Manitoba.

Fort William, meanwhile, fell into disuse after 1821 when the Hudson Bay Company absorbed the Northwest Company. By the late 1800s, with construction of the Canadian Pacific Railway connecting Fort William (now Thunder Bay) with Selkirk, Manitoba, the Kam-Dog as a Canadian waterway for commerce was dead. Fort William would have completely died, too, around the turn of the century, but Canadians preserved its memory by reconstructing the fort as a living-history museum at Pointe de Meuron on the outskirts of Thunder Bay.

Fort William, Ray and I figured, would be the 1981 Kam-Dog Expedition's first stop.

 за за за

The Sleeping Giant, a large island shaped like a prone body, floated on the waters of Lake Superior as we loaded our aluminum 18-foot, five-inch "Big Brother" Beaver canoe and set off up the Kaministikwia in the heart of industrial Thunder Bay.

A tugboat towing a platform to a dredging site overtook us quickly, sending us scuttling toward shore in fear of being swamped by its large waves. The water, a dark brown with an oily surface film, foamed over as the tug went by. The air stank of chlorine from processed wood, and soon we were passing a Shell oil tanker from Toronto, a junkyard for cars, large grain elevators, a man busy with a sandblaster, and a rusty barge with disassembled bow. As jets took off and descended overhead, roaring with the power and thrust of ignited fuel, Ray spotted a pink liquid draining out of a pipe into the river.

We checked our map. The liquid came from a chemical plant.

It was an inauspicious start for strangers in a strange land but we put the poison behind us, trusting in wilder, cleaner country further upriver, as we headed for Fort William beneath sun. The fort's publicity director knew of our trip and had arranged for a traditional voyageur welcome. We were greeted with musket fire and bagpipe music. After Ahkash, the fort's staff photographer (a Toronto student originally from India), finished with us, he took us to the Cantine Salope for voyageur era food: pork and baked beans, apple juice, biscuits, whole wheat bread and slices of cheese. Afterwards we meandered around the fort's forty or more buildings, pausing at the canoe sheds and naval yard where a shipwright, in period costume like everyone else, was working on a schooner scheduled to sail two years later.

Identical ships, he said, were used during the fur trade heyday for shipping furs from Fort William to Montreal because too much of normal canoe loads was the voyageurs' own food.

We were back on the river shortly after noon, little fanfare this time, sun still shining. We headed for a section of the Kaministikwia that had tested the grit of voyageurs. Fortunately, we had with us a small booklet about the Kam-Dog canoe route published by Ontario's Ministry of Natural Resources. The booklet had surfaced in an uncanny way. The previous summer, while frantically searching for information about the Kam-Dog's rapids, waterfalls and portages, we had tried a combination of word-of-mouth inquiry and a classified ad in the widely read *Ely Echo*, learning little. I was astonished, therefore, when Alex Stig of Moorhead, Minnesota—who was camped on Moose Lake near Ely while leading a canoe trip to raise money for cancer research—walked into the *Echo* office where I was working and handed me the Kam-Dog booklet.

The booklet, albeit helpful, sketched forthcoming trouble.

"Between Pointe de Meuron [Fort William] and Kakabeka Falls," it said, "during periods of normal water level, you can expect to wade or line your canoe about two miles out of every three."

Sure enough. Our meal at Fort William wasn't even digested when we ran into shallow water and fast current. At first, resisting the obvious, we tried poling the canoe with our paddles, and lining the canoe, but we finally gave up and simply pulled the canoe, muscling it upriver, as we waded knee-to-crotch deep. By nightfall we had camped at the mouth of a small creek, taken naps, and bathed naked in the river. Supper, packed by Chris, was Rock Gut Stew: noodles, peas, potatoes and rice, sloshed down with Columbian coffee and hot chocolate.

## Chapter Five MEANING AND MISERY ON THE KAM-DOG

I washed dishes as Ray split wood.

"Now we both sit in the light of the fire," I noted in my journal before bed. "It is too dark to walk in the woods. A jet passes overhead occasionally. A two-thirds-full moon is at my back, the Big Dipper ahead over our dome tent. Blue-black sky. Silhouettes of elm treetops. The sound of vehicles on the distant Trans-Canada Highway. Twelve miles behind us. Close at hand: campfire light.
"We are on our way."

≈ ≈ ≈

Within two days we had not only bitten the Kam-Dog bullet, we had chipped our teeth. It was nine o'clock in the morning. Ray lay in the tent reading a hypothermia manual from the medical kit. We had awakened to thunder, fog and rain at our camp on a sandbar near Corbett Creek after a full day of exhausting paddling.

Paddling, however, stretches the meaning of the word.

Although we managed to cover seven or eight miles, we waded five of them, water to our thighs. The river bottom was uniform most of the distance but became bouldery near Roselyn Village. Wading was difficult as we constantly slipped on the submerged boulders, twisting and jarring our legs, and soon my knee, which I had strained the previous summer while jogging, began to hurt. Worse, my heart had a strange arrhythmia; it would inexplicably speed up, flutter, leave me faint, then resume a normal beat. When we became tired of wading, or when we reached our limit of frustration, whatever came first, we'd get back in the canoe to pole with our paddles, push with tiring arms against the current. Still, we covered ground. When we looked back we could see the drop in elevation as the Kam's banks of ash trees with gold leaves twisted and disappeared toward Lake Superior.

The rainy cloud cover over Ray's tented reading broke softly, just faint sunlight at first, but as the fog and mist dissipated, the day swelled into glorious, hazy sunshine.

## OPEN SPACES

We packed the canoe, paddled against a strong headwind past Stanley and tracked the canoe around four islands. More paddling beneath a bridge and past grazing cows led to more wading. Wading, paddling, wading: it was our karma. The wind grew stronger, and as a hawk circled on air currents in sunny haze above rippling aspen leaves, we found a white porcelain chip of a plate with blue markings, which we later learned resembled dinner ware the voyageurs sometimes freighted on the Kam-Dog. Not for themselves, of course; for the bigwigs.

Unaware of this, we tossed the chip back into the river.

The land continued to slope behind us into rugged high hills and ridges blued by distance as we approached 128-foot Kakabeka (Cleft Rock) Falls, once called Grand. Ahead of us lay the rock escarpments forming Kakabeka while on the riverbanks, beneath the September sun, cedar trees grew on duff above shale outcrops flowered with white and purple asters, blue forget-me-nots, yellow daisies and red poison ivy, the latter's leaves having lost green to frost. The last two miles to Kakabeka were the hardest of the day, all waded, sometimes down the middle of the river against strong wind.

The current at the base of Kakabeka Falls was fast, roiling with motion, as we waded around a small island on the west side of the river. No sooner did we have our lifejackets on, the trip's first time, than we found the portage: flat at first but then climbing at a steep grade. Pack on back, I crawled the last section on my hands and knees, careful not to grab the abundant trailside poison ivy for support. Ray and I had battled the Kam for three days, getting dirtier, smellier and tougher by the hour, and so we were not prepared for what awaited us at portage's end. As I crawled out of the bushes, the woods turned into clipped grass, a deck, and two clean-machine older folks (straight from their RV), standing at a railing overlooking the waterfalls. One of them held a trim poodle which began to yap at us. Even its owner appeared nervous, likely not knowing quite what to think about two men crazy enough to be traveling *up* a river with a waterfall comparable in height to Niagara.

We made campsite #153 of Kakabeka Falls Provincial Park our home for

116

the night, right next to the RVs, fluorescent bug-killers, and among roaming skunks. The distant sound of highway traffic blended with the roar of the falls as a park ranger showed up to collect three dollars for our camping permit. Under the permit's Vehicle License Number he printed "No Vehicle" (not quite true, I thought) and then he asked about our journey.

"I hope you make it," he said.

"What do you mean *hope* we make it?" I replied. "You're supposed to say 'Have a good trip.' The worst part could be over."

"Yah," he said laughing. "You can really motor from here, eh? If it doesn't turn cold and freeze up."

೫ ೫ ೫

Like the Holy Landers we were, we walked to the falls twice, pilgrims to beauty. The first time we went at night, despite the chill, to see the Kaministikwia snake away toward Lake Superior beneath a crescent moon. Although physically weary our spirits felt strong. We could sense how we were ascending the Canadian Shield, gaining elevation fast, and how we would eventually be among granite outcrops, red pine, and the dance of whitewater flowing with us, not against us.

We visited Kakabeka a second time in the morning, frost stinging fingers, and watched a rainbow form in the spray as a rising sun cleared eastbank trees. I was reminded of some of the Kam's earlier visitors like artist Kane who, in May, 1846, thought the falls of Kakabeka surpassed "even those of Niagara in picturesque beauty." Geologist Hind in 1857 also found the falls "extremely beautiful." The river's yellowish-brown water, he wrote in his later narrative, plummets over "a sharp ledge into a narrow and profound gorge. The plateau above the portage cliff, and nearly on a level with the summit of the falls, is covered with a profusion of blueberries, strawberries, raspberries, pigeon cherry, and various flowering plants, among which the bluebell was most conspicuous. On the left side of the falls a loose talus is covered with wild mint and grasses which grow luxuriantly under the spray." Hind found many springs, 20 degrees cooler than the river water, trickling down a cliff and he drank from them: "a delicious beverage." He described the 100-foot cliff on the east side of the falls as having "perfect fidelity" because of the exposed geological stratification. Hind had a strange way with words yet he didn't finish commenting on Kakabeka without remarking on its beautiful rainbows "of very intense colour. . . continually projected on this talus."

According to Denis in his *Canoe Trails Through Quetico* (we were far from Quetico), another Kaministikwia traveler, Catherine Moodie Vickers, visited Kakabeka in August, 1873. She, too, was struck by the beauty of a rainbow, although below the falls, not—as Ray and I saw—above it.

"Gilded and burnished by the morning sun," she wrote her mother, Susanna Moodie, an author, "the great current of water came rushing down nearly two hundred feet, the whole breadth of the river, no island or stone to break the outline—one pure torrent of snow-white foam, not clear or crystalline, but like a continuous mass of cream. As it reaches the rapids below it breaks over the rocks. . .There is a little island. . .and here we landed. . .we were in the loveliest rainbow—the stones, the trees, everything gloriously colored with it."

⁓ ⁓ ⁓

"We're missing what?" I asked Ray.

We were packing up, breaking camp, getting ready to leave Kakabeka's campground.

"We're missing a map," he said.

"Which one?"

"Southwest Windigoostigwan. We'll need it to reach Quetico's French Lake."

After discussing options, we decided to write Peter Sturdy, a parks and recreation planner for Ontario's Ministry of Natural Resources, whom we had visited in Thunder Bay, and ask him to send us a Windigoostigwan map in care of the post office at Owakonze, Ontario, which we would pass through. But when Ray walked into the village of Kakabeka to mail our letter he learned there was no post office in Owakonze. He sent the letter anyhow, adding a postscript to mail the map to a gas station, grocery store, whatever in Owakonze.

It was a long shot, and we would miss.

ૐ ૐ ૐ

By the time Ray and I gained almost a thousand feet of elevation, nine days and 100 miles from Lake Superior, we were convinced the Kam-Dog Expedition was reducible to one obstacle and challenge after another.

When we left Kakabeka, for example, we had a short paddle across quiet water but soon had to wrestle the half-mile Rocky (or Ecarte) Portage around rapids and a dam. We rode whitecaps above the dam for two miles beneath sunny skies, shirtless weather, but— despite beautiful rock shores with jackpine on one side of us, and tamarack, sedge grass and aspen with gold leaves on the other—our fortune was short-lived. We had to pull the canoe up a mile of swift rapids. The water was crotch-deep, the boulders large and slippery. Ray slipped once and fell backwards. Near the top of the rapids we had to unload the canoe, pull it several feet at a time across rocks, secure the canoe, then go back to get the packs, all the while balancing on boulders as water swirled around our shins and thighs.

We stopped to watch an osprey ride air currents against blue sky over a nearby island. Sometimes, despite the strong wind, it remained stationary, flapping furiously for fixed position. It dove once into shallow water, missed the fish, rose, then soared overhead past us.

Within a quarter mile after reaching calm water near Hume we had another portage, this one 250 yards long around a series of falls where the river dropped 15 feet. Ray broke the drudgery and tedium by swimming briefly above the falls in an amphitheater of granite walls. A short paddle led to another portage, more tracking, waist-deep wading and, as day waned, a mile of rapids as high forested hills appeared in the direction we were going. Uncle. We had had enough. We camped on the east shore of the rapids, Ray making a lean-to shelter with canoe and tarp as I cooked herbed vegetables over a fire of bone-dry driftwood. We ate the trip's first dessert—dates and apples in brown sugar with cinnamon—while sitting on the rock shore at sunset. Cooling dusk brought peace filled with the inescapable roar of whitewater. By dark we were huddled next to a campfire.

"Now the full moon swinging over the Kaministikwia," I scribbled in my journal, my back against a log: "Trudgery. Despite the perfect weather we are covering half the needed distance each day."

This changed the next day when we covered 16 miles despite more portaging, wading and morning rain. We passed Brule Creek, the town of Kaministikwia and the mouth of Shebandowan River. Skies cleared. The sunshine felt warm as homes appeared along the shore. We stopped paddling near a wooden bridge to drift and watch unseen as a girl riding a bike—three dogs following her—stopped to chat with a beautiful young woman on a narrow gravel road along the river. They laughed, enjoying company in sun. As they spoke in French the scene seemed part of a foreign land, as if we were paddling in France itself, a slice of beauty we could see and hear but not enter or touch. For we were invisible. We were voyageurs of an earlier time. The girl and woman could not see through the afternoon's slant of historical light, the tunnel of time connecting their presence on the Kam with the men in canoes of a previous age doggedly journeying upstream.

We reached Little Dog Lake, source of the Kaministikwia, by nightfall, spent the night, then fought head-on wind to the bouldery start of the infamous Great Dog portage. The two-mile portage gained 500 feet in elevation while bypassing a series of waterfalls to the west that, in Hind's opinion, surpassed the beauty of Kakabeka. There was a legend rooted here that the Dog lakes were named after an effigy of a dog made with sand in troughs of excavated clay by the Sioux following a battle with Ojibway. The effigy teased the defeated Ojibway and, although discovered later, was almost obliterated by 1823.

## Chapter Five MEANING AND MISERY ON THE KAM-DOG

We climbed the portage in two hours despite seven stops but could go no further. Dog Lake, 12 miles long, was wild with wind.

What now?

Windbound, we surrendered to weather.

Stopped in our tracks, we relaxed.

As whitecapped rollers continued to crash against Dog's pebbly crescent shore all afternoon, we sipped tea and coffee, burned brownies and put up clotheslines to dry damp gear. We napped, lazing in sun like turtles. Later, still waiting for Dog to calm, I swam in the cold lake as Ray read Sig Olson's essay "Spiritual Aspects of Wilderness." Both of us knew we were biding time, edging ever closer to an old voyageur trick. If the day's winds diminished at sunset we were going to head out on the water, paddle in darkness, and sneak across Dog for Dog River.

It didn't quite work out that way.

Although we broke camp at seven o'clock to paddle twilight's moderate chop, darkness slowed us down. We had forgotten batteries for our flashlight. We couldn't read the map. Not until a full moon rose reddish-orange through broken clouds above islands could we continue forward confidently. I could read the map by angling it against the moonlight, and as the moon rose we could see Dog's west shore which we paralleled. So far, so good. But as we headed northwest a wind from the northeast began to brew, sweeping across Dog's expanse.

We could feel it on our skin and in our hair. Wavelets licked the starboard bow.

We made an important decision when we came to a large bay. We could continue following the shoreline, or take a beeline across open water to a small island, then scoot another mile north of it to the far shore. I agreed with Ray the island way would be shorter, no doubt, but I also thought it would be safer—should a squall strike—to hug the shore of the bay.

## OPEN SPACES

We took the bay, caution proving wiser than valor.

An hour later the wind reached gale force. Large swells rolled under our canoe which, knifing through whitecaps, slammed down hard into troughs. We realized as spray wet our faces it was time to get off the water. Camp or die. We searched the shoreline, squinting in the moonlight at its rocky, forested features, but not until the last minute—paddling desperately, wind still building—did we spot a relatively flat point with a clearing large enough for a tent. Wave spray shot six feet into the air off rocks as we beached the canoe, unloaded, and put up the tent. We moved quickly, our motions habit, caring little when we discovered close-up that the ground beneath the tent was rough with rocks and roots. It was simply good to be on ground, any ground.

As we crawled into our sleeping bags, warm and dry, I positioned my head so I could look out the tent door. The full moon shone on my face. Outside, beyond silhouetted jackpines, the restless lake flashed liquid silver: a flood of silver as my eyes closed, Dog swelling and surging, the shoreline awash and swept, the Kaministikwia behind us, the Dog River ahead.

It was midnight.

❧ ❧ ❧

Hind, while crossing Dog Lake 124 years earlier, had timed his voyageurs whom he called, in a thoughtless moment, "the strange companions with whom necessity compels you to associate." They made one paddle stroke a second, 60 a minute. "This," Hind explained to Provincial Secretary R.L. Terrill, "would give for a day's work, from 5 a.m. to 7 p.m., with two hours stoppage, 12 hours, at 3600 strokes per hour, or 43,200 strokes a day."

❧ ❧ ❧

The pace of our journey changed dramatically as we ascended the alluvial Dog River, the French's Riviere des Chiens. It hadn't changed much since L'Abbe Belcourt in 1831 found it "torturous" and "very dirty" or, even earlier in 1823, when Major Delafield found it to be a "dreary scene" of muddy water, floating and falling trees, and "almost insupportable" mosquitos throughout the day. We didn't have to worry about the mosquitos—it was the third week of September—but the 35 miles of the Dog River we had to cover before heading westward overland tested our navigational skills.

Go left. . .left, no, right. . .right, no, straight ahead.

The river, banked with alders, tamarack, willows and Labrador tea, meandered back and forth through flatlands. Sometimes it widened into marshes, other times narrowed into channels with equal-sized fingers of water leading to dead ends. Relying on map, compass and luck, we probed our way up the maze yet covered 19 miles our second day before camping on a rough moose path next to Little Rapids.

We put a tarp up when night skies began to sprinkle.

"Imagine it," Ray joked later in the tent as we adjusted our bodies to the moose-tracked ground. "Some bull will come by tonight, tangle its antlers in the tarp, then, spooked, it'll come charging down the path, tarp streaming behind, and trample us."

It was more possible than I cared to admit but I was anxious about something else. I was worried about running out of water. We were approaching the Kam-Dog's height-of-land, and I could recall a dream I'd had months earlier of canoeing up a serpentine river twisting through dense vegetation. The river eventually narrowed into a stream, then a brook which, in turn, possibly disappeared in a spring bubbling out of a peat pocket. I wasn't sure. I couldn't remember the dream's ending. But the dream itself, flowing into its dim conclusion, had undertones of landscape closure and claustrophobia.

I mean, what do you do when you're on a canoe trip and, separated from home by 200 miles of wild country, you run out of water?

Do you call the cops? Radio the water patrol? Dial 911?

## OPEN SPACES

Summer had been unusually dry.

Worry gnawed at me as we continued up the Dog the next day. We saw a gray-white wolf dash along the riverbank at noon, then turned west into Jourdain (or Prairie) Creek. The creek was only five feet wide in places and getting narrower. If not for beaver dams it would have been dry, perhaps ending our trip, but the backed-up water, cold and tap-clear, granted passage. Windfallen jackpine and balsam fir criss-crossed the creek, and if we couldn't pull our canoe out of the water and around the trees we cut our way through them.

My Hudson Bay axe, with its 27 inch oak handle, began to get a workout.

Jourdain led to Coldwater Creek, several marshy lakes (including Viscous, or Muddy Lake, where the voyageurs complained of hard paddling due to the lake's shallow, slimy bottom) and, at the top of the Kam-Dog watershed, Coldwater Lake, originally L'eau Froide, once thought too cold to drink. We drank. We filled our water bottles. Soon we were scrambling through the woods looking for the beginning of Prairie Portage: the longest, hardest, most never-give-an-inch portage of our lives.

ও ও ও

The Kam-Dog guidebook, which Alex Stig had given us, claimed Prairie Portage was marked well. It wasn't.

Once we found its faint trail with occasional blazed trees it quickly disappeared into windfalls which we bulled or chopped through. The axe again. It became clear we would either have to bushwhack a couple miles west to Dog River Road or turn around.

Go back.

And going back, well, as any true Kam-Dog voyageur knew, going back was absolutely out of the question.

The portage we were looking for had changed much since the early voyageurs, artists and government travelers like Hind. The original portage led two miles to Height of Land Lake, Lac du Milieu and, replete with a Northwest Company walkway of hewn logs, to Savanne River, a total portaging distance of about five miles. By 1981, however, the original portages were so obliterated by disuse, logging and natural decay they were considered impassable. Instead, canoeists were advised to follow Prairie Portage to Dog River Road, take the road five miles south to the Trans-Canada Highway, then follow that a mile and a half west to a roadside park on Savanne River near Argon.

Total portaging distance? 8.1 miles rather than the original five.

"However," the Ministry's guidebook warned, "logging trucks and heavy traffic on these roads make portaging this stretch extremely dangerous, if not impossible. Arrangements should be made to transport canoes and equipment with an appropriate vehicle."

*Non*, Pierre and I had thought: legs would do. Long before we reached the Kam-Dog's height-of-land, probably back on Burntside Lake in a moment of bravado, we had agreed to portage the entire distance come hell or low water, which, as long as we insisted, is exactly what came.

Having lost all signs of the portage, Ray climbed a birch and jackpine to scan the western horizon in hopes of locating an old clearcut where the portage was supposed to lead. I searched for an abandoned logging road marked on our map. Drifting apart, we periodically called to each other, our responses keeping us in touch, oriented. The only thing worse than being lost was getting lost from each other, or separated from our gear. It was a windless, quiet late afternoon, and as we called to each other the shouts became fainter and fainter, swallowed by forest, mere audible threads a step from snapping. The persistent nagging of my pre-trip claustrophobia dream returned.

It had—in a slightly altered version—come true.

Anxious moments. Hard-fought miles.

Out of options, day aging, we had no choice but to review our map, shoulder the canoe and packs, and head cross-country. Bushwhack. As the sun began to set we found the old logging road, portaged a mile and a half west, then pitched camp in a gravel pit next to Dog River Road. It wasn't our idea of a wilderness experience, the pit ran against our romantic grain, but there were no campsites along Dog River Road. No rock points with needle duff and pine. What you found is what you got. This was logging country, the cellulose trough of Thunder Bay's timber empire, and the road—gravel, wide, mostly flat—was a trucker's "Move over I'm coming" north-south trunk where loaded trucks had a penchant for losing logs on—oops—sharp curves.

Logs lay scattered in the ditches and the pit was all we had. We'd make the best of it, rest up, and portage to Savanne in the morning.

I heard a train whistle in the south as I walked away from camp at dusk to fetch water. We were thirsty, and our Spanish Rice dinner required more water than we had. Having lived on water, or next to it, for many days, we hadn't given its availability much thought. Little concern. This changed as I searched the countryside. The best water I could find was in a ditch, the water brown, its edge scummed, its surface rippled by scuttling beetles. I knelt next to it, started filling my water bottle, then emptied the bottle out.

I stood up.

For Ray in the pit, and for the long portage ahead, I had bad news.

&#10086; &#10086; &#10086;

There was no usual coffee or hot chocolate with breakfast the next morning, and, like our disgustingly crunchy rice supper after I'd hiked to the ditch, our dawn fuel was dry: nuts, raisins, figs and peanut butter.

We didn't speak much as we packed. Circumstances didn't favor enthusiasm. Nor did we have to consult a book by Cliff Jacobson or Bill Mason about canoe traveling to know portaging six miles without water was going to be a severe test of endurance.

One of us carried the 60-pound canoe and a light pack while the other carried two packs weighing, stuffed and strapped, about 80 pounds. We exchanged loads every half mile or two rests. Logging trucks, barrelling down Dog River Road, passed us, sending us to the ditch in clouds of dust for clearance and safety. A lone car stopped to offer us a ride. No thanks. I was exhausted after five miles when we reached the Trans-Canada Highway near the railroad stop of Argon. Not only couldn't I tolerate the canoe pressing down on my shoulders, its weight augmented by life jackets and paddles, but a strong northwest wind buffeted the canoe, twisting it sideways.

My lips and mouth were dry, my tongue thick. I felt lightheaded. My knee, now in an Ace bandage, hurt with every step.

Ray, getting a surge of strength when we reached the Trans-Canada, carried the canoe the last half mile. As fleets of semi-trailer trucks, logging trucks, and cars approached us at 70 miles per hour, he would stop, spread his legs apart, and put the bow of the canoe on the highway's shoulder to brace himself against the onrushing blasts of air. I held onto my hat and leaned forward beneath the packs. I pitied Ray. I pitied myself. It was easy to question our wisdom. Somewhere along the line we had put sanity on hold.

We were both weak when we reached a small picnic area on the Savanne River, the end of our portage. We had declined another ride and, despite profuse sweating under sunny skies, we hadn't drunk any water for almost 24 hours. We were ready to dive into the Savanne, to splash our faces, drink deeply and thank our ever-giving *manitos*, but when we reached the river we found boulders, bear tracks and a few inches of muddy water heading, at least, downhill. We were over the Kam-Dog's height-of-land. Over but dry.

We had to find water. Water wasn't a trivial question; it was the single, most important thing in our lives. We would find it, buy it, or steal it. We stashed our gear and began our hunt, Ray heading downstream, me to the picnic area.

There was no well, no pump, no public water. An old phone booth, its door ajar, had no phone to call for help if it came to that. I passed a large sign commemorating the Kam-Dog as Canada's first trans-highway then came upon a picnic table where a couple families had bailed out of their RVs to eat bratwurst, chips, and to drink cold beer. Cold beer. I felt conspicuous. I was dirty, disheveled and desperate. I suppose I appeared capable of crime. I was. The women looked up. Someone call the cops I imagined them thinking. There, to the side, was another RV, its owner bent over a jack to change a tire.

"Excuse me, sir," I said dryly, hoping to elevate politeness over appearance. "You wouldn't happen to have some water?"

Before he could say no I explained our expedition and situation. He looked me over. He was from Utah, he said, an ex-fireman. He knew the value of water. He led me to the side of his camper and opened the door. His wife was standing next to a five-gallon glass container of water replete with bottom spigot.

He filled a glass. I drank it. I drank another.

"You wouldn't have some water I could take with me?" I said. "I have a partner who is dry as a bone."

He rinsed a half-gallon milk container, filled it with water, and did the same to an empty bottle of vodka.

I was already feeling spry as I headed back to Ray. We had agreed to rendezvous at the canoe and, given my initial lack of success in finding water, I reasoned Ray had come up empty-handed. I quickened my steps, crossed a ditch and headed down a trail to our gear. Ray was sitting against the canoe, his back to me. Without so much as a glance over his shoulder as I approached he raised a can of cold beer and took a long swig.

We made good time on the Savanne.

## Chapter Five MEANING AND MISERY ON THE KAM-DOG

Although we awoke to frost after a restless night of hearing Canadian Pacific Railway trains, the tracks paralleling the Trans-Canada, we were able to fight our way through the upper river's windfalls and beaver dams to cover 22 miles by dark. The river was marshy, meandering, flanked by willow, alder, dogwood and tamarack. We saw a bull moose as we struggled against a head-on wind, and we stopped briefly at the village of Savanne for supplies, netting little. But progress was good.

The next day, riding a soft breeze from the northwest beneath sun, we paddled 15 miles down island-studded Lac des Mille Lacs. Here the Seine River flowed west to Rainy Lake but the voyageurs avoided it because of its steep drop and rugged portages.

They, like us, veered southwest to Brule and Windigoostigwan.

"Dad burn it!" Ray cussed. "What would people say?"

We had reached a small island campsite—rock, red pines, caribou moss— in Baril Bay of Lac des Mille Lacs and, nights freezing regularly, Ray was again wrestling with his sleeping bag. Along with the fishing rod to accompany his expensive Canadian fishing license, he had forgotten the zipper for his sleeping bag. At first he had coped by putting the zipper runners beneath him, letting the weight of his body hold the bag shut. As the nights became colder, he invented new, more complicated methods of trying to stay warm. On Baril Bay's island he had laid spare clothes on his foam pad, put wool socks on his hands, wool-lined winter mittens on his feet, a wool balaclava on his head, and he had put my spare down jacket on backwards, an arm up each sleeve but with the zipper at the back, unzipped.

I didn't question Ray's ingenuity as I lay snug in my subzero-rated REI down bag. I had to laugh at Ray's fussing, and I did, and as I laughed, Ray's humor—such a blessing on the trail when things got tough—multiplied upon itself, approaching slapstick.

"I swear it, Jacques," Ray said as he finally settled down, "if that big pine outside the tent draws lightning tonight, and we get fried, some good old boys are going to find our bodies, see the socks on my hands, the gloves on my feet, the jacket on backwards, and they're going to mutter for weeks that we were a couple of American freaks zippin' on drugs back in the bush."

It could have happened. Ray was right. And we could have been the gossip of the province. But morning brought more sunshine as we portaged into Baril Lake and paddled past Camp Owakonze—a Jesuit boys camp closed for the season.

We met Joe Kreis at Brule Lake portage. Kreis, about fifty years old and one of Owakonze's population of two, was working on an outboard motor. Originally from Luxembourg, he had lived in Owakonze for 20 years. In summer he took care of the Jesuit camp. In winter he trapped beaver and marten, using a snowmobile to cover his 30 mile trapline.

Joe put down his tools and invited us to his cabin where we met the woman he lived with. Nicknamed Dink, she was from Denver, liked Winston cigarettes and was quick to offer coffee. She and Joe went to Atikokan every three weeks for supplies and mail. No, she said, they hadn't received a map for us. Yes, Joe said, our general overview map should get us to Quetico.

I asked about the crank telephone on the wall.

"Help yourself," they chimed.

As Dink poured more coffee I called a friend near Ely to inform Chris, who was scheduled to replace Ray, that we would be at Quetico's French Lake in the park's northeast corner the next day. Ray phoned friends in Sleepy Eye, Minnesota, to say he'd likely be able to be best man at their wedding the following weekend.

Everything, it seemed, was falling into place.

From Kreis's we portaged a half-mile to eight mile-long Brule Lake and then paddled west to Windigoostigwan. The shimmering sunlight on the water was bright, burning our eyes as we searched for a campsite—the day's 20 miles behind us—on a crescent sand beach. The campsite faced southwest and was roomy enough for several tents, but it had been used many times before: rusty lard cans, fish skeletons and fish heads were scattered everywhere. Ray started a fire, gathered the fish remains, and burned them. I walked the beach to find firewood, but as I walked, the stench of Ray's fish-burning fire followed me, deepening my anger at slob campers, and reminding me of a grim tale Hind had told in his 1857 narrative.

Windigoostigwan, he explained, was once called Cannibal Lake because of an "unnatural deed" in 1811. As a band of 40 Ojibway starved, survivors ate the bodies of the dead. Eventually only a woman remained, she living because she murdered the second-to-last survivor, whom she ate.

"Meeting with another party of Indians," Hind said, "who drew the dreadful secret from her, she was put to death, under the impression that those who have once fed on human flesh always retain a desire for it, which they are not unscrupulous in gratifying when opportunity offers. Several instances of cannibalism were mentioned to us by the voyageurs as having occurred on this route. . . Both voyageurs and Indians always spoke of these horrible deeds in subdued tones and with an expression of anxiety and alarm."

I said nothing to Ray about this when I returned to camp for supper of Rock Gut Stew, nor, later, after paddling alone on the Windigoostigwan to drift in dusk silence. Hind's tale had begun to pall, to seem unimportant and trivial. Under the circumstances it barely applied.

What applied, what mattered, was the closeness I felt to Ray on this our last night together.

As we sat in the firelight, our spark against the arctic, we spoke about simplicity, labor-intensive cultures, and the differences between wilderness travel and the button-and-switch hubbub of city life. The dropping out and tuning in. They were worlds apart, we agreed, yet connected now by the passing of fragile flesh and the sweep of personal vision. Behind us lay the lives we led before departing Thunder Bay. Ahead of us lay new lives with unknown trajectories. Between the past and future we had canoed out of time to camp in the middle of things. Ray, I sensed, needed this, not permanently like a few people, but periodically like most of us. He needed the timeless perspective of the trail, or the promise of the trail, and without either his spirit was starved, weakened and susceptible to technological cannibalism.

Ray threw another stick on the fire and I could see—in the brightened, ensuing silence—he had little to fear at the moment. He was where he wanted to be. He had proposed doing the Kam-Dog, paddled its hardest section and, en route, accomplished a journey some of the original voyageurs refused to do.

I would miss him.

Without saying a word, by surrendering to an interior fire with its own glow and arc, I wished him well.

ᣚ ᣚ ᣚ

Ray left me in good company at French Lake where, just like that, he was gone.

We had paddled the foggy waters of calm Windigoostigwan at dawn, worked our way down the bouldery shallows of French River, then portaged two miles down the old Dawson Road, now a nature trail, to a campground along Quetico Park's French Lake. Chris, shuttling Ray's car 270 miles from Ely, arrived a few hours later bearing fresh steak, apples, cookies and Molson's beer. The three of us spent the evening swapping news and stories next to a star-capped campfire, cementing camaraderie, but by morning—with Ray's departure—the Kam-Dog had taken a subtle turn.

I had known Chris for less than a year, yet I knew her aspirations were close to my own. She had the canoeing skills, experience and enthusiasm to complete the Kam-Dog, and the endurance, I hoped, to paddle another fifty miles to my cabin, near her own, on Burntside Lake. One of my goals was to connect Lake Superior and the Kam-Dog to my home. I was counting on Chris to quicken the current.

She had already contributed much. She had chosen the expedition's menu of whole foods, making sure proteins and nutrients complemented one another; she had packaged individual meals, separating breakfasts and lunches from dinners; and she had tucked longhand quotes by Sigurd F. Olson, Calvin Rutstrum, Wendell Berry and other naturalists in with each meal: food for thought while nourishing our bodies, or when just paddling along, mulling things, as Sig Olson did by keeping similar quotes in accessible pockets. Chris had, moreover, dropped Ray and me off at Thunder Bay.

But there was more to Chris than Kam-Dog support.

She had environmental knowledge and outdoor savvy. Born in Rochester, Minnesota, she was the daughter of a dentist who liked nothing more than to hunt elk in Wyoming. When Jim returned home he brought meat for the family and stories about wild country for whomever wanted to listen, like Chris. In 1976 she earned a degree at the University of Minnesota, Twin cities, before working as an extension agent for Minnesota's Ramsey County, a plant information specialist for Chicago's Botanic Garden, and in customer relations for Eddie Bauer in Minneapolis. She got a good discount on clothing and recreational equipment at Eddie Bauer, and when we met she had better canoeing equipment than my own.

This mattered. It caught my eye. It led to further inquiry.

Chris moved from Minneapolis to Burntside Lake in May 1981 to work as staff naturalist at a YMCA facility on the lake's North Arm. The following August she made arrangements to move into a slab-sided, 15 x 27-foot cabin on St. Louis county land surrounded by Superior National Forest. The cabin was heated with wood, had no electricity, telephone or plumbing, and required a mile walk between car and cabin. Once Chris had fully settled in—after the floor-to-ceiling bookcase was up and filled; after the Monarch cookstove and Jotul woodburner were connected—she returned to the Twin Cities to get her black cat, Fatima, to be her companion and expert in-house mouser.

Clearly Chris had made a commitment to living in the Northwoods.

# OPEN SPACES

I asked her, back then, why.

"The singing wilderness," she said, paraphrasing the first of Sig Olson's nine books focusing on the natural beauty and mystique of the Quetico-Superior. "Sig was probably the most influential person in my life."

Chris also wanted to get to know the old voyageur waterways and, when canoeing, to simplify her life.

"When people talk about simplifying," she explained, "and stay within their usual surroundings, especially within a city, I find it almost humorous. I think for practical purposes my life is very simple now, but I still have a comfortable bed, comfortable chairs, all my books. I like, for a part of every year, to really simplify: to sleep on the ground, to carry my belongings with me, and to manage to live with those belongings. And I hope that the reminder of that style of life will carry with me through the year until I travel another route the next year."

I was convinced that Chris Trost, albeit only five-foot-one and 105 pounds, was—as a voyageur and woodswoman—a woman after my own heart. She belonged on the Kam-Dog.

ཿ ཿ ཿ

Weather, not terrain, was the persistent obstacle for Chris and me on the last leg of the Kam-Dog. Eight of its nine days were overcast, rainy, sleety and, inevitably, blasted by snow. Autumn was at hand. Winter approached. As they met we had to make several decisions that not only influenced the outcome of the expedition but flowed far beyond the Kam-Dog to ripple against beaches of future years: clear to the shores of Hocoka.

The rain began on 13-mile-long Pickerel Lake southwest of French our first day out together. There, huddled next to a lunch campfire, I was forced to re-examine and clarify one of the precise purposes of the trip: route fidelity. I was studying maps when I noticed that Deux Rivieres, part of the original Kam-Dog route, lay a day away.

## Chapter Five MEANING AND MISERY ON THE KAM-DOG

*Deux Rivieres?* I asked myself, my French rusty.

Earlier on Pickerel a passing canoeist had asked us if we were going to Two Rivers.

"No," I said, not yet familiar with the name.

"Good," he replied. "The water's terribly low. Gotta wade in muck."

As I looked at the map I began to make a simple linguistic connection. Chris knew French. I asked her the meaning of "deux rivieres."

"Two rivers," she confirmed.

At that point we had a choice: do the Doré Lake and Deux Rivieres route, or veer south on Pickerel River via Beg, Bud and Olifaunt lakes, bypassing what promised to be a muck-slogging experience. Chris and I discussed options, she leaving the decision to me. I weighed the decision for the rest of the day, that night, and again the next morning.

Who, after all, likes misery?

Who wouldn't be weary after 17 straight days of wading up rapids and making countless portages including a dehydrating eight- miler?

Who wouldn't be tempted to take the easiest way out to avoid downstream muck, maybe leeches and bloodsuckers?

Contrary to evidence, we weren't masochists. We didn't get our kicks from pain.

Yet when we broke camp the next morning beneath gray skies, my mind was made up. I wasn't doing the Kam-Dog to do what a conniving voyageur might have done (take the high water of Beg-Olifaunt). I was retracing a historic waterway or the natural lack of it. We would stay the course.

Ray, I knew, would have been proud.

The sky was beginning to clear in the northwest as we paddled south of Emerald Island on calm water to the 108 rod portage to Doré Lake, a portage Hind and his voyageurs called *Portage des Morts:* portage of death. It was named in memory of a voyageur who, Hind said, "being overanxious to cross the portage while supporting the bow of a north canoe [weighing, when wet, 300-400 pounds and carried by two voyageurs], lost his footing, and was so much injured by the heavy burden crushing him as he sank to the ground, that he died after the lapse of a few hours." Our own portaging went well (no falls) and on Doré we detoured to two pictographs: one appropriately of a canoe with two people in it, the other resembling an animal.

Deux Rivieres was more a mental than physical challenge, but just to be prepared, Chris and I changed into old clothes at an unnamed lake south of Doré before doing the river. There the sun shone as we paddled from beaver dam to beaver dam, their walls of intertwined sticks and mud keeping the river's north end deep. After four dams, however, the water was too shallow, a mere four inches, to float the canoe. We surrendered to the inevitable, got out and—Chris guiding the stern, me steering the bow— pulled the canoe downriver while wading knee-deep in muddy water and weeds. Midday passed sluggishly as we sloshed from bend to bend. Ducks burst into the air from russet riverside grass, their sudden eruption startling us, keeping us watchful. After a half-mile we were able to paddle more than walk. When Deux Rivieres debauched into Sturgeon Lake, us afloat, all was right with the world.

At least momentarily.

I could sense the end of the Kam-Dog, could feel the pull of open waters, and so I agreed to a layover day along Sturgeon Narrows. We napped, hiked up a section of the Maligne River to Russell Lake, and generally lounged around. Chris occasionally read Farley Mowat's *Never Cry Wolf,* and I browsed Schwarz's anthology, *Voices for the Wilderness*. Meals were fried bass and walleye caught with a Mepps spinner. Chickadees flitted among bushes throughout the day, their black and white feathers mingling with scarlet leaves. Pileated woodpeckers hammered distant trees. Black ravens swooped and banked beyond the red tops of maples while whiskeyjacks, the Canadian jays of the Quetico-Superior, whistled as they glided to our campsite, landed on overhead pine boughs, then fluttered to the ground. They hopped around on needle duff and rock while hunting flakes of cheese or chasing tossed bread crumbs. By evening, as a southeast wind buffeted our campfire, falling leaves swirled among falling leaves, maple's red mixing with aspen's gold, the hours showered by the finest colors of ripe September.

It was a lovely, lonely land, and before I slept I had to add a final touch. I reached into my pocket for a quote by Thomas Wolfe, taken from *The Hills Beyond*, which Chris had included with a meal. I unfolded the gray notepaper and read Wolfe's words in the firelight:

*And time still passing. . . passing like a leaf. . . time passing, fading like a flower. . . time passing like a river flowing. . . time passing as men pass who never will come again. And leaving us, Great God, with only this. . . knowing that this earth, this time, this life, are stranger than a dream.*

It was perfect. It was about as perfect as anything on the Kam-Dog was going to get.

≈ ≈ ≈

Two days later we were trapped on haunted Sturgeon Lake by gale-force winds.

Perhaps we should have sensed the storm coming. Shortly after leaving Sturgeon Narrows we passed Scripture Island then turned southwest down Sturgeon's trunk. Skies began to sprinkle, then pour, as winds blew from the southeast. Seeking shelter, we paddled to a sand beach, hastily put up the tarp, and then sat beneath it, read, and ate lunch. Chris, wet, walked the shore restlessly during lulls in the rain, but she couldn't get warm. Nothing helped her spirits. Not my woolen sweater, not seeing a moose swim between two islands, and certainly not the thought of staying where we were with no tent site in sight.

# OPEN SPACES

When Chris ended up hugging her knees, hunched in a ball on a damp log, I knew I was looking at misery. It was time to act.

The wind swung around to the west, head-on, as we paddled furiously for a mile—partly to warm up, partly to beat the wind— along Sturgeon's south shore to a sand peninsula with large pine and fir trees. We hit the beach like Marines, put the tarp up again, cached the packs under it, then built a stubborn fire. Once the tent was up I walked to the windward side of the peninsula and faced the wind. I was fed up with the weather and Chris's moroseness. I wanted to be alone. I couldn't help Chris, and in the obstinacy of my mission I couldn't reach out and tenderly touch her, returning more of the love and care she had so graciously given.

I felt for her and resisted her at the same time. I was frustrated.

The weather matched my mood. As the wind grew, gusting to 40 miles per hour or more, it blew whitecaps, swells and clouds down the main body of Sturgeon towards me. Anyone on that water, I thought, is dead. When tears came to my eyes I blamed it on the wind, which, gusting, blew the tears sideways across my temples and down the backs of my cheeks. Low clouds scudded among and above distant islands, some wisps of clouds at treetop level. Black clouds mixed with sunlit clouds mixing with rain clouds. They merged, tore apart, and merged again.

The roar of the wind fused with the roar of crashing surf at my feet. Looking down I saw the head and skeleton of a large northern pike. It was another omen to add to the growing list.

We were windbound. Nothing else to call it.

Night brought fear. After a supper of bulgar and vegetables with mint and rosehip tea, the wind increased in intensity. Darkness deepened. As we lay in the tent unable to sleep, we listened to the large pines crack and snap around us. Trees broke in the distance. The wind waxed and waned, grew strong and ebbed. It began like a roar in a distant mountain canyon, came closer, then washed over us with the force of a freight train as the forest canopy twisted and groaned. We feared a tree, like the cracked pine next to the tent, would fall on us, perhaps kill us, or smash our canoe leaving us stranded. There was no escape. No safer place to go.

Morning brought little relief from the wind although sunshine appeared in the afternoon. The sunlight, glorious in its cool brilliance, made the frothing crests of large waves look laced with snow. By evening the wind began to ebb. Sitting around the campfire, Chris told me she heard voices the night before.

"They mingled with the wind," she said. "It sounded like some canoeists, trying to escape the storm, beached their canoe where we did."

Weeks later, when I mentioned this to Mike Manlove who worked for Superior National Forest adjacent to Quetico, he told me of another odd Sturgeon story. A group of canoeists had camped Sturgeon not far from where Chris and I had sat out the storm. During the night they heard other canoeists pitch camp on a shore nearby, saw their fire, and listened to them sing voyageur songs. The next morning the canoeists paddled by the camp of the late-arriving songsters. They saw no sign of them. Stopping, they looked for remains of a campfire.

They found none.

ða ða ða

Hoping to recoup the two days storm bound on Sturgeon, Chris and I put the last of the lake's west end behind us by dashing five pre-breakfast miles on choppy water to the Maligne River.

The next 15 miles went quickly as we paddled and portaged five times down the Maligne, crossed Tanner Lake, then portaged around the ten-foot drop of Twin Falls on the east side of Lou Island. As we reached Lac la Croix, the day's brief sun — which had fired red maples and gold birch with light, doubling the beauty with shoreline reflections — disappeared behind solid overcast. Pellet-sized sleet began to fall. Although chilled, I was excited because Lac la Croix was technically the end of the 230-mile

Kam-Dog. Here it joined the Pigeon River route heading west to Rainy Lake and beyond.

I could almost feel Hind leave me, almost see the ghost of his back fade into western gray.

We turned south the next day and paddled past Warrior Hill to rendezvous with Ken MacDonald in Boulder Bay. Ken, a musician and photographer from northwestern Minnesota, had canoed the Red Lake River and parts of Voyageurs National Park with me, and we wanted to expand plans to canoe the Little Missouri River in western North Dakota's badlands. As Chris and I reached his campsite, he met us at the shore to show us what previous campers had left.

A chunk of bear scat was duct-taped to a paper plate. On the plate was scribbled one word: Warning.

It was getting late in the season for bears but not, certainly, for rain. As we parted the next morning, Ken for his car on the Nina-Moose River, Chris and I for our cabins on Burntside, the overcast let loose with drenching rain. The rain was steady, waves high, as we angled across a bay to Bottle Portage connecting Lac la Croix with Bottle Lake, Iron, Crooked and the Horse River: homeward.

Wet and cold, we bivouacked along Bottle Portage. We erected a tarp back in the woods, nursed a smoky fire, pitched our tent at nightfall and crawled into our sleeping bags. Our bags, the only gear still dry, were our last defense. Again we lay sleepless in the dark. Lordy but it had been a long journey. Old Never-Give-An- Inch, or whatever the responsible *manito's* name was, had barely budged from Thunder Bay to Bottle. Chris ever-so-carefully reminded me we could paddle out the way Ken did, hop a ride on the Echo Trail to our cabins, save 40 miles or more of paddling, and call it quits. I agreed. We could. Possibly. Maybe. Then I ever-so-carefully suggested we wait until morning to make a decision.

The wind was dead at dawn leaving an uncanny calm. It was October 1st. Chris tapped her side of the tent. Something slid down its outside wall. I tapped my side. More sliding. I unzipped the tent door and stuck my head out.

Snow.

During the night, rain had turned to snow which clung two-inches thick to bushes, trees, rocks and everything else. It was a heavy wet snow demanding, for comfort, a roof and stove. As we packed wet gear I remembered my promise to Chris about a decision the previous night. Go on, try to finish the expedition by following its waters to my cabin, or bail-out to the Echo Trail.

We walked to the Lac la Croix end of the portage. Chris stood at the edge of the water, her arms at her sides, a wool cap on here head, as she gazed out over the gray water beneath low scudding clouds. I stood behind her, studying here silhouette, and in the anxiety of my decision could feel the full weight of possible failure.

Turning, I walked to the other end of the portage and scanned Bottle Lake. I strolled the shore, looked at the clouds, and listened to the chatter of squirrels and calls of bluejays. I needed a sign that the low-pressure weather system was dissipating, that our luck was shifting, that we had passed through a crucible and there were good days ahead. Days of tailwinds. Days of sunshine.

"Well, Jacques?" Chris asked as Ray had in the beginning.

She stood behind me next to the packs.

I looked at her, felt for her, and knew I'd be responsible for what was about to happen.

The squirrels seemed a little louder, the jays and chickadees frisker, all life busier with post-snow activity.

"Let's go on," I said. "Let's risk it."

It was to be the story of our life.

# CHAPTER SIX
# GOOD MEDICINE
# IN THE BADLANDS

When gold suns rise over western North Dakota's Little Missouri River, there stands — silhouetted against the dawning light — a line of buttes and bluffs speaking of a land everlasting:

A land where titanotheres, rhinoceros-sized prehistoric creatures, roamed the ranges, giving rise to the legend of Thunderhorse.

A land where Indians huddled in earthen lodges against winter's snow-whipped night.

A land where conservationist and naturalist Theodore Roosevelt ranched cattle en route to a daring national vision and, later, more than a few dark hours on Brazil's River of Doubt.

And a land — if I could help it — where paddles would flash in April sun on a good river through an alleged bad land.

Surely the badlands, with their sand, clay and shale, comprise an uncanny region in which to take a canoe trip. Its topography doesn't usually favor boats. It favors well-watered horses, rattlesnakes, cactus and coyotes. It favors loneliness, dehydration and old bones. Its name alone intimidates.

The Sioux called the badlands *mako sica:* "land bad," "a vicious place to chase life-sustaining bison. Early French trappers called it *les mauvaises terres a' traverser:* "the bad lands to cross." In 1852, U.S. geologist Professor Owens compared its gullies, gulches and eroded slopes to a "magnificent city of the dead."

Twelve years later, General Alfred Sully halted his 2,500 soldiers near today's Painted Canyon Overlook while on a retaliatory mission against

142

the Sioux. There, Sully fed, gestering to the Badlands, is "hell with the fire put out."

Strong words, these. Not exactly flattery. There were other memorable comments.

"They are somewhat as Doré pictured hell," painter Frederic Remington said of the badlands. "One set of buttes, with cones and minarets, gives place in the next mile to natural freaks of a different variety, never dreamed of by mortal men."

Even naturalist John Burroughs, usually quick to herald natural beauty, was shocked by the badlands. They made a "strange, forbidding-looking landscape," he said in 1903, "hills and valleys to eastern eyes, utterly demoralized and gone to the bad — flayed, fantastic, treeless, a riot of naked clay slopes, chimney-like buttes, and dry coulees."

Such verbal slander, however, could not and cannot mask the magic and mystery of a landscape that is large enough, wild enough, and powerful enough to fan sparks of curiosity. Once the badlands enter the spirit, they can't be forgotten, cannot be ignored. They stick to the soul like dust on wet lips. Call the region central North America; the badlands could hardly be farther from the sea. Or call it the western edge of the Midwest, the great gouged moat between the prairies and the Rocky Mountains. It is a country immemorially fluted and periodically flooded. Acres are countless. Sky, grass, wind: infinite.

But not water.

Water can be about as common in the badlands as crocodiles in Connecticut, yet what little water there is flows into the Little Missouri River. Beginning in northeastern Wyoming at the base of Devil's Tower, the Little Missouri meanders north-northeast through a slice of South Dakota into North Dakota's Bowman and Slope counties. There it gathers volume and force. By the time it reaches Medora, gateway to Theodore Roosevelt National Park's south unit, it is — particularly in spring after hard rains — sometimes navigable. Like rivers in arroyos, the Little Missouri rises and shallows with precipitation or dry spells. It is a liquid barometer of the weather. For a canoeist or kayaker, when the level of the Little Missouri is high it is simply time to go. The serpentine river flushes you down. And you ride it.

I learned this truth the hard way in 1982 when I tried to organize a canoe trip down the Little Missouri, scheduled for May. I wasn't a badlands greenhorn. I had visited the badlands now and then by car and foot for ten years. But I had never paddled in the badlands, never floated through its backcountry. The Little Missouri and its wild banks remained incognito. Slowly, with each passing year, my passion to paddle the Little Missouri grew; I wanted that country in my spirit. I wanted to sniff its air and rub against its sands. Only by doing so, I figured, would the badlands bare their best. Yet two days before my 1982 group was set to leave, I called park headquarters at Medora and was told there were only 16 inches of water in the river.

Paddlers were turning back. Others were forced to portage long sandbars along the 120-mile route to the park's north unit.

I canceled the trip.

April 1983 had its own problems. Again I organized a trip. Again the water was low. A solo canoe I intended to use arrived in Ely with four holes in it the size of a shipper's boot. I seethed. A new canoe: ruined in transit. Trip members, too, dropped out. One minute I was ready to go, alone if necessary. Moments later — knowing Ken MacDonald would come — I would change my mind. I became incapacitated with ambivalence. I couldn't work, couldn't plan, couldn't even unpack and accept failure.

The only constant from hour to hour was a vision. Relaxing, or closing my eyes, I imagined bison coming down grassy slopes to drink in a river. I couldn't help it. It was a timeless scene, an icon of the Old West. Lewis and Clark had seen it. So had Crow, Cheyenne, Arikara, Gros Ventre, Hidatsa, Mandan and Sioux Indians.

Perhaps it was part of one of Custer's last peaceful panoramas. Yet the experience was practically unknown in 1983, especially from a canoe. I couldn't tell whether my imagination was playing with pure fantasy or whether it was aflame with premonition, but I was restless. I was on edge, my mood testy, and the bison wouldn't leave me alone.

Maybe I had cabin fever.

For five months I had skied, snowshoed, read books, written magazine articles, burned wood and skied more. During winter's dark hours I lingered over Quetico-Superior maps, marking the routes I had paddled the previous summer while guiding, canoeing with friends, or traveling alone. As a canoeist — thanks to winter — I felt stalled in my prime. Even the meaning and misery of the Kam-Dog was whiting-out into snow-devils of time. I had shoveled snow, scraped snow off the cabin roof, sucked on snow during five-mile road hikes, melted snow on the woodstove, got stuck in snow, and squinted into snow: snow on the ground or coming down. Always.

Twenty weeks of this.

Enough snow, let's go.

This seemed a simple solar prescription, with the added medicine of buttes and bison, when I finally grabbed a shovel and stepped up to Chris's 16-foot Old Town canoe buried in snow along the path to my cabin. We had kept it there over winter, partly because it was harder to get the canoe to Chris's cabin, but largely because we were consolidating resources. We were getting married. The canoe, made of ABS royalex, would be perfect for sliding over shallow, gravel shoals. As I shoveled I thought of the foot or more of solid ice on Burntside by my cabin. A nervy local could have put his four-wheel-drive pickup into low gear, driven out on the lake, and left the pickup out there for a week. Yet at the same time, having phoned Medora again, I knew the Little Missouri was flowing in a thawed, sunlit land 600 miles west of where I stooped.

Out there. Past the west edge of the Quetico-Superior, beyond northwestern Minnesota's Red River Valley where I'd pick up Ken, across North

Dakota's undulating plains and geese-filled potholes, back where the prairie was gutted and gullied, was a river flowing.

It was just what the doctor ordered.

᳓ ᳓ ᳓

"The river's pretty low right now," Ranger Micki Hellickson told Ken and me when we reached the south unit of Theodore Roosevelt National Park on April 19th. She was writing us a backcountry permit. "Maybe too low for paddling. This past winter was the driest since 1931. How far did you say you came from?"

᳓ ᳓ ᳓

What's this, I thought, some kind of re-enactment of the Kam-Dog's height-of-land? The sequel?

Discouraged but stubborn, having made a hefty mileage investment, Ken and I drove to Cottonwood Campground, unloaded the canoe, slipped it into the river, filled it with packs, and launched. It was 4:30 p.m. I switched immediately from a new wood bent-shaft paddle to one with an aluminum shaft, a $7 special: better to pole with. The river was two feet deep, often less. We could touch bottom. Dirty ice, remnants of winter, melted on the sandbars as flocks of sandhill cranes flew north overhead. A rising half-moon loomed porcelain bright. At dusk, shortly before camping on the north boundary of the park's south unit, we startled three mule deer on a steep grassy slope. They leapt—nimble as goats—among juniper, then stopped to watch us drift by.

We were finally, irrevocably, on the river.

᳓ ᳓ ᳓

Quietly, gently, our canoe moved out into the current of the river the next morning as the sun rose above Pikes Peak. The notched stick I had used to mark water depth showed no change overnight. It was a good sign but we weren't relieved. Any less water and we would have been wading. As it was we kept to the outside of bends where the river was deepest.

My thoughts were stark, words spare, as the river rationed buoyancy.

Ken, in the bow, assumed most of the navigation and when he stood to scan the river for shoals he cut a strange figure: yellow wingtips on his blue cap, hip boots rolled down thigh-high, Silva compass hanging behind his back. He sat down. We shot a bend's rock-riven riffles. Ken the Navigator stood up. I, too, could see the reddish and blackish shoals ahead of us or to the side but Ken more often than not called the correct channel. So I kept my mouth shut.

I glanced at Ken sometimes and thought of the years we had known each other, and I wondered what it is that brings men, women and their destinies together on canoe trips. It is one of the advantages of being in the canoe's stern—this staring and studying.

I had known Ken when he was a high school halfback in Crookston, Minnesota. He played both folk and electric guitar, drove a motorcycle, pumped iron—muscles, man—and grew his hair long. Cool. The nuns would let him get away with it. Ken was a musician, they said, and long hair was part of his off-school uniform. The rest of us had to keep trimmed or as I discovered, get expelled. It was discrimination, black and white, yet everyone liked Ken. Discrimination just made him groovier.

Then college came — those intellectual years when Oriental metaphysics and theosophy, not canoeing, certainly not football, were uppermost in our minds. Ken studied architecture before dropping out of the University of Minnesota; he couldn't fully get with what others deemed the Wright program. I studied theology and psychology, political demonstrations (We Want Peace!) and full moons above campus backwoods. Ken and I would meet back in Crookston during semester breaks: midnight coffee-quaffing time at Country Kitchen. Discussing reality. Chewing the contagious cud of intellectuality. Ken eventually chose music for his daily bread with photography as dessert. Reclusive yet amiable, he married a woman whose love was deep and he continued to find life curious right down to the Little Missouri.

"Curious," he would say when intrigued by something, which was almost everything. "Curious, wouldn't you say?"

Here, then, was my paddling partner: Ken the Navigator MacDonald. He was a river rat on an annual lark.

Ken stood up, gave directions through shoals, and then sat down.

Killdeers cried and western meadowlarks called, mallards took off, quacking, and Canada geese honked heavily as the miles of shoreline twisted and turned. We waded occasionally. Sometimes we scraped rocks in riffles. Day's warmth turned to heat. Wolf Draw was dry, as were Wannagan Creek, Crooked Creek, Ash Coulee and Roosevelt Creek. I, too, felt drained and dry.

It is a story whose first and last words are water. The badlands, for all their dryness, are the ancient pancaked beds of inland seas. Water covered the badlands for a half billion years while eroded debris from adjacent terrain mixed with marine organisms to blanket the seabeds. Slowly, inexorably, the area's last seabed continued to fill until it was elevated above sea level to form a broad, featureless coastal plain. Rivers writhed across the face of the plain for the next 15 million years; they dumped silt and sand, and eroded deep channels in the landscape. Plant life took root on high ground: cedar, cypress, poplar and sequoia. Organic litter accumulated. This, too, was again inundated and then compacted by deposited mineral strata until, in some cases, what was once a redwood tree metamorphosed into lignite coal.

The badlands were alive as layer upon layer of river deposits formed like striated skins on the face of primordial time.

Yet the show wasn't over.

During the Eocene epoch, about 50 million years ago, the Rocky Mountains continued to rise in elevation as did western North Dakota. The climate of the badlands became semi-arid, yet rich enough to support, by the Oligocene epoch, bear-sized carnivores with large fangs. There were oreodonts in twenty-two varieties. Some were as small as opossums, others as large as sheep; all had piglike bodies, ratlike tails and chewed cuds like cows. There were 12 foot-long turtles. There were collie-sized horses. There were sheep-sized camels. There were ten-foot-long enteledonts: root eaters six-feet tall with a humped back like a giant pig. There were saber-toothed cats whose jaws with three-inch teeth could open 90 degrees.

Perhaps the most amazing of all these prehistoric animals were the titanotheres. They weighed five tons, stood eight feet tall, had heads three feet long with horns on their snouts shaped like Vs, and they had fist-sized brains. Indians, Champ Clark wrote in *The Badlands*, occasionally found petrified titanothere bones which they thought were the remains of Thunderhorse, a stallion of legends.

According to one story the giant horse roamed earth during thunderstorms to kill bison. A variation on this theme had Thunderhorse driving a bison herd conveniently close to a camp of starving Sioux, thus assuring their survival.

Climatological time, meanwhile, worked the land. The rivers and creeks of the late Pleistocene epoch a million years ago merged slowly to form the ancestral Little Missouri. Meandering from side to side with a gentle gradient, it leveled and widened its valley on the way to Hudson Bay. It eventually changed course eastward when headward erosion opened a new channel through the Killdeer Mountains.

The Little Missouri: gnawing, nibbling, nagging at obstructions. Not even the Ice Age, which dammed the Little Missouri 25,000 years ago, could squelch the river's force.

It was on this million-year-old river that the Navigator and I paddled to our second night's camp. We found it on a bend among cottonwoods opposite a 75-foot cliff. Two wild turkeys in trees were silhouetted against approaching overcast. We erected a tarp for a windbreak, drank brandy, shared a rice-tuna supper, and finished with strong Sumatran coffee strained through a bandana. I walked down to river's edge at dusk where I fingered pebbles, splintered bones and a coyote track in dry, cracked mud.

OPEN SPACES

The land felt solid. Despite its continuum of change, the land—at least for the moment—felt as solid as a bison hoof on sun-baked clay.

⊰ ⊰ ⊰

Six miles after leaving our cottonwood camp, and as another seventy degree sunny day evaporated dew, Ken and I paddled up to the bank of Theodore Roosevelt's historic Elkhorn Ranch site west of Black Top Butte. Small Park Service signs and barbed wire marked the site. As Ken elbowed his way through juniper, hunting remnants of Roosevelt's ranch, I stood on the riverbank to gaze east and try to feel what Roosevelt must have felt on similar mornings.

This was, after all, a sacred place to him, as were all the badlands north of Medora.

Here his love of natural history, hunting, and wilderness adventure solidified. It was here his political personality— Bully, bully! he used to say—developed a backbone. It was here he assuaged grief that would have crippled a lesser man.

Roosevelt (1858-1919) first visited the badlands in 1883 to hunt bison, but before he shot his first bull he became so enamored of the environment he dished out $14,000 to Howley and Wadsworth for 400 cattle and the Maltese Cross ranch. His plans to be an absentee rancher were shattered the following February when his wife, Alice Lee, and his mother died the same night. Roosevelt needed peace, solitude and the close-to-the-bone light of wide open spaces. He returned to the badlands the following summer, bought the Elkhorn ranch, and built a herd of 8,500 cattle.

It was the fourth largest herd in the county.

Just as tragedy implanted Roosevelt in the badlands, it also ousted him. He lost 60 percent of his herd to starvation in the winter of 1886-87. He visited the badlands occasionally for the next ten years, but by 1898—the year he served as Assistant Secretary of the Navy and formed the Rough Riders to fight in the Spanish-American War—he had liquidated his ranching interests in favor of politics.

150

And in politics he shone.

Roosevelt's career stepladdered to the 26th Presidency of the United States by 1901, a position he said he never would have attained if it hadn't been for his experience in North Dakota. As President for two terms (1901-1909) he built a record of conservation leadership second to none.

He established the National Forest Service under the Department of Agriculture, eventually adding over 150 million acres to the national forests. He established 16 national monuments including the Grand Canyon, now a national park. He increased wildlife refuges from one to 51. He doubled the number of national parks from five to ten. And he encouraged, through correspondence, the work of naturalists like John Muir, John Burroughs and William Beebe.

"No nation," Roosevelt believed, "facing the unhealthy softening and relaxation of fibre that tends to accompany civilization can afford to neglect anything that will develop hardihood, resolution, and the scorn of discomfort and danger." Wilderness experience fought cowardice and exposed people to the "silent places: the wide waste places of earth, unworn of man, and changed only by the slow change of the ages through time everlasting."

In 1914, after Roosevelt served as the nation's top executive, he led a canoe expedition down Brazil's River of Doubt, a 1,000-mile tributary of the Amazon river. It was an expedition of the most remarkable and vicious kind. There were hordes of bees, flies, and ants that bit flesh, sucked blood and ate clothing. Rapids destroyed five of seven canoes. One man drowned. Another was murdered.

As for Roosevelt, the trip nearly cost him his life.

Self-sacrifice in the headwaters of the Amazon must have seemed like a nightmare to Roosevelt whose original intentions to tour Brazil's hinterlands had been full of his characteristic love of life. Some biographers claim he was poorly prepared for the trip, yet circumstances fueling the adventure were many. There was Fr. John Zahm, a South American explorer, who had encouraged him to visit the Brazilian outback. There were upcoming speaking engagements at universities in Brazil, Argentina and Chile. Plus Kermit, his son, was working in Brazil as a construction engineer.

At first Roosevelt wanted to ascend the Paraguay River to its headwaters, cross a continental divide, then float down one of the Amazon's large southern tributaries, possibly the Tapajos. From there he thought of visiting the Rio Negro, Casiquaire country, and the Orinoco River. But plans changed drastically once Roosevelt was in Brazil.

There he was told by Lauro Miller, Brazilian Minister of Foreign Affairs, that a Colonel Candido Mariano da Silva Rondon had found the headwaters of a large unmapped river. Miller asked Roosevelt if he was interested in exploring it.

"We will go down that unknown river!" Roosevelt said.

His change of plans brought immediate protest from American associates. Henry Fairfield Osborn told Roosevelt that the American Museum of Natural History, an expedition sponsor, would never consent to the museum's flag on a River of Doubt trip. They wanted no responsibility for what might happen if Roosevelt didn't return.

Another friend, Henry Cabot Lodge, wrote Roosevelt that the region he wished to explore was, like other remote parts of South America, one of the most unhealthy places on earth.

"I have already lived and enjoyed as much life as any other nine men I know," Roosevelt responded to such complaints. "I have had my full share, and if it is necessary for me to leave my remains in South America, I am quite ready to do so."

The River of Doubt, the Rio da Duvida, was literally terra incognito. Large-scale maps showed a blank space the size of Nevada through which the river ran. Some maps showed imaginary streams or mountain ranges.

Roosevelt knew that to canoe the River of Doubt would be exploration of the purest kind.

"If Roosevelt had made a deliberate attempt to choose the most perilous route anywhere on the face of the earth," biographer Paul Russell Cutright wrote in *Theodore Roosevelt. The Naturalist,* "he could not have done much better."

The expedition, which Roosevelt called a "zoogeographic reconnaissance," consisted of 22 men. Included was ornithologist Dr. George K. Cherrie, Kermit Roosevelt, Rondon, Dr. Cajazeira, and seventeen camaradas: various olive-skinned canoemen Roosevelt likened to pirates but who were, he said, strapping, expert rivermen, skilled in wilderness work, brawny as bears, lithe like panthers, and who could swim like "water-dogs." Canoes consisted of seven dugouts carved from single trunks of trees. One was small and cranky, two were "old, water-logged, and leaky." The lightest was 900 pounds. They were loaded with food, surveying equipment, personal gear and tools.

"Our heavily laden, clumsy dugouts," Roosevelt recalled in *Through the Brazilian Wilderness,* "were sunk to within three or four inches of the surface of the river, and, although they were buoyed on each side with bundles of burity-palm branch stems, they shipped a great deal of water in the rapids."

The expedition began February 27th, 1914, and ran into trouble immediately. There were stubs jutting up from sunken trees. Other trees, uprooted, jackstrawed across the water and had to be cut through. Dense riverside brush and trees had to be cut for campsites. Hacking and hewing in the rain became the norm.

Bell-birds called in the distance. Signs of agouti, peccary, tapir and paca were found along the river.

Insects, meanwhile, feasted.

There were horseflies the size of bumblebees. There were polvoras (sand

153

flies), small stinging bees, and pium flies. The worst were boroshuda flies in daylight; their bites caused instant bleeding and left marks for weeks. There were forest ticks and biting ants crawling inside clothes. Carragadores ants ate holes in mosquito netting, the straps of a gun case, the doctor's undershirt, boots, handkerchiefs, and one of the legs of Roosevelt's underwear. Termites ate holes in Roosevelt's helmet and cot. Venomous snakes, scorpions and centipedes were killed around camp.

Portages were hellish.

The first major portage paralleled a mile of rapids with some six-foot-high falls. It took the men over two days to chop a route through the forest and fell a couple hundred six-foot poles to use as rollers on the ground spaced two yards apart. The men used block and tackle to hoist the dugouts up the riverbank.

"Then the men," Roosevelt recalled, "harnessed themselves two by two on the drag rope, while one of their number pried behind with a lever, and the canoe, bumping and sliding, was twitched through the woods."

The expedition's biggest concern was doubt. They didn't know if they had 60 miles to go, or 500.

"We had entered a land of unknown possibilities," Roosevelt said.

One possibility was disaster.

On the night of March 10th, two moored canoes filled with water broke loose and were destroyed among rocks. Several days were spent adzing and launching a new dugout.

Disaster struck again when Kermit's canoe filled with water and capsized as Kermit and his bowman, Simplicio, scouted a passage through rapids. Simplicio disappeared beneath waves. Kermit, clutching his .405 Winchester rifle, was swept downstream. Roiling water sucked him under. He surfaced, gasped for breath, went under again. With his last strength he clutched a branch overhanging the river and pulled himself onto land.

Simplicio was never seen again.

March 16th was another bad day for the Expedicao Scientifica Roosevelt-Rondon, as the Brazilian government dubbed the expedition. While the crew lined the dugouts down more rapids, Rondon explored the riverbank with his dog. Lobo ran ahead. Moments later Lobo started howling in pain. Rondon suspected hostile Indians, sought backup, then returned with a posse to the riverbank. Lobo was dead: killed by two arrows.

Meanwhile, back at the rapids, one of the lining ropes broke. The new canoe with its load of ropes, pulleys, adzes and axes was destroyed.

Situation: grim.

In 18 days the expedition had lost three canoes. They had no way of portaging the large dugouts without the pulleys, yet they possibly had three times as many rapids to descend. They were among hostile Indians so they couldn't stop to build new canoes anyway. Some of the men who had gone barefoot, or who wore only sandals, were bitten so badly by insects their legs had to be wrapped in pieces of hide or canvas; still, they could barely walk. A third of the group's food was gone, yet they might have five times as far to go.

Time to tighten ship. The expedition abandoned two tents and a box of surveying equipment. They winnowed personal belongings to what they had on their backs and could fit in small duffel bags. They began eating monkeys, piranhas, and palm tops which tasted like celery.

"There was no longer any question that the Duvida was a big river," Roosevelt wrote, "a river of real importance. It was not a minor affluent or some other affluent. But we were still wholly in the dark as to where it came out."

The crewmen used what tools they still had to build two more canoes. More rapids passed beneath their hulls. Gear was portaged overland at the worst rapids while the canoes were run down empty. Food rations were cut in half. More men came down with fever. Fun became a word in someone else's vocabulary; it didn't fit the Duvida. As Roosevelt paddled and portaged, doing the best he could to deal with horrid adversity, never shirking work, he reconfirmed an earlier comment of his that genuine wilderness exploration is as dangerous as warfare.

Still, he wasn't blind to the River of Doubt's beauty.

"The day was overcast," he wrote of one morning, "and the air was heavy with vapor. Ahead of us the shrouded river stretched between dim walls of forest, half seen in the mist. Then the sun burned up the fog and loomed through it in a red splendor that changed first to gold and then to molten white. In the dazzling light, under the brilliant blue of the sky, every detail of the magnificent forest was vivid to the eye: the great trees, the network of bushropes, the caverns of greenery where thick-leaved vines covered all things else. Wherever there was a hidden boulder the surface of the current was broken by waves."

A few days later, after the expedition passed petroglyphs of unknown origin, Roosevelt injured his leg when two canoes being lined down the rapids were caught in a whirlpool. They filled with water, sank, then were held fast by the current against rocks. Two canoemen jumped in waist-deep to hold the canoes in place. Dr. Cherrie ran down the slashed-out portage to the bottom of the rapids and called the rest of the group to help.

Roosevelt, 56 years old, was the first man back to the canoes. He leapt into the river. Working in water up to his armpits, he used what energy he had despite low-grade malaria to help raise the canoes and save them.

But not without injury. Roosevelt bruised his leg while floundering in the rapids. An abscess developed. His malaria grew worse. His temperature rose to 105 degrees. Gravely ill, and seemingly a burden on the expedition, he made a difficult decision. He called Dr. Cherrie and Kermit, his son, to his side.

"I want you and Kermit to go on," he told Cherrie. "You can get out. I will stop here."

They said no.

156

Roosevelt stumbled on, his heart paining him. When too weak to help portage gear, he sat against trees reading Gibbon's *Decline and Fall of the Roman Empire* or the *Oxford Book of French Verse*. At night, wearing headnet and gauntlets, he wrote articles about the expedition for *Scribner's Magazine*. He thought of suicide but dismissed it; he figured Kermit would insist on hauling his father's body out, thus aggravating their already perilous situation.

Roosevelt's condition didn't get better.

"There was a good many days," Dr. Cherrie wrote in *Dark Trails*, "a good many mornings, when I looked at Colonel Roosevelt and said to myself, he won't be with us tonight; and I would say the same thing in the evening, he can't possibly live until morning. . .[yet] the fact that the Colonel was with us gave us energy to do things we couldn't possibly have done otherwise."

Perhaps Dr. Cherrie was referring to the gorge they reached the last few days of March. Here the river constricted into rapids and waterfalls among mountainous shores. Rondon scouted it out and returned with bad news.

"We will have to abandon all our canoes," he said. "And every man fight for himself."

Bullshit, Kermit and Dr. Cherrie thought. Abandoning the boats meant certain death.

The group tossed away more baggage before spending three days lining the empty canoes down the gorge. A few miles later they negotiated another canyon which at one place narrowed into a rock gash 30-feet wide. Some of the camaradas voiced their fear of getting out alive. Everyone was wet. Shoes rotted. Bruises became sores. Insect bites became oozing wounds.

Julio, a camarada, was caught shirking work and stealing food. Corporal Paishon reprimanded him with a punch in the mouth. Again Julio was caught stealing food. Paishon scolded him. Julio cracked. He nonchalantly grabbed a rifle, followed Paishon down a portage, and shot him through the heart. After chasing Julio, the group abandoned him, yet when they spotted him along the river a few days later they decided to take him captive.

Julio resisted, escaped and was never seen again.

Slowly the hills on both sides of the River of Doubt began to draw back into level plains as the expedition fought onward. There were more rapids: what Roosevelt called "by far the most dangerous enemies of explorers and travelers." The canoemen took risks. Possible consequences were obvious. But if they took no risks their caution could prolong the trip to the point of starvation.

Roosevelt viewed their progress as a "perpetual working compromise between rashness and overcaution."

Terrain continued to flatten as water smoothed into tranquil stretches. The expedition covered nine miles, then 22, on single days. At night—for the first time in weeks—they slept beyond the sound of rapids. "For the first time we had open space in front of and above us," Roosevelt said, "so that after nightfall the stars, and the great waxing moon, were gorgeous overhead, and against the rocks in mid-stream the broken water gleamed like tossing silver."

On April 15th they found a sign initialed "J.A." and a few miles later they discovered thatched houses belonging to rubber cutters and homesteaders. That night they slept with the first people they had seen in 48 days.

They had made contact. They were back in the mapped world.

Best of all, perhaps, the Expedicao Scientifica Roosevelt-Rondon finally knew where it was. From knowledge to the unknown and back to knowledge. From the thatched houses of the rubber cutters, the expedition continued down to the Airpuana River which, in turn, let to the Madeira River draining into the Amazon. A steamer hauled the crew down the Madeira and up the Amazon and Rio Negro to Manaus, reached April 30th.

## Chapter Six GOOD MEDICINE IN THE BADLANDS

The expedition, despite its difficulties, was a success. About 200 miles of unknown river were explored, another 800 miles mapped. (The River of Doubt was renamed Rio Roosevelt against his wishes.) About 2,000 birds and many mammals were collected for the American Museum of Natural History (having relented on its expedition fears). Eleven of the species were new to science. Roosevelt's zoological observations contributed much to what was known about the Amazon's watershed.

But there was more to the trip for Roosevelt than mere accumulation of scientific knowledge. He had been a man of action. He liked grit (he once gave an hour speech with a would-be assassin's bullet in his chest). He hated cowardice and admired courage. And when it came to comrades, nothing pleased him more than roaming the world's wild places with fellow naturalists.

No matter that in Brazil he lost 35 pounds and permanently maimed his leg.

"I am always willing," he once said, "to pay the piper when I have a good dance."

He paid the piper on the River of Doubt. It would be the last dance of his kind. Five years later Roosevelt was dead.
*****
Roosevelt was dead but not forgotten as the Navigator and I left Elkhorn and paddled north toward Buckhorn Butte where a bald eagle cast shadows against riverside sandstone. Large S-curves sloped downward and spun us centrifugally around bends as the valley widened and horizons withdrew. Dust devils danced on dry sandbars. An east wind waxed. Past North Fork Creek we wove through a stretch of bone-white cottonwoods jutting out of the river.

We were quiet, saying little, mesmerized by the badlands and our paddle strokes.

No. Something new was happening. Recognition of it came slowly. The river, despite its dry tributary creeks, was inexplicably deeper. We no longer worried about water depth. Without this nagging concern halfway to Theodore Roosevelt National Park's north unit, we were free men. We were liberated by water, freed by flow.

Four mule deer suddenly ran across the river in front of us, their hooves splashing gold water in evening's slanted sunlight.

&#9756; &#9756; &#9756;

Sometime during the night, on the heels of coyote calls, I awoke to find the river and its butte banks bathed in moonlight. A high slope across the river was dotted with cows. There was a scent of sage in the still air. Lunar sage silence. Not even the river murmured as I sank back into sleep, my body conforming to dried cattle tracks beneath the tent, my parting glance stippled with stars.

Spring death was on our minds after we broke camp. Near the mouth of Bear Creek we watched a vulture pick at a dead fish on a sandbar. It rose and circled us as another joined it. Both glided black with fingered pinions against morning's blue sky.

Moments later we smelled the stench of putrefying flesh. A dead coyote lay rotting in the mud of a cutbank.

Death seemed incongruous in the hour's live light, yet its aura remained with us past French Creek, Ice Box Canyon, Bridger Creek and Bummer Creek. It circled in and out of our thoughts, strafed our feelings, or simply hovered—mortality's vulture— awaiting a mammal's mistake.

Like Jim Anderson's.

Anderson, 30, was fishing for catfish in the Little Missouri as we paddled in sunshine past his ranch. It was a Huck Finn scene in the badlands: line/pole/man held in a riverbank idyll on an impeccable day. Anderson called us over. Talk turned to tales. Anderson, no stranger to the river's moods, had one of the best.

Chapter Six GOOD MEDICINE IN THE BADLANDS

One spring day, after the Little Missouri had flooded in freshet, Anderson took his canoe and dog four miles upriver from the ranch and shoved off. Ice still clung to banks. Chunks floated in midstream. As he rounded riverbends, Anderson noticed more ice floes catching up with him. They surrounded him and began to squeeze in on him on the outside of riverbends. Ice pushed his canoe up out of the water. He slashed and pushed at the ice with his paddle, working feverishly.

"I couldn't land because of ice along the riverbank," he said. "So I jumped out of the canoe into chest-deep water near the ranch. I grabbed for a hand-hold to get up on the icy bank. When I made it, I started pulling the canoe out of the water. The rope broke. The canoe with my dog slid back into the river."

Anderson called his dog which jumped out of the canoe and swam to shore. They scrambled up the riverbank and ran back to the ranch. The canoe, empty but undamaged, was eventually found by Boy Scouts. It was snagged among cottonwoods on a high bank about 18 miles downriver from where Anderson last saw it.

Anderson, meanwhile, had grown wiser in the ways of the Little Missouri.

Ken and I shoved off.

"Find any buffalo skulls?" Anderson called. He had begun to dissolve behind us in a blast of river-reflected sunlight. "You can find them sometimes after spring floods wear away the cutbanks!"

Buffalo skulls or, more precisely, bison skulls in canoe country. A canoe in bison country. It was a curious juxtaposition to mull as Ken and I nosed our canoe past Sheep Creek, Bennett Creek and north toward Corral Creek. Certainly bison were indigenous to the badlands, as much a product of the geology and climate as the 40 species of grass bison ate. But the history of *pte*—as the Sioux called bison—was a sad, haunting one, not one easily reconciled by two paddlers wending through a bison graveyard.

*Bison bison bison,* as plains buffalo are scientifically called (distinguishing

them from *Bison bison athabascae,* Canada's wood buffalo), once num-
bered up to 60 million in North America. They grazed as far east as the
Atlantic. Herds on the plains occupied as much as 50 square miles. Bulls
weighed a ton: the largest land animal in North America.

They were sacred to Sioux. As with Indian tribes before them, Sioux not
only used all of *pte's* flesh but also all the animal's parts: from the brains for
dressing skin to the tail used as a fly brush. It was a predator-prey cycle of
survival. A holy cycle. One to note on shields and pipes. One to dance and
sing about.

It nevertheless presaged disaster.

First came the white man as meat hunter and skin hunter, then rancher and
railroader. Bison were killed by the hundreds of thousands, a man's
reputation sometimes staked on how many bison he could gun down in an
hour. So prolific was the felled game—as white men impersonated the dark
side of Thunderhorse—that by 1873 a bison hide cost 60 cents. Soon
professional hunters and skinners began butchering the herds for a new
reason: the military realized it could subjugate the Sioux by cutting off their
main source of food—the axis of their sacred cycle.

For bison, not to mention the Sioux, it was a slaughter damn near to
annihilation. Eighty years ago there were only a couple thousand bison left
on all the great plains. None in the badlands.

*Bison bison bison* bellowed on the cliff of extinction.

The killing finally stopped. Blood dried. The sands of Little Missouri
freshets buried skeletons. Surface bones bleached and decayed, gnawed by
rodents. Skins rotted. Then *pte*—historic purveyors of life—were reintro-
duced to the badlands.

They were brought home out of the graciousness of the responsible
culture's guilt.

Agitated by the slaughter of an animal asking no harm, I wanted a fire to dance around when Ken and I pitched camp in another grove of cotton-woods. I wanted a war dance: paint, feathers, drums and weapons. But the warm night with its circumstances wouldn't have it. I stood by the river. Cirrus clouds hung over a peach-colored western horizon. Beyond the river curving toward us from the northwest: was a ridge of buttes, their gray-and-mauve hues dimming in the dusk. An owl hooted. Frogs thrumped in a distant swamp. A kingfisher rattled. Gravel and clay occasionally slid down red and brown cliffs on the outside of a nearby riverbend. It was a quintessential badlands campsite, the prettiest of the journey: remote, wild, relatively untracked. Things were sharp as they cut teeth on the primordial present.

But something was stirring. It was pawing. . .pawing on the edge of time, haunting my mind, trying to get in.

More clay cut loose within earshot.

Startled, I looked toward the water-browsed bank and could almost see a bison skull breaking free and rolling, horn-over-horn, to river's edge. Its empty eyesockets brimmed with moonlight. And the air turned cold.

ﻉ ﻉ ﻉ

Dawn brought life, not lingering shadows of death, to our last day on the Little Missouri as my Burntside premonition followed Ken the Navigator and I, seeking morning's first warmth, from one sunny spot on the river to another. After 120 miles we were aware of our good fortune: not a drop of rain in five days, warm temperatures, not a single mosquito, no bad head winds, and just enough water in the river to squeak by.

Everything—the route's geology, its prehistoric backdrop, Roosevelt's legacy, even the river-revealing rendezvous with Anderson—seemed to have conspired to grant us easy and pleasant passage.

But my Burntside premonition of seeing bison was still with me. It seemed to paw and scrape, like the ghostly bison the night before, on the crust of possibility. Finally it broke through.

OPEN SPACES

I noticed dark objects on a grassy hillside beneath Sperati Point shortly after we paddled into the park's north unit. We were over a half degree further north in latitude now: near Watford City in McKenzie County, just west of Fort Berthold Indian Reservation and adjacent Lake Sakakawea, a Missouri River reservoir where white people, using the Garrison Dam, saw fit to flood Indian land; traditional graveyards, birthplaces and villages notwithstanding. We stopped the canoe in view of Sperati Point, paddled backwards against the current, and grabbed a stout branch of a midriver cottonwood sweeper, its trunk anchored on the bottom of the river. Out came the binoculars.

Bison. Six of them.

We beached the canoe, grabbed our cameras, and stalked the bison like Mandan or Sioux. Lewis and Clark would have taken aim. We hadn't gone far, however, when we were stopped in our tracks by the gaze of one-ton bulls. They had turned to face us, sunlight glinting in their black eyes, a link with the past shining there, perhaps a touch of vengeance in genetic memory, staring us down. My hackles rose as the herd—grown to a dozen—ran toward us. Ken and I backed off, scampering toward the river, but the bison were bluffing, buffaloing us, and they swerved away to the southwest. We lost sight of them yet heard their hooves pounding dry ground, the sound thundering, the passing of bison trailed by dust.

We saw another bison near noon as we approached our take-out at Squaw Creek. A lone bull taking its time—nothing to fear, no plains grizzlies left, no sign of rifle-toting market hunters— shuffled down a clay bank in front of the canoe, waded belly-deep to the middle of the river, drank, then climbed back up the bank. It's hard to say if it even noticed us or, for that matter, whether it was real. It came, it drank, it left. We came, we canoed, we left.

We didn't touch a hair.

Maybe Thunderhorse was playing with us.

Maybe the great legendary stallion—nostrils flaring, mane flying, hooves sparking on bones and clouds—was deadly serious.

It didn't seem to matter.

Thunderhorse wasn't killing bison any more. It wasn't driving bison close to camps of starving Sioux. Thunderhorse was making one of its last runs through the soul of man. It was closing a circle in a land everlasting and its medicine, like the myth, tasted good.

# CHAPTER SEVEN
# THE
# WABAKIMI-KOPKA CAPERS

There is something about a $1,000 kevlar canoe smacking rocks in rapids on a wilderness river that excites great expectations. It was autumn, five months after canoeing the Little Missouri River in the badlands, and I was on a small section of wildwater in northwestern Ontario. This was Wabakimi country, specifically the Ogoki River south of Kenoji Lake, and at the moment I was caught in the grip of a reasonable fear born of trying to maneuver an 18 foot canoe loaded with three weeks of food through the kind of rapids good whitewater rivers are famed for.

Bowman Ray Niedzielski and I would start down the rapids fine, cross-ferrying or backpaddling where necessary, but eventually the Ogoki's current would win control and heave us over mounds of water that made my stomach crawl.

We weren't in complete control and we knew it. And we weren't near a road if a rock punched a hole in our Wenonah *Odyssey* on her maiden voyage. Like the Kam-Dog, the Ogoki River was at times almost more than a man could stand.

But whitewater thrills came with the terrain. Ray, Kerry Donars and I had chosen to check out two controversial wilderness areas northeast of Quetico Park: Wabakimi, smaller than Quetico but richer in whitewater rivers, and the proposed Kopka River Provincial Waterway, a little-known route of incredible beauty whose bridgeless character faced an end.

"There is a fascinating parks crisis brewing about the Kopka River Waterway," Bruce Hyer of Thunder Bay, Ontario, had written me the previous July. "It is an exceptional canoe trip and this perhaps is its last season to be seen in its natural state."

166

Hyer had reason to know. He had operated Wildwaters Wilderness Shop and Expeditions using Kopka country for a fly-in base camp and the locus of most of his outfitted trips. He had been chairman of Ontario's Environmental Concerns Committee and an executive member of the Ontario Wilderness Guides Association. In 1982 he received the "Conservationist of the Year" trophy from the Federation of Ontario Naturalists.

Hyer's remark, therefore, about the Kopka offering exceptional canoeing opportunities had bite to it. I had also heard rumors about the Kopka from contacts in northern Minnesota. Praise was common. There were high waterfalls. Cliff portages. "The kinds of rapids you don't run in a canoe." Here, I figured, was a river of lore and legend.

Ray, of course, was ready to go.

The route to Kopka country was circuitous, a large figure- eight loop beginning appropriately on Little Caribou Lake west of Armstrong, Ontario: 75 miles north of Thunder Bay. The forest around Armstrong was, almost unbelievably, caribou country — a mere 400 miles northeast of Minneapolis - St. Paul. In 1981, wildlife biologist H. G. Cumming of Thunder Bay's Lakehead University had counted 41 caribou bedded down at the snowy end of Armstrong's abandoned airport runway. Cumming had seen caribou on Lake Nipigon to the southeast, and he knew there were scattered bands of caribou to the west, but only after seeing those at Armstrong and Elf Lake was he convinced a sizable and soon-to-be controversial herd lived in Wabakimi country.

These were Rangifer caribou, creatures of woodland, and they were the primary reason Wabakimi Provincial Park was created in the first place. According to Cumming there were about 13,000 woodland caribou left in Ontario, most of them in the northern section of the province. A large bull weighed 350 pounds.

Winter diet: mostly lichens. Preferred range: undisturbed wild areas.

Like timber wolves, grizzlies and bison, caribou carry a mystique — symbols of wilderness. They enliven landscapes. Caribou carry with them the ambience of the far north's boreal forest: that swath of spruce, birch and jackpine that thins and opens like a vestibule to the treeless arctic. But caribou also symbolize something other than wilderness. Their presence represents man's willingness to protect places of extraordinary natural beauty: oases where wildlife like caribou can make their stand while the forest around these oases is literally reduced to pulp.

About the time Cumming was studying near Armstrong, Hyer and a consortium of wilderness preservation organizations were trying to persuade Ontario's Ministry of Natural Resources to set aside about 1.3 million acres of wilderness to protect both caribou and wilderness recreation opportunities. The proposed area was known at first as Whitewater Park after large Whitewater Lake which it would encompass, then by Hyer and others as the Ogoki-Albany Wilderness, named after the Ogoki and Albany rivers. The northern perimeter of the proposed wilderness included part of the Albany River's watershed, the Albany flowing into James Bay of Hudson Bay.

"In 16 years," Hyer said in a report to the Ontario Provincial Parks Council, "and over ten thousand miles of wilderness travel, mostly by canoe, throughout northern Canada, I have never encountered a wilderness area that offers more diversity, richness, and challenge of wilderness experience, together with reasonable accessibility."

The proposed Ogoki-Albany Wilderness was a third larger than Quetico's million acres, a third smaller than Algonquin Provincial Park north of Toronto, and a quarter the size of Polar Bear Provincial Park along the southwest coast of Hudson Bay. It was, furthermore, Ontario's last opportunity to preserve a virgin chunk of boreal forest which was a Ministry of Natural Resources objective in light of its desire to preserve representative landforms of the huge province's diverse environment. The Ogoki-Albany Wilderness was endorsed by the Federation of Ontario Naturalists, Sierra Club of Ontario, the Wilderness Canoe Association, Canoe Ontario, Algonquin Wildlands League, the National and Provincial Parks Association, the Conservation Council of Ontario, and other groups.

There was just one catch.

Great Lakes Forest Products of Thunder Bay had held a license to log the area since 1957. They had expanded mill operations and employed 2,800 people on the premise all Ogoki-Albany's wood would be available.

A classic environmental battle erupted. Full-page newspaper ads placed by the logging industry accused canoeists of elitism. Virgin forests were called "green deserts." GLFP threatened to shut down its facilities part of each year. Environmentalists, meanwhile, cited various Ontario forestry reports indicating Ogoki-Albany soils were thin, growth rates were slow, and haul distances for trucks would be costly. They quoted expert foresters George Marek and Andrew Gordon who said large clear-cutting operations in the area "could be disastrous" while tree planting would be costly, wasteful, often impossible.

As the upshot of Cumming's research became clear, he realized one of the largest and most southerly aggregations of woodland caribou occurred "squarely in the middle of the disputed parcel of land." Giving his discovery urgency was a proposal by the Department of Regional Economic Expansion to push a road through the caribou's wintering area and the heart of the Ogoki-Albany. Cumming recommended establishing a Caribou Management Area where tree cutting, cabin building and road construction would be prohibited. The proposed Caribou Management Area was bounded by Elf, Smoothrock and Wabakimi lakes.

Both sides of the controversy arrived at a resolution in 1983: the 383,000-acre Wabakimi Provincial Park. Yet it disappointed the wilderness consortium. As Hyer put it, "Most of the key natural features and recreational highlights were omitted."
Places like the sand dunes and peatlands near Whitewater Lake.

The wildlife habitats of Berg and Misehkow rivers.

Wild rice stands of Metig and Rockcliffe lakes.

The corridor connecting Wabakimi Lake and Albany River.

# OPEN SPACES

The good news was that 65 to 150 caribou had received a sanctuary in line with Cumming's suggestion. What irked Hyer, besides the severe reduction in size of the proposed area, was the potential concentration of activity in Wabakimi's most fragile zone, exactly where Ray, Kerry and I intended to take a look.

❧ ❧ ❧

Cumming had told me caribou might be seen on Elf Lake. Elf, at least in winter, had a herd equal in size to the whole caribou population Cumming stalked around the north end of Lake Nipigon. Elf Lake, hence, was the axle, the caribou crux, and so after leaving Little Caribou Lake we veered toward Elf via glass-calm Caribou Lake, Smoothrock and Lower Wabakimi. As a campfire ebbed on our fourth night out, a single band of northern lights grew progressively brighter against a starry backdrop, the band twisting, stretching and undulating like a marble's curlicue from horizon to horizon in the glass expanse of space.

It was a good omen as beams of light shot upwards to silhouette spruce along opposite shores. We lay on our backs on granite, the same Precambrian shield underlying the Quetico-Superior to the southwest, and for the moment — free of maps, free of clear-cut proposals — we acquiesced to innocence in the face of the fabulous.

Drop the timber percentages, I thought. Drop the wildlife counts. Forget heated arguments at public hearings. Be Here now.

Time stood at a standstill following dawn's moonlit fog, as it often does after days in the outback: beyond roads, beyond the steel of railroad tracks, and beyond the nightly glow of urban areas. As we canoed and portaged to Roberts Lake, approaching Elf, we felt as if we were finally entering remote country. The deeper, the wilder. Sunlight sparkled on small waves. We spoke in whispers as our canoes cut water in a rockbound channel opening wide onto Elf's two-mile expanse.

The joke was on us.

We might as well have junked our hushed respect, our quiet hope of seeing caribou, and yelled at the top of our lungs.

Someone else did.

Ray spotted the floating cigarette butt first. A Winston. I then spotted the red cabin to our left. Offshore, straight in front of us, a fat man in white shorts stood in the back of an anchored motorboat. Alone, not seeing us, he muttered like an excited kid as he landed a big northern pike. He held it up by the gills and shouted, yanked the cord of his motor, adjusted the throttle and roared east.

When he realized he was going in the wrong direction he slowed and turned north toward the cabin.

Our feeling of remoteness: shattered. Our hopes of wild country: throttled.

We decided to paddle to a rock shore a mile away and leave the fly-in fishing camp behind.

A different motorboat bore down on us.

"How the hell did you get in here?" a man asked, ignoring the obvious.

"Paddled," Kerry said.

"Where from?"

"Little Caribou."

"Where you going to camp?"

"Not sure yet," I said.

"Well, come on over for a drink later on if you want. There's always a boat at the cabin. Play some cards. Someone'll be there, eh?"

The shore was almost a perfect campsite. We swam in hot sun and washed sweaty clothes. I picked blueberries and wrote in a journal as Ray and Kerry caught four walleyes for supper. An orange sunset, silhouetting islands at dusk, was followed by more northern lights. Ray took our solo canoe, a Wenonah *Solitude*, out on the night water to watch the lights. Vertical auroral beams reflected off the lake as he drifted near shore, the beams moving east to west.

"They're like marching spirits," Ray said.

Yes, I thought. Spirits marching away.

We could hear the fishermen laughing at the cabin, the coolness and calm of the night air carrying the laughter our way. Perhaps we should have paddled over to meet them; should have had a drink and eaten some fish, but I was disappointed. I hadn't come to Elf to play cards and sip scotch. We would see no caribou in fisherman's paradise.

&a &a &a

There were signs of caribou the next day, however, as we canoed northwest. We found the twin inward-facing crescent shapes of caribou tracks in green moss along a portage. Then Ray, near Granite Falls on Allen Water River, found a lone caribou antler dropped among blueberry bushes.

We stopped, picked the antler up, looked it over, noticed the toothy nibblings of calcium-hungry mice, then set the antler back down. We debated bringing it home where it might grace a fireplace mantel, but, no, another canoeist might find it as sun warmed his shoulders and sparkled on offshore waters.

Why rob someone of discovery? Why abort later delight?

We paddled down the Allen Water, camped in the roar of an S-shaped rapids and then crossed wind-whipped Wabakimi Lake's east end, careful not to broach in large waves quartering us from the rear. A long portage led around Ogoki River rapids to more rocks and powerful currents where the

Ogoki flowed into Kenoji. It was here Ray and I fought to keep the heavily laden *Odyssey* off the rocks, testing skill, stretching luck.

We camped on a small rock island near the mouth of the river. A storm squall passed and then an airplane. It wasn't the first airplane we had seen in the area, and it wouldn't be the last. It reminded me of how airplanes had been outlawed in Quetico Park and the Boundary Waters Canoe Area since 1949 as the result of a bitter wilderness battle led, to a great extent, by Ely's Sigurd F. Olson. The airplane ban helped to preserve the Quetico-Superior's silence and its precious, albeit sometimes elusive, sense of remoteness. The same couldn't be said of Wabakimi-Kenoji country. The passing airplane's high droning, carried for miles by the wind, rooted consciousness in the mechanized present, destroying—with engine roar and aluminum, the suggestion of quick entry/exit—the arena of remoteness and timelessness that wildernesses should be designated, in part, to protect.

Airplanes, according to new park plans, would be allowed indefinitely in Wabakimi Provincial Park. Although on Kenoji we were further north than Quetico, and logically in a wilder place (the further north, common assumption went, the fewer the people and machines, hence wilder conditions), I could nevertheless hear and understand more deeply than ever that where there are airplanes there can be no long lasting, no deepening, of wilderness feelings. Silence is a part of wilderness. As Olson wrote in *Reflections From the North Country*, it is one of the most important parts: "Without it the land is nothing more than rocks, trees, and water." So Sig had fought for silence in the Quetico-Superior, his most beloved of wildernesses. Who would do so for Wabakimi country or, for that matter, most other wilderness areas in North America?

Should airplanes be allowed? Ray later asked, playing devil's advocate. Should a Thunder Bay surgeon stressed from five days at the operating table be denied air access to a cabin on Elf Lake or Kenoji?

Are we talking wilderness playground, I rebutted, accessible to people with short-term commitments? Or is something possibly more valuable at stake?

Must airplanes forever cast their shadows across caribou which, like wolves and other wild animals, are sensitive to machine-caused stress?

And what of people who hunger silence? Where will they find it if not in places like Wabakimi? The Boundary Waters to the southwest, rich in silence, was visited to capacity on many summer days.

We moved on. We covered water and ground, passing another fly-in fishing camp. Once up small rapids to Palisade River, with cliffs closing in, the water channel deepening, and our paddles slowing to a rest on gunwales, our eyes searched a cliff. I had been told there were pictographs along the Palisade.

We looked closer. There: smears of red ochre, three vertical tally marks and what looked like an "H" with elongated horizontal line extending to the right. Like at Darky, Crooked and Lac la Croix, there was mystery here where fingers once stroked rock. Compared to the moose, hourglass and man-smoking-a-pipe figures of Lac la Croix Narrows, however, or the horse, ship and serpent figures of Lake Superior's Agawa site, the Palisade pictographs seemed unremarkable.

Perhaps it was the place that was important.

Across the river was an old campsite with a fire ring overgrown with caribou moss. It had been years since the ring was used. Nearby, rotting among bearberries, a moose antler lay white beneath autumn sun. We stayed there two nights, spending the layover day searching shores.

Something subtle and fine, a vibratory dancing of atoms, seemed to emanate from the rocks.

While canoeing alone in a rockbound bay of the Palisade, Ray found a log structure shaped like a large coffin. It was wider at the top than bottom, just large enough for one person to sleep in, or prop himself up on one arm to read a book or stir soup. Outside near the doorway was a campfire ring. Inside was a small shelf. Layered moss provided cushioning from the ground. The structure inclined narrow-end downward on a slight slope facing south. Jackpines, born of past fire, cast shade. There was no litter. Whoever built the log tent, for that's what it essentially was, did so for an unusual purpose and kept his act clean.

"Maybe it's the site of a vision quest," I told Ray who was standing bare-chested in the sun.

Anthropologist Selwyn Dewdney had found evidence linking pictograph sites with shaman retreats where they fasted to the limits of solitary endurance. The shaman's purpose was to contact spiritual guardians by unleashing, as Dewdney once wrote, "a flood of images and sequences that reveal the rich resources of the inner man." Dewdney located such a site on Picture Rock Island in Whitefish Bay on the east side of Lake of the Woods on the Minnesota-Ontario border. A ledge 20 feet above the water provided sleeping space and a stable platform on which to stand while painting pictographs: a rectangle divided by horizontal lines, a hand print, a female genital sign, and what looked like a dog or wolf.

Dewdney's point, and one apparently confirmed by Ray's discovery on the Palisade, was that there are connections to be made between place, shelter and spiritual power.

It was my turn to paddle alone in the *Solitude* a few hours later. I returned to the pictographs and slowly worked my way along the rock face. I peered closely, touching granite and lichens with my fingertips. Grit and flakes fell loosely into the river. A faint image caught my eye. I splashed water on the image and then watched as a painting of a four-legged animal with short, upright tail and long vertical antlers darkened on the rock.

The pictograph would have been easy to miss, and it had been. Archeologists and anthropologists had hitherto been unaware of this caribou painting. I took a few photos and made a sketch.

Then I remembered.

On the night before I left the Quetico-Superior for Wabakimi country, I had dreamt of searching a rock cliff among rock shores, islands, and the sight and sound of waterfalls. I was standing in chest-deep water and running my fingers along a lichen-encrusted cliff similar to the one on the Palisade. And the cliff began to sing. Liquid bubbles of rock ten feet above my head began to swell and burst. From each burst came a musical note. An orchestra of sound. The tempo quickened like mud bubbling to a boil. It was then I noticed an opening in the cliff at water level. I looked in. A cave, unknown to anthropologists, was covered with red pictographs. Cave art in canoe country. I was stunned, baffled. . .water licking at my chin. Should the cave be kept a secret? Nothing among Canadian Shield pictograph sites could compare to it. Hell, it'd be a grotto. The sound of flowing water in the distance, where a river tumbled over rocks to fill the lake in which I stooped, swelled like a growing wind.

Now, on the Palisade, in the clear light of afternoon, I saw someone had honored Rangifer caribou. The pictograph, bridging past and present, was fitting. It symbolized in a visual manner the controversy that had raged, and still lingered, over Wabakimi Provincial Park and its endangered clutches of caribou.

ᐧ ᐧ ᐧ

My dream of the cave filled with pictographs, accompanied by orchestral granite music, intrigued me. Ever since I had dreamt of a man's suicide prior to meeting him, I had learned to watch out for dreams. Rarely do their meanings make sharp-edged sense. Yet sometimes meaning strikes unexpectedly like lightning, arriving with a jolt and packing more force than a deja vu. It hits behind the sternum as the dreamer realizes he has stood in the face of premonition.

Are we dealing with mere synchronicity, or are we subtly connected to all time and unknown things, immeasurable and logically fathomless? Can the future reach back and touch us? More than rest, I suspect, lurks beneath moon and stars as people lie lost to their wakeful selves.

Again, a dream:

I am watching a boy sledding down a high roof and hitting a roof-edge

176

snowdrift. He launches into the air like a ski-jumper. He—on red sled in exploding snow—is silhouetted against a glowing yellow sun. Suddenly I am standing by ice: a rink? frozen river? A boy has fallen through. I see his mitten next to a hole. I break away snow and ice to reach shoulder-deep into the water. I grab the kid by the shoulder of his coat. I pull him out and hold him upside down. I press his stomach firmly with my hand. The boy vomits water.

He lives.

I awaken, descend the ladder of my cabin's loft, and turn on the radio. Immediately I hear of a boy who had fallen in the Red River of the North near Fargo-Moorhead 250 miles away. Yanked out of the river, he regained consciousness in the hospital. He was home by Christmas.

Synchronicity? Intercepted airwaves? I'm not convinced.

Let people who are not haunted by dream premonitions extol answers. I have none. I never asked for the doors beneath blankets that I sometimes have through. But I watch out.

ॐ ॐ ॐ

After the pictograph layover on Palisade River we ventured east to Whitewater Lake, pausing briefly on Greyson Lake, the furthest point north of our trip. Greyson was calm as its far northern end faded into the bluish haze of distance. There was a way down that end to the Misehkow River. The Misehkow flowed into the Albany River, the Albany east to the sea of James Bay. Big distance. Big water.

Our canoes bobbed on the lake as we looked long and hard, tugged by a restless yearning to continue north. Yet ever so slowly our paddles pulled against water and we rounded the last rock point to turn south.

Some other time, I thought. Some other time I'll come back and keep going.

ॐ ॐ ॐ

## OPEN SPACES

While portaging from Greyson Lake to Greyson River, Ray slipped moose turds ("mumbles" he called them) into Kerry's plastic map holder. When we were all together, ready to launch the canoes, Ray asked Kerry to check the map. . .see where we were.

"What the hell?" Kerry said, breaking into a grin.

We laughed like kids.

❧ ❧ ❧

By sunset I was on my knees looking for a tent spot near a rapids of Greyson River. The site had promise: a clearing of spongy, green-gold moss striped with shadows of jackpines. I felt the moss with my fingers, sinking my hands wrist-deep, probing for rocks, pine cones, sticks, the flotsam of forest floor that rips tent floors and pains backs. The spot was round, level, freshened with breeze and the soft sound of distant rapids. Perfect. I spread the tent out and started fitting the poles together when I noticed boulders in an evenly spaced circle around the clearing. Most of them were covered with moss, some just a hump beneath the mat. Another people at another time had camped along the Greyson. Perhaps they had used skins to cover the sapling framework of their tent, and boulders to hold down the skins.

Nomads, like us, passing through. Energy changing form. Skin changing color.

I knelt in the sun, listened to the rapids run, and hesitated to put up the tent. But there was no other place. How would I tell Ray and Kerry we would be sharing the bed of the dead?

❧ ❧ ❧

Thanks to Ray we ate walleye that night. Fishing for walleye was an addiction Ray condemned one moment but couldn't resist the next. Sometimes he criticized fishing even while doing it.

"I don't know why people have to fish all the time," he said back on Lower

Wabakimi the evening of our first northern lights. "Wherever they go, to lakes, to rivers, to rapids, to waterfalls, they gotta get out their rod and reel. They gotta fish."

Ray cast.

"It even hurts the fish. They snap at a lure and get this barbed piece of steel stuck in their jaws, tongues or gills. They get hauled in and half the time you have to rip the hook out."

He had a bite.

He set the hook.

Grudgingly he reeled the walleye to the sloping rock beneath his feet, carried it up the shore. The walleye was too small to keep. Besides, we already had enough walleyes for dinner. This was one of those fisherman's fantasy campsites where you set up the tent, cast from shore, and reel-in dinner in less than 15 minutes.

I looked at Ray. He was hooked by conscience. His hands were streaked with blood. He was grumbling to himself. His face bore a grimace rare to his nature.

He stood up, held the fish in one hand and his rod in the other, and faced me.

"Perfect example," he said. "Walleye butchery."

He squatted next to the lake, held the fish upright in the water, and watched as the fish—with a flick of its tailfin— disappeared into deep water despite lost blood.

Ray stood up, stepped along the shore, cast, reeled in, and cast again. He still wasn't resigned to what he was doing. He looked like a Shakespeare Tackle junkie holding a hook to his forearm: I hate it but I gotta do it. Not until we sat next to the evening campfire did Ray reach a compromise his conscience could live with.

## OPEN SPACES

As we talked, Ray—pliers in hand—nipped hook barbs off lures into the
fire's gathering ashes.

ᴣ̀ ᴣ̀ ᴣ̀

Even with barbless hooks Ray could catch fish as he proved on Greyson
River while I was putting up the tent. But there was something odd about
one of the walleyes. Its fillets were pink. We nevertheless rolled them in
batter and browned them in butter over an open fire, the pink fillets
blending into the batch.

We ate well, slept as dew froze, and for the next five days I was sick.

I felt nauseous, lethargic, my energy gone, yet we had to continue on.
Beyond Greyson we crossed Whitewater, Smoothrock and Onamakawash
lakes, stopping once in the middle of an afternoon for a shoreline rest when
I was too weak to go on. I lay balled up on a rock in the sunshine. Floating.
Unable to focus. When I felt better, at least stubborn and pressed for time,
we headed down Lonebreast Bay, worked our way up a small river, then
portaged across the Canadian National Railway tracks to Beagle Lake.
Along the way, by the tracks, we found a ramshackle cabin. In the old days,
Calvin Rutstrum's time, such places were open to visitors. There was a
traveler's code of welcome, as long as burned wood was replaced and no
damage was done. We stopped to investigate.

The place was a mess. Rusty cans were scattered around the cabin among
rotting mattresses. We opened the door. Several traps—for mink? marten?
now people?—were set by the doorsill. An old parka hung on the wall above
a dilapidated bed. The floor had rotten boards. On a counter next to open
cans was an unwashed frying pan filled with dirty water. It looked like it
had been weeks, if not months, since anyone had used the place.

We found a small note on the outside of the door.

"Gone to get my things," it said.

But why the set traps? What other surprises awaited someone rash enough

180

to set foot in the wreckage of some backwoodsman's Lonely Hearts Club schemes?

We closed the door and left.

I still felt nauseous and jittery when we reached LaParde Lake, but I was eating blueberries, the bushes so laden with fruit—a month later than the Quetico-Superior's blueberries—that they sprawled flat on carpets of moss. With my appetite back, I fed it. This was good. I would need to feel strong, if not cocksure, to deal with the Kopka in Lake Nipigon's western watershed.

⁂

We reached the Kopka River after a dawn quarrel (Should we, or should we not, dismantle our fire ring on Aldridge Lake? We did.) and after a run-in with a bull moose (No argument there; we gave the moose freeway rights on the portage). Being on the Kopka meant we would flow east and south toward Nipigon which, in turn, flowed south to Lake Superior. The geographical shift was barely perceptible. The canoe trip simply took on a new dimension, a changing of tone and cadence well-known to canoeists who have been too long on large lakes and now sniff the dance of flowing water.

Where scenery constantly changes.

Where water speaks at rapids.

Where shorelines expand and contract, look far away and then close at hand, as if the river corridor is breathing, paddlers riding air in the lungs of the landscape.

The dawn sun was in our face. Visored cap time. Sunglasses. With breakfast granola barely filling our stomachs, and as the caffeine of strong Sumatran coffee began to kick in, we rode the sunlit pulse of a new waterway, a shining trail of power. . .onward, onward, lining our canoes through boulder gardens, running what rapids we dared, onward toward Nipigon, smacking, scraping, flowing with the Kopka's bridgeless flow.

Technically, the Kopka River is in both the Thunder Bay and Nipigon districts of Ontario's north central region. The river encompasses, in Nipigon District alone, 18,000 acres. At the head of the river's 75 miles is a nest of lakes: Uneven, Waterhouse, Redsand, Sparkling and, with a portage or three, Brightsand. The Kopka was one of Ontario's 155 recommended provincial park candidates in 1983. Logging isn't normally permitted in provincial parks. The Kopka was to be different. It wasn't, as far as I knew, going to be logged, but land use guidelines stated specifically that the Kopka would be "bridged to access forested areas."

The Kopka wasn't bridged anywhere in the hinterlands west of the Armstrong Road along Lake Nipigon, but it was the threat of a bridge, and everything its road might bring, that had irked Hyer. A bridge, he and other wilderness preservationists had said, would change irrevocably the Kopka's natural condition. One bridge might lead to two bridges, or three.

Jim Jackson, senior planner for the Ministry of Natural Resources' North Central Region, admitted there might eventually be other bridges spanning the Kopka.

"We have to cross the river," he told me in his Thunder Bay office before the trip. "You can't put it off forever. The trees are there to be cut. The logging companies have an agreement and license to manage that area, and so we're coming up with the best possible solution right now in that particular waterway."

The bridge and road, he said, would be built "conscientiously."

Specifications called for a tight right-of-way and "whatever is necessary" to discourage parking spaces from developing along the river. Ditto for a boat launching site. The bridge, moreover, would be located at a riverbend so it wouldn't be seen until the last moment by approaching canoeists. A portage would pass beneath the bridge so canoeists wouldn't "have to lug their canoes over a road with a pulp truck coming down on them at 50 miles an hour."

I listened but I didn't agree. I had portaged Dog River Road on the Kam-Dog Expedition, and what I understood in reference to logging roads was this:

First, a logging truck loaded to the max and moving at 50 miles per hour was not, and never would be, low impact on a wilderness visitor, bridge at riverbend or not. Besides, on a cool day or when wind carried sounds, the noise of logging trucks would be like airplanes: silence one minute, modern man's mechanical intrusion the next. You're ripped right out of silence. You're raped by sound. And wilderness takes flight.

Secondly, what Jim Jackson was referring to were industry's concessions to wilderness "elitists." Industry was conceding what allegedly belonged to *it*.

Elitists: get on your knees: be reasonable: give thanks for concessions to your play.

There's real work, the subtext said, and then there's recreation.

I wanted to remind Jackson that intangible values were becoming increasingly important as the last of North America's wild areas were being ravaged. . .changed forever. Unlike a logging road which can be designed, admittedly sometimes more expensively, to bypass a virgin waterway, a cost rightfully passed to the consumer, an intangible value—silence, timelessness, the sensation of being encompassed by natural beauty—cannot be drafted, constructed, easily restored or reduced to abstract numbers on paper shuffled between banks. But I said nothing to Jackson.

He probably knew. Even on the job side of his desk he probably knew, in his best hours, that putting a bridge across the Kopka was like putting a scar on a beautiful woman's face: right across the bridge of her nose.

Rapids on the Kopka, like those on the Ogoki, came with the terrain. As we descended the river, we often had to get out of our canoes to line them down rapids or through boulder gardens where the Kopka bottlenecked.

Other parts of the river widened into long, narrow rockbound lakes. Sheer beauty. We heard logging trucks near Sandison Lake, but the rest of the river was silent. As aspen leaves glowed gold in evening sunlight, we paddled in anticipation, stroke after stroke, switch after switch, of what lay downstream at the south end of Kenakskaniss Lake.

First the river fanned out, flowed through an unnavigable stretch of rocks, then plunged over a granite shelf to a pool below. An island split the river downstream where water roared around rock before fusing into a cataract gushing down a gorge. Despite its small size, the Kopka dropped 200 feet in a little over a mile. Portages were rocky and steep. Canoes were sometimes handed down to partners, not carried. Packs were lowered with ropes; bodies belayed. The Kopka had opened like a gaping cut through a granite canyon.

I paused to take photos. Ray, along a steep rapids with a series of waterfalls beyond him, drank water with his hands, scooping the Kopka to his lips, an appropriate gesture. We pitched the trip's last camp on a shoreline point of a cliff-ringed lake. There were no pictographs here, no wolves howling in the evening air, no visible woodland caribou, certainly no bison like in the badlands, but we could see, yes, there's beauty left in the world. We needed it, wanted it, and we had it.

I understood why Hyer, unlike people less knowledgeable of the Kopka's beauty, felt a parks crisis was at hand. A road and bridge upstream from the falls section, where it was planned, could make the Kopka's most beautiful stretch easy to reach. It could become a holiday picnic site. Catch a couple fish, drink beer, roast wieners from Thunder Bay, chomp chips. . .

Shame on me.

But I hurt. Just like Hyer and the rest of the wilderness consortium hurt.

It was especially frustrating to know the Kopka might be diminished because, as a proposed provincial waterway, it still hadn't reached the master plan stage. Zoning restrictions hadn't been finalized. Regulations hadn't been fully determined. Meanwhile logging trucks, as Jackson said, rode a license to penetrate the Kopka's corridor at 50 miles per hour.

This was a heavy stew to chew, a bit like pulpwood, as a full moon rose to light our camp's arena of rock. The Kopka filled the arena with a canyon's waterfall at one end and drained it with a larger waterfall at the other. Landscape connections. Expansions and contractions. Despite the Kopka's political problems you didn't need to be a diehard romantic, an alleged wilderness elitist from adjacent northern Minnesota, or a foreigner, for crying out loud, to know there was magic in the night.

Ray felt it coming. He had climbed cliffs as the sun set to struggle within himself—now at trip's end—not over walleyes or environmental battles but whether his next adventure, sacrificing some voyageur freedom, should include marriage.

It did, along with two baby boys.

Kerry, who would later become an outstanding instructor for Minnesota's Voyageur Outward Bound School, and who would canoe more remote rivers including Ontario's Albany and Manitoba's Bloodvein, had studied topographical maps as night neared. Kerry had glanced up occasionally to put the 500-foot hills to the east into perspective. The maps showed small lakes squiggled into yonder ranges: places of difficult passage: temporary homes for the likes of Kerry in spirit if not body.

I, too, looked at maps.

I had grown thin. My ribs were fatless beneath my shirt, my pants loose around the waist. Despite the late hour I sipped the last of the day's coffee. I had no intention of early sleep. I was going to savor the night. A fog was gathering. Something was coming. I thought of how good it felt along the Kopka. Something. I thought of Wabakimi's caribou, and how the new park, so beautiful, needed all the protection it could get. Was coming. I stirred the campfire's coals, fed it more firewood, and looked up at the moon: round, full, orange-paling-to-white.

If only I could stay here long enough, I thought. Some realization, some epiphany of insight about our Wabakimi-Kopka capers, might circle around me with wings of freedom before swooping and clutching my soul like an angel with talons.

An angel, I hoped, of mercy.

Take me.

Ray and Kerry went to bed leaving me to my prose and dreams, and I waited for that angel. She was a quiet one. Nothing but northern lights again. Nothing but the sound and cool breath of the waterfalls on a brisk, calm night after 22 days of canoeing.

Perhaps this—the crystalline clarity of flowing water, the solidity and security of ancient bedrock, silence, solitude, a flickering campfire, a star-rimmed moon, and thoughts wending toward wordlessness—maybe this is what the Kopka River and other trails of power are all about. You shuck phone, job, debts, politics and stand exposed to primordial time. You become a synthesis of prehistoric and modern man on a wild shore, truly ecumenical, catholic in its most universal sense. Paddle at hand, you have walked the evolutionary path. You have followed the meltdown of glacial ice in a renewed land, sniffing its cool till edge, tracking sign, and sensing the long road, our organic heritage, up which people of all races have come.

You feel it in your gut. You hear it in the silence. You find it in the night or it's born of light. It is a song of wonder that knows no end but is joyous in the singing.

As for my angel of mercy, I'm still waiting for her. But if that angel has anything to do with pure wilderness—with land unlogged, unroaded and unbridged—she's going to remain, if anything, more evasive.

The Kopka is now bridged.

# PART III
# ASSIGNMENT:
# PARK RANGER

*One of the reasons to have national parks is to give people an opportunity to change their ways, to assume a new humility, a new self-restraint, a new willingness to face risks. But if we no longer expect that of the ranger, we no longer expect it of the parks or of ourselves.*

— *Peter Steinhart*
*"Surviving on Sunsets"*
*Audubon*

# CHAPTER EIGHT
# THE RANGER ZONE

The adrenaline was flowing as I stood in the marijuana garden looking at Ranger Bob D'Alessandro in late summer, 1986. It was harvest season in northern California's Humboldt County, locus of Redwood National Park. Times were tense. Marijuana growers — counting on sinsemilla plants worth $1,000 to $2,000 apiece, and no harder to grow than tomatoes — were taking their work seriously. Many of them were armed. Some used face-to-face threats to frighten people off public land. Redwood rangers, meanwhile, had located the largest of three known gardens in the park. They were small by non-park standards, yet the garden we stood in could have grossed $80,000. Worth working. Worth stealing. Despite stake-outs by D'Alessandro and Ranger Chuck Carlson, we didn't know who the growers were. And we didn't know if we would be out-armed.

Car doors had startled us. After Ranger Carlson had dropped us off, we had bulled through wet brush down to a ravine where fenced clumps of marijuana were watered by PVC hose funnelling water from a nearby creek. Given a choice by District Ranger Steve Hurd, I had taken a low profile in the operation but had decided to tag along with D'Alessandro to see what he was dealing with. It had just rained and growers like to shake rain off their plants to prevent mildew. The access road near the garden had a locked gate. No one was expected to pass through that gate this day except, possibly, growers with an illicit key. When we heard the car doors we radioed Carlson to see if he had seen anyone pass through the gate.

He hadn't. Bob and I unsnapped our holsters.

The gun.

As a seasonal National Park Service ranger, I wore a Smith & Wesson .357, with .38 +P+ ammunition. It was stainless steel and my own. Outside of rifles it was the deadliest weapon I had ever held. I hoped it would never be used.

It was my first year with the Park Service, and what I found en route to Redwood, there, and afterwards intrigued me. Not only had rangers adopted law enforcement responsibilities over the years but in northern California there was a little-known guerrilla war going on. On one side were the marijuana growers; on the other were state and federal agents including park rangers.

People were getting killed in the woods. A helicopter belonging to CAMP, the multi-agency Campaign Against Marijuana Planting, had crashed during operations, and another was grazed mid-air by a bullet. One night a California game warden told me of a shooting the previous summer within two miles of where I lived: one man killed, the other shot and crawling to help. Both men were growers. The year I was at Redwood looked worse. Officials suspected over 20 deaths that summer related to marijuana growing.

"A body can be ditched in the ravines around here," the warden had told me, "and never be found."

Most of the fighting was among growers. They couldn't, of course, turn to police if their gardens were robbed. If a bad friend of a friend knew of a $100,000 garden worth taking (better yet, a dried stash in a cabin), top gun could have it.

The gravity of the situation was easy to sense with Ranger D'Alessandro. There was the adrenaline, the fragrant foot-long sinsemilla buds, and Bob—with his gray NPS shirt, green nylon jacket, and bronze ranger badge—reaching for his revolver.

I also couldn't forget the brochure I found in a van on an orientation tour. Published by CAMP and titled *Outdoor Alert*, it warned hikers, fishermen, boaters, hunters and birdwatchers about the marijuana gardens. The tourism industry in northern California hated the brochure. It frightened people away, partly with its map of northern California counties where sinsemilla production was big-time and where, the implication was, dangers to the public were highest.

Humboldt County led the pack. There was a warning to readers who stumbled across gardens to assume armed guards were near.

"I didn't mean to do this," they were supposed to say loudly, even if no one was in sight. "And I'm leaving right now."

As if they didn't belong on public land. But, of course, they did. That was the problem. It wasn't whether marijuana was good or bad, or should be legal or illegal. The gardens didn't belong in a national park, nor did corn, hay or alfalfa. People, meanwhile, were getting injured and killed.

There were warnings of trails with trap-guns, fishhooks dangling at eye level, deadfalls, bear traps and snares. Not for me alone did paranoia pervade the air during harvest time.

Someone like myself, wearing a uniform and gun, could end up dead.

Imagine a dark night. I did.

I'm alone in my patrol pickup. There's a gun inside the cellar, Mike and the Mechanics sing on the radio, use it only in emergency. In my headlights I see an old pickup on the side of the road, its hood up. There's a tarp over the pickup bed. I stop. Suppose the driver is a wanted felon. Or perhaps he's been busted before, granted probation, and now faces prison. All that separates him from freedom is the man with uniform, gun and badge walking toward him. If I were smart I would radio the vehicle's license number to the park's dispatcher, stating location and action.

But maybe I'll forget.

Maybe it is the last thing I will ever forget as the man aims a gun and night explodes.

Pure paranoia, perhaps, but it was the possibility of injury or death in the course of routine ranger duties that led the National Park Service to train and equip many of its rangers to protect themselves, visitors, and parkland resources. Over 300 million people visited the parks each summer, and among them were a small percentage that not only were outlaws, they were dangerous: car burglars, poachers, rapists, a few murderers and a handful of marijuana growers serious about making money.

Forget the peace and love of the 1969s hippie movement. Just add the fertilizer.

For D'Alessandro, me, and the marijuana growers, this was everyone's lucky day. The occupants of the car were unexpected park maintenance personnel. Only later did Redwood rangers arrest the two gardeners in whose fragrant crop we stood.

&#10086; &#10086; &#10086;

Two things had happened by the time I became a ranger. I had come to see that while it's one thing to support park and wilderness legislation with organization membership, donations, writing, speeches, and active lobby work in rooms of marble and oak, it's something altogether different to enforce that legislation in the field: to confront abusers face-to-face, changing ways.

Rangers, moreover, had come under the gun. They were controversial.

Alston Chase in *Playing God in Yellowstone* had no end of negative things to say about rangers being "policemen rather than wildlife scientists or historians." At one time, Chase said, rangers epitomized everything good about the Park Service whose goals—to preserve parklands—were beyond reproach. Rangers were the "incorruptible guardians of our precious national heritage, and they encouraged an impression of complete competence. They were Smoky the Bear, Sergeant Preston, and Ranger Rick rolled into one."

But rangers, Chase argued, had changed over the years. Most were "gumshoes" immersed in law enforcement. Visitor safety and protection had become an indelible part of the "ranger mentality." Gumshoes, in fact, were the NPS personnel most likely to advance into superintendent positions. Meanwhile,

Chase alleged, resource research and management suffered.

Bernard Shanks in *This Land is Your Land* agreed. The new rangers were "more interested in firearms than flowers, more oriented to hand-to-hand combat than mountain climbing or hiking... Instead of protecting people from the park's environment and the environment from people, the new rangers concentrated on conflicts *among* people. They were more suited to be urban police than resource managers or conservation officers."

Even the late incorrigible Edward Abbey, himself once a ranger, took a shot at rangers in his novel *The Monkey Wrench Gang*. He describes Ranger Edwin P. Abbott, Jr. as looking like a ranger should: "tall, slim, able, not too bright." After Abbott searched monkeywrenchers Doc and Bonnie, the ranger's friendly tone of voice "sank to a snarl." The gun, handcuffs and leather belt/holster, Abbey says, had gotten in Ranger Abbott's "eyes, in his heart."

So why did rangers begin toting guns instead of being the botanists and Mark Trails of yesteryear, what writer Jeff Copeland of *Newsweek* described as "Boy Scouts whose most heroic poses are struck on horseback for tourist cameras"?

The change accelerated around Independence Day, 1970, when 500 campers in Stoneman Meadows at California's Yosemite National Park got unruly. The riot has been described as a "crucible in rangering experience." The first park rangers, after all, were U.S. Cavalrymen valued for their woods and firearms savvy, but after the National Park Service was established in 1916 it developed its own cadre of rangers. Most were generalists doing everything from handling bears and arresting poachers to collecting garbage and entrance fees. Many, with strong backgrounds in natural sciences, became naturalists and interpreted the parks to visitors. Only a few rangers practiced law enforcement. Hence, at Stoneman Meadows, where generalist rangers—called *tree fuzz* and *pine pigs* by the rebels—were given guns, Mace and told to quell the disturbance, the Park Service realized it was caught off-guard. The result by 1976 was Congress' General Authorities Act mandating NPS to take greater responsibility for law enforcement within its jurisdiction.

More and more rangers went through law enforcement training, wore guns, wrote tickets and made arrests.

This was especially true in the larger parks like Yosemite (where, with its own jail, and where visitation reached two million people a year, 800 to 900 annual arrests were not uncommon) and Death Valley National Monument (where rangers in 1969 helped to capture mass-murderer Charlie Manson). As park visitation increased from 10.7 million people in 1960 to 344.4 million in 1982, crime rose proportionately. By 1982 there were 87,153 annual offenses in the parks. By 1986: 127,322. Fortunately, serious offenses increased infinitesimally compared to lesser offenses like vandalism, drug and alcohol incidents, natural resource violations and traffic violations.

When dealing with crime, rangering became touch-and-go, sometimes dangerous. In 1989, for the first time in NPS history, rangers killed assailants in three incidents.

In March a man at Lake Mead National Recreation Area in northwestern Arizona pulled a gun on a ranger, threatened to kill him and then advanced until the ranger stopped him with a 12 gauge shotgun.

Two months later a suspected car burglar, Phillip Claw, was shot by Chief Ranger John Miller while Claw fought him and several rangers at Canyon de Chelly National Monument in northwestern New Mexico. Claw, shot twice, carried Miller with him in a 30-foot fall down a steep embankment to a talus slope. Claw fell another 30 feet. Rangers bandaged Claw and administered cardiopulmonary resuscitation for fifteen minutes until a rescue squad arrived, but Claw died.

In a third incident, knife-wielding David Noftser of Westoff, Texas, attacked rangers John Peterson of Grand Canyon and Don McBee of Lake Mead on May 13th. Noftser had been squatting in a hut on parkland, staying beyond a 90 day backcountry limit, and once had been heard chanting near a self-made altar. Shortly before the rangers had their run-in with him, he had gone fishing with two acquaintances, pointed a rifle at one of the men's heads and fired wildly at the other.

After Ranger Peterson confiscated the rifle, the boats headed for shore where Noftser brandished a knife and threatened the rangers. The rangers drew their weapons and tried to talk Noftser out of his knife, but Noftser jumped onto the bow of the NPS's twenty-foot Boston Whaler. Suddenly Noftser jumped into the cabin and threatened to cut out McBee's guts.

McBee fought him off with a life ring and scrambled onto the bow of the boat. Noftser followed. McBee—using deadly force in self-defense—shot him four times. Noftser kept coming. McBee shot him two more times, as did Ranger Peterson.

The county coroner and NPS investigated the incident. Both ruled it justifiable homicide.

Death in the ranger zone.

What might have happened to the rangers if they hadn't been armed?

As if the Lake Mead incident wasn't enough, rangers at Yellowstone in early June, 1989, had to deal with a man using a .30 caliber Ruger to hold eight hostages in a visitor center at Old Faithful Geyser. Fortunately the man, Bret Hartley, 18, of Baton Rouge, Louisiana, let the hostages go before surrendering to rangers after a five hour ordeal.

♨ ♨ ♨

"If you look for trouble hard enough," Ely's Fred Rayman, a friend and fellow ranger trainee, warned me, "you're going to find it."

For rangers there's trouble to be found among drug runners in Florida's Everglades National Park and along the Mexican border in Texas's Big Bend National Park. Handling irate drunks, as Ranger D'Alessandro discovered, is common in places such as Whiskeytown-Shasta-Trinity National Recreation Area in California. There's trouble in remote Alaskan parks where trophy hunting sometimes leads to game violations, and where locals have traditionally despised any representative of the federal government. In the mid-1980s, for example, Ranger Marty Stage documented several threats on his life in Alaska's Kobuk Valley National Park. There and elsewhere poachers are armed.

More trouble:

1984: Operation Trophy Kill: rangers joined local sheriffs and U.S. Marshals to bust a syndicate killing grizzlies, elk and bighorn sheep for paws, antlers and horns.

1985: Rangers and county deputies stopped thieves stealing artifacts from Civil War graves at Virginia's Richmond National Battlefield Park. The arrest resulted in the first convictions under the Archeological Resources Protection Act.

1985-1988: Operation Smoky: Rangers helped bust a black bear poaching ring in, and near, Tennessee's Great Smoky Mountains National Park. More than 60 people were arrested; they had killed 368 of the park's 500 bears, leaving the smaller ones. They were vicious poachers who used dogs to chase and tree bears, or they would capture bears, remove their teeth and claws, tie them to trees and then sic their dogs on them so the dogs could develop a taste for bear blood. At least one ranger had to leave the Smokies because of threats on her life.

At least three rangers have died in the line of duty.

James Cary, who was to testify against Arkansas bootleggers, was ambushed and killed in 1927. In 1973 Ranger Ken Patrick was killed by poachers at California's Point Reyes National Seashore. In May, 1990, Robert L. McGhee, Jr., 50, was shot to death by escaped felons at Gulf Islands National Seashore. At Redwood National Park, I saw a poster seeking a ranger missing in the Southwest for over six years.

Although 1989's shootings and the murders of Cary, Patrick and McGhee were unusual incidents, there have always been sporadic assaults on rangers, increasing over the years. In 1986 there were 31 assaults on rangers, 86 in 1988. In response, and due in part to 1989's shooting incidents, the National Park Service issued regulations in late 1989 requiring law enforcement rangers to move-up from .38 caliber revolvers to .357s. The Park Service put the regulations on hold by 1990-91, however, as NPS—on the heels of other federal land management agencies—weighed the merits of nine millimeter and ten millimeter automatics.

For seasonal ranger Chris Schmidt of California's Lassen Volcanic National Park, wearing a sidearm took getting used to. Although she received her law enforcement commission (allowing rangers to wear sidearms) from California's Santa Rosa Criminal Justice Program, she resisted putting on the gun and even imagined ways to circumvent it.

"I nevertheless wore the gun," she told me in 1986, "and when people asked me why I'd tell them it's to protect the park visitor, because there are crazies out there. If something goes wrong, I can respond. And when they realized it was for their own safety, it was okay."

Schmidt sensed the effectiveness of her added authority:

"Last year, as a non-commissioned ranger, I could say to people 'Your dog needs to be on a leash, those are the rules,' and they'd go 'Okay,' and this year I say 'Your dog needs to be on a leash,' and they say 'Yes, Ma'am, we'll do it right away.' And they do it."

According to Schmidt, however, it's not authority that makes the best ranger but concern for the environment. They weave this care into effective communication skills.

Permanent Ranger Larry Kangas of Isle Royale National Park agrees. In a career spanning Everglades National Park, Rocky Mountain National Park, Tennessee and Kentucky's Big South Fork National River and Recreation Area, and Michigan's Pictured Rocks National Lakeshore, Kangas has found that public relations abilities are *the* priority when hiring someone. Next is a ranger's sensitivity to the resource and an ability to observe changes (natural? man-made?) in parklands.

"Law enforcement," Kangas told me one evening, "is just another tool to accomplish our mission which is to protect the parks and visitors. Wearing a gun enables a ranger to get through a higher risk situation safely."

Armed rangers have outnumbered naturalists and generalists since 1977. In 1990 there were about 2,500 armed rangers compared to 1,100 naturalists.

ɹ᷈ ɹ᷈ ɹ᷈

As rangers Schmidt and Kangas know, rangers complete specific training and undergo a background search to get a law enforcement commission. Permanent rangers (3,182 in 1989 out of NPS's total permanent work force of 12,634) go through nine weeks of training at FLETC, Georgia's Federal Law Enforcement Training Center. Seasonal rangers, at their own expense, attend similar programs at approximately a dozen schools nationwide. I went through a program at Vermilion Community College in Ely, hoping to be employed outdoors where the action is: where eagles soar, where grizzlies roam sandbars, and where I'd be in daily contact with the natural beauty national parks are designated to protect. The required 200+ hour ranger course (often supplementing self-acquired outdoor skills and emergency medical training) covered everything from jurisdiction and crime scene management to defensive tactics. There was no history of John Muir or Stephen Mather, the spiritual and founding fathers, respectively, of the National Park Service. Nothing about trapping grizzlies or the latest brouhaha over the reintroduction of wolves to Yellowstone.

Firearm proficiency is vital. Prospective rangers must go through 40 to 50 hours of firearms training and then pass a qualifying shoot.

There's a peculiar perversity to shooting a .357 at a human silhouette. Instead of the traditional bulls-eye target there's the shape of a person's head, shoulders and torso. A kill zone, worth five points, is shown in shades of green or blue. The object, of course, is to hit the kill zone enough times to qualify.

There are also low-light and shotgun qualifications.

I asked Rayman, an ex-machine gunner in the Army, to help me learn to shoot. Before long I had bought squeeze-grips to strengthen my fingers, was dry-firing at my cabin's clock and one of Dan Metz's grouse paintings (to develop a smooth trigger-pull), and I had invested a small fortune in ammunition. Like I say, a peculiar perversity, but a necessary one. If I were going to carry a gun, I wanted to be faster with it than the other guy, and I wanted to be comfortable with it. Respect it, yes, but not fear it. Same as with a canoe paddle.

Getting top score didn't matter. I had to requalify at Redwood and, like all rangers, on subsequent years. Seasonal rangers also go through 40 hours of annual refreshment training (varying from death scene management and juvenile procedures to wildlife issues) to keep a commission.

As far as seasonal ranger Steve Spickerman was concerned when I spoke to him in 1989, the NPS's commissioning of rangers as law enforcement officers had gone too far. It was a conviction he arrived at while working at several NPS units. Spickerman was a generalist ranger. He didn't have a commission. Despite his outdoor skills, good rapport with people, and a deep love of the land, everywhere he worked there was talk of replacing him.

"The ranger position should not be dependent on a commission," he explained. "People who want to become rangers are going to law enforcement school, getting their commission, but nevertheless are not 100% committed to being a law enforcement person. They're not going to react properly if they must face a drunk with a shotgun. Eventually you're going to see rangers either being killed or hurt."

"Or you're going to see the public hurt."

Spickerman, who had hunted most of his life and enjoyed shooting guns, insisted on the difference between being commissioned and being law enforcement-oriented. He once heard of an incident where a frightened female ranger in the Southwest failed to respond to a report of gunfire.

"I'm not saying there isn't a need for law enforcement officers in national parks," he said. "I think there definitely is. But it doesn't have to be every field ranger position."

Spickerman was like a few other rangers I met: hanging onto, other rangers said, the old days. His idea of a ranger had to do with living in the backcountry and wearing flannel shirts: "Somebody like Bob Marshall walking across the crest of the Brooks Range."

Steve paused.

"I'm trying to keep that vision alive. By not getting a commission."

Although commissioned rangers will likely continue to have the lion's share of the NPS ranger job market, variety remains the spice of life. Ranger Butch Farabee once described a day when he rescued a stranded climber, pulled a human corpse out of the Merced River, and helped with a night-time drug bust.

Other rangers have done artificial respiration on deer and closed-chest heart massages on grizzlies. Still others, like Ranger Bill Wade, have tracked down frozen people.

Wade's assignment, according to Jay Heinrichs in *National Wildlife*, was a grisly one. Over ten years ago Wade and other rangers were asked to locate a man who was terminally ill and who, with son and daughter, wanted to spend some of his last days at Camp Muir. A snowstorm hit. The man dug a snowcave and sealed it with his body. As Ranger Wade discovered, the son and daughter lived but had to watch their father die.

Rangers have realized all along that risk is sometimes the name of the game. Most rangers, like urban police, often patrol alone even during night's more hazardous hours. Some sleep alone in grizzly bear country where they throw their fate to the wind (or gun, as need be). Park pilots, like Ranger Larry Van Slyke, play their own game of hardball. When Van Slyke was stationed at Lake Clark National Park in Alaska, he had to make an emergency landing on a remote lake when his airborne Beaver blew a cylinder.

For all their risk taking, law enforcement situations, and interpretive work, rangers are paid relatively little. In 1988 the Association of National Park Rangers (ANPR) surveyed its members and discovered pay rates had declined to a level "which often makes them uncompetitive with even the lowest salaried employees in the private sector." Most rangers made less than the average salary of a fulltime American worker ($26,000). Almost half of all rangers made less than $20,000 a year.

In a comparison with city and state park rangers, and with officers of the U.S. Fish & Wildlife Service, Immigration and Naturalization Service, U.S. Marshals and U.S. Park Police, NPS rangers were invariably paid least. Many depended on working spouses, overtime pay, shared residences and old cars. Few could afford to buy homes.

Perhaps seasonal "temporary fulltime" rangers (about 5,158 in 1989) are particularly hamstrung. They can only apply to two parks out of several hundred a year (albeit with rehire rights if they've worked at a park before); they're locked into a government pay scale of less than $8 an hour; they get no health insurance; and they're laid off every autumn to face the paper music of state unemployment agencies.

Perhaps the most startling statistic in ANPR's survey was that 64% of its members were thinking about leaving the National Park Service because of inadequate money. ANPR in 1989-90 was backing legislation calling for "just compensation" in the fear good rangers leaving the Service might result in "mediocrity in carrying out the essential tasks of government."

If ranger pay is so low, what's the draw?

Many rangers are simply committed to the Park Service's mission of preserving parklands, monuments, historical sites, and recreation areas. Others like helping visitors by enforcing safety regulations, handling emergencies, or working in a beautiful and nationally significant environment.

"I'm not in it for the money," District Ranger Larry Johnson of Apostle Islands National Lakeshore told me. "I'm in it to touch the land."

Ranger Dave Mihalic claims rangering can be reduced to "a glimpse of a grizzly with its fur shining against a stand of spruce." And there's adventure: airplane patrols above glaciers, dogsledding in the shadow of Denali, sitting in candlelight in a fire tower of Isle Royale National Park, or snowmobile patrols near the sand dunes of Pictured Rocks. There's also, as I discovered in the Apostle Islands in the late 1980s, the challenge of boating in gale force winds or rescuing sailors aground at sea.

ﯤ ﯤ ﯤ

Wind was whistling through the halyards of the sailboat *Synergism* when Lead Park Ranger Jeff Hepner and I pulled up to her in the NPS <u>Gull</u>, a 21-foot Boston Whaler. We were on the north side of Stockton Island off Wisconsin's Bayfield Peninsula. Lake Superior—the largest body of freshwater in the world—was whipped with 30-knot winds out of the northwest. Three-foot waves beat on the hull of the grounded *Synergism*, certainly not big waves by Superior's stormy standards (10 to 40 feet), but choppy enough to make vessel rescue questionable. A half hour earlier, Hepner and I, while cooking duck in my ranger cabin on South Twin Island, overheard *Synergism's* distress call to the U.S. Coast Guard.

We had wanted to beat the Coast Guard to the scene, and we did. What happened next wasn't part of the plan.

It had to do, I suppose, with the side of a ranger's life the public rarely sees. Rangers with sidearms appear to be doing only hardcover law enforcement work, but rangers have always been, and remain, multi-faceted. They are not simply misplaced urban cops or adjuncts to sheriffs' departments. They act as ambassadors or emissaries between the landscape and public. They range around, functioning as the eyes and ears of desk-bound administration. They fight structural fires and forest wildfires. And they monitor wildlife activities.

One night in the Apostle Islands, for example, as dusk brought fog and mist, I had to make a sudden boat run to Devils Island where lighthouse volunteers had what they thought might be an immature bald eagle. It was attacked by an owl in mid-flight: taloned in the chest, but dropped. My assignment was to identify the bird, take appropriate action (more care, possibly professional, if it was an eagle), and then get back to South Twin before darkness made navigation with compass and depth-finder a painstakingly slow, hazardous necessity. The bird turned out to be a marsh hawk, was kept in an open box on the lighthouse keeper's porch, and it flew away the following morning.

Rangers also save lives. They evacuate park visitors with serious medical problems and search for missing persons. When barefoot Shane Justice, 6, for instance, became lost in the Great Smokies in the summer of 1989, rangers set out and found him. He had slept in a hollow log and used leaves and his dog for warmth.

Smart kid.

Also that year rangers conducted a successful search for actress Jane Fonda, the beautiful aerobics queen, when she became separated from friends in California's Sequoia-Kings Canyon parks and had to spend the night alone in the backcountry.

Rough ranger assignment, I joked with Hepner. Let's invite Jane to the Apostles.

Even without Jane, rangers have been busy. In 1988 they responded to 3,551 search and rescue incidents. Although there were 174 fatalities, 1,327 sick or injured people were rescued. According to Butch Farabee, Emergency Medical Services Coordinator for NPS, the statistics were similar in 1989. Over 600 people would have died without ranger intervention.

Conducting a successful search can make a ranger's day. I've seen a glow in Ranger Hepner's eyes after he found, in the middle of the night, an overdue family near Squaw Bay. "Job security," he said, but I could tell it was more than that. Of all his functions in the Apostles (including handling a knifing incident at Otter Island in 1987), Hepner likes nothing better than a rescue.

I know the feeling. On my first day back in the Apostles in 1989, I joined Hepner in rescuing a marooned family from York Island. Their new boat had been swamped and destroyed in six-foot waves Memorial Day. I had to crawl from Hepner's NPS *Osprey* into a fishing boat, and then, with hip waders, into the lake which was deeper near shore than I expected. The waders filled with May-cold water. Once on shore I guided the family of four, including two-year-old Matthew in my arms, along the tops of low cliffs with waves crashing below to a boat-boarding sandstone ledge in the lee of York.

As for the grounded *Synergism* near Stockton Island, the Coast Guard was right behind us. We relinquished command. Unfortunately, and unlike the Coast Guard's customary display of skill, Murphy's law about things going wrong, if they can, danced on the water. The Coast Guard's 41-footer was blown into shallow water where its propellers churned sand; soon a towing line was wrapped in one of the propellers. The Coast Guard pulled out into deeper water and decided, along with Hepner and Ranger Larry Johnson, to abandon trying to tow the sailboat off the sandbar. Instead the crew of five would be evacuated. I was given the job of using the *Synergism's* unsteady dinghy to ferry three of the crewmen, one at a time, from the sailboat to the NPS *Gull* which, in turn, took them to the Coast Guard vessel.

It was a bad way for sailors to end a vacation but the day wasn't over for Hepner and me. After leaving the *Synergism* we searched for a missing kayaker, finding him safe near Stockton's Julien Bay. As Edward Abbey wrote in *The Journey Home*, "One calamity after another. One mishap after another. A ranger's work is never done." Darkness settled. Soon we rode waves—spray splashing in our faces, Hepner humming a tune—back to South Twin Island.

The duck, which hunter Hepner had shot the previous autumn and brought to my cabin, was more than done. During our search and rescue it had sat in wine and its own fat for over six hours.

"Tastes strange," Hepner said. "What do you think?"

(I had been rangering on adrenaline. I was famished.)

"Tastes fine," I said.

Truth was, it was almost midnight. The marine radio was momentarily silent. It was time, quite simply, to fuel up and power down on the nearest food available. It was time to dine on poorly-cooked ranger zone duck.

# CHAPTER NINE
# FOREVER BRANDED

I remember well. My back ached as I sat on a log on the fire line massaging toes that had mysteriously become numb. It was my eighth day fighting western Montana's Red Bench Fire. This wasn't Yellowstone—summer's big gun when it came to wildfires—but the danger and pain of fighting wildfire was the same. I added fresh moleskin to foot blisters and then slipped my socks and boots back on.

Suddenly a gust of wind fanned nearby flames. The fire leapt up dead branches into the crowns of pines and flashed overhead. Treetops behind me, preheated by the thrashing fire, also burst into flame.

"Get the hell out of there!" my squad boss yelled. "Run!"

I didn't need to be told. As embers and flaming branches fell around me I was already on my sore feet, grabbing my half-empty Fedco water bag, and hustling down the bulldozed trail. Walled and roofed by fire, this was as close as I ever wanted to get to being fried.

Fighting wildfire wasn't among my normal ranger duties. Although I was involved with prescribed burns at Redwood National Park in 1986, and was certified to fight fires while a ranger in the Apostle Islands, not until 1988's western fire situation reached national emergency proportions was I yanked from South Twin Island on Lake Superior and flown from Duluth to Montana.

Destination, my original National Park Service travel voucher read: unknown. Length of stay: unknown.

I joined a crew of 20 NPS firefighters from the Midwest at Kalispell. We boarded a school bus, stopped at a restaurant for midnight food and paperwork check-in, then drove northwest beneath clouds tinged orange by flames.

I had grabbed a local newspaper from a coin machine at the restaurant. The front page was all Red Bench.

Smoldering forest duff, supposedly ignited by lightning, had crept alive the previous afternoon, September 6th, near Red Meadow Creek in Flathead National Forest seven miles northwest of Polebridge. Fed by 30 mile-per-hour winds, the fire grew to 3,000 acres in four hours and formed a fiery wall 200 feet high. Embers flew two miles ahead of the flames. Logs, rocks and dirt were hurled into the air. Flames made an explosive run eastward, jumped the North Fork of the Flathead River, burned a bridge and over 20 buildings near Polebridge, then consumed 1,000 acres of Big Prairie's grass and trees in ten minutes on the way to Glacier National Park's Bowman Creek Drainage.

Officials said the fire, unlike the onset of Yellowstone's, would be "aggressively suppressed."

We were one of the first of 75 firefighting crews at Red Bench. A man with a flashlight met our bus on a gravel road by a cattle pasture destined to become our Moran Creek base camp. Time: 3:30 a.m. or 0330, military time, as it would go on reports. We spread our sleeping bags on frosted grass and slept restlessly until dawn.

Day air was thick with smoke as the fire grew to 18,000 acres beneath noon's red sun. Assigned night duty, we were supposed to rest throughout the day, but the excitement and machinery made sleep impossible. A bulldozer built fire lines around camp. More fire crews arrived. DC-4 and DC-6 fire retardant bombers circled overhead. By dusk we had our fire gear ready: Nomex fireproof clothes, hardhats with goggles and headlamps, extra clothes, batteries and water bottles. Within minutes of boarding a camouflaged National Guard truck we were lost. Our driver, yet to learn the local road layout, had taken a wrong turn. The result was a baptismal tour through the heart of the fire. Flames licked trees alongside the road. Clumps of pine burned on the edges of meadows. We passed the remains of cabins burned to the ground and others with lights on as nearby trees stood silhouetted against an orange wall of approaching flame.

The truck returned to base camp, reconnoitered, then took us to a large spot fire near Hay Creek.

For 11 hours we fought a six-acre blaze and, when that spread, a second fire. We built fire lines with shovels and pulaskis (a combination axe/hoe): cutting brush, removing dead branches, and scraping away forest debris to make dirt trenches a few feet wide to keep the fire from spreading. We worked single file: chopping, digging, whacking, uprooting, grunting our way up hillsides.

Not until sunrise, with help from a long but leaky hose connected to a tanker truck, did we have the fires under control.

There was no climax. No one thanked us for doing a good job, working our backs to pain, or successfully dodging rolling trees— on fire—somewhere around two in the morning. Instead we ended up waiting for over an hour for a ride back to base camp. The road ditch was cold as we sat on its bank, waiting, and some of us began to shiver uncontrollably as our joints grew stiff.

"I'm getting too old for this shit," Tim Mason of Effigy Mounds National Monument said. "Our limo should be here any minute, wouldn't you say Jim?"

Our limousine was again the back end of a National Guard diesel truck where it was colder still, and where fumes of diesel exhaust caught up with us whenever the truck slowed. Arriving at base camp we hacked away some brush in the cattle pasture and set up a canvas tent. Some of the crew slept in two-man tents off to the side. No matter where we slept we all crawled unbathed into our sleeping bags for six hours of sleep. This, after working all night in smoke and ash.

The noon sun was hot when we awoke. Rain wasn't even a consideration. The reason the Red Bench area was burning in the first place was due to weeks, if not months, of drought. Things weren't going to change with the day's blue skies hazy with smoke. Plus the wind was picking up. When you've got a fire, drought and wind, you have an inferno.

Dusk found us riding through cold air up a winding road, arriving at our drop-off point in the dark. Trouble. We couldn't — because of the darkness—see the surrounding terrain to pick out an escape route, one of a firefighter's Ten Commandments. Complicating matters, we had a poor map, our crew's radio didn't work (we couldn't call for a truck to evacuate us if we needed it), and spot fires, although subdued by the night's humidity, burned around us on nearby mountainsides. The crown-outs were beautiful: giant Fourth of July sparklers. You'd see a small flame in the distance working at the bottom of a tree then, when the tree was sufficiently dried out by the flames below, fire would race up through the branches until the entire tree was engulfed in candle-shaped flame. Sometimes two or three trees at various dark distances would torch-up at the same time. When the fire was close we would occasionally stand in its heat, flames being both foe and ally. Still, the flare-ups could explode into rampant wildfire at any moment. Night winds of 30 miles-per-hour were in the forecast, and we were positioned upslope from some fires. The situation was grim. We discussed it, mumbled strategy, and then the crew boss took control and we began climbing a bulldozed fire line. Dozer tracks and torn roots of trees appeared in the light of our headlamps.

Up was steep.

Bears, possibly grizzlies, had been seen in the area.

Grizz in wildfire country. On the edge.

Ranger D'Alessandro, an adrenaline junkie, would have loved this place.

We trudged on. Firefighting is paramilitaristic and you do what you're told. Whenever we stopped, "Bump up!" got us going again. The chain of command, from the fire line to unseen overhead, is clear. Our job at the bottom end of the command chain was to patrol a dozed fire line to ensure, or try to ensure, fire didn't jump across to fresh fuel. If it did, the previous day's work, including the expense of bulldozers and the destruction they caused, would be for nothing.

We patrolled in pairs a shout's distance apart. More trees, like random hillside candles, torched into flame before ebbing in showers of sparks. Temperatures continued to drop. Near midnight, with winds remaining calm, we gathered on the side of a ridge and built a campfire for warmth: a "warming fire" in firefighting's vernacular. What irony, we thought, to build a fire for heat when our purpose was to put fire out. We became Red Bench sentinels, eyes in the night, forming small groups to periodically patrol the fire line but otherwise lingering near our makeshift camp. Most of us were cold from lack of clothes and groggy from lack of sleep. After a meal of burritos wrapped in tinfoil and cooked with a shovel, some of us lay in the dirt to rest, dozed from exhaustion, awakened, then dozed more.

On the way back to base camp, with a pink sun rising over Glacier's Livingstone Range, I studied the faces of my fellow firefighters, barely recognizing anyone. To protect themselves from road dust they wore bandanas and respirator masks on their mouths, dirty goggles over eyes, hardhats pulled down over foreheads. Some were nodding asleep as they sat, half falling to the truck bed.

Yet, later: singing, laughter, helping hands, cuss words understood, comforting words timely said, jokes.

"Well, Tim," I asked one day in the foodline. "How was your day?"

He reached for a second bun.

"I had a little trouble with the secretary," he said, "but I took care of that. Remember the helicopter I told you about; the one that was supposed to pick us up and take us to the command center in Boise, Idaho, for lunch? That didn't show either. It should come tomorrow, though. I'll check into it."

Playful illusions of grandeur.

Base camp, meanwhile, grew into a village of over 1,500 firefighters plus overhead personnel. Looking like a M*A*S*H compound, there was a supply tent area, a medical services tent, trailers for finance and security, a communications center, a bulletin board with news clippings (What? NPS director Mott resign?), three phones mounted on trunks of pines, a truck trailer with showers (at first we just rinsed face and hands in a cold creek), and portable latrines ripe with human waste. Tents for firefighters were scattered in the surrounding woods. Food was served from a trailer with attached wall tent: 650 meals an hour, 4,000 meals a day. Fare included barbecued ribs, pork chops, eight-ounce top sirloin steaks, salad and vegetables: all we could eat. Cost of one food shipment: $75,000. Within six days of our arrival, base camp had the largest kitchen and was the fourth largest community in Flathead County.

Contact with loved ones was minimal. Alternatives: Stand in the phone line for a half hour (instead of getting much-needed sleep) or write, not get, letters. My letters, written while sitting against a log, usually went unfinished, tucked in an unfinished book (Louis Erdrich's *Beet Queen*) stuffed in a pack serving as a pillow.

I thought of that pillow when doing mop-up, the calisthenics of Filth City: hosing down burning trees and brush, hacking at smoking stumps with pulaskis, and stirring ashes with shovels to uncover coals which, in turn, were hosed down again. Smoky steam with ash particles, seen in the beams of headlamps, wafted up from wet coals into our eyes, noses, lungs. In mornings to come, when we awakened at 5:00 a.m. to dress in the cold, some of us coughed chronically, barking up phlegm, the tent sounding like a frontier tuberculosis ward.

Colds and flu were epidemic. Hotshot firefighters—members of Indian crews that roam the West every summer to fight fires—were suddenly gone, their immune systems given out.

With fire duty ranging from 12 to 16 hours a day, we stole sleep when and where we could. I saw firefighters, awaiting transport, dozing in empty cardboard tool boxes resembling coffins. Others wrapped themselves in sheets of clear plastic and curled up in ditches.

To the comedians among us, this was home-sweet-home except for the fire's worst hazard: widow-makers, snags with burnt root systems that fell unexpectedly. Snags resulted in at least ten serious injuries. Patrick David,

26, a Native American firefighter from Bonners Ferry, Idaho, was killed near Red Meadow Road. According to Don Overly, an administrative officer for Flathead National Forest and a member of a team investigating the accident, David and four other firefighters were waiting for transport at a pick-up point when a western larch fell on the group. The tree was alive but its three-foot, seven-inch diameter base had been hollowed out by fire. Injuries to David's companions included a broken ankle, wrist, arm, bruises and head lacerations.

Night was especially dangerous. You couldn't see the trees coming. Some would just give way at the roots, begin to fall, hit other trees and knock off branches then crash to the ground. It didn't take much of a branch or tree trunk to crush a skull, so when we heard them falling our hackles were up.

Roaming the woods was like playing Red Bench roulette with cocked cellulose guns.

A similar situation could have been created by walking into a large stand of trees, taking a chainsaw and cutting through the trunks to various depths, some trees practically held in place by bark on one side, and then whacking away at them with axes, rakes, and the sharp edges of shovels as the wind brews.

Not smart. Not what you'd tell your children to do.

We got hazard pay, of course, but in light of serious injury, possible death, or just the grueling nature of the work it seemed insignificant. . .something to compute when the fire was over. Fortunately, because of the nighttime dangers of falling snags and increased nocturnal activity by grizzlies, all night duties were canceled.

After being switched to day duty, and after spending parts of two days "rehabilitating" bulldozer scars east of Glacier's Big Prairie (helicopters with water buckets whizzing by overhead), we were sent to a nearby fire line as the Red Bench Fire, its head blown into Glacier National Park, grew to

32,200 acres. Assignment? Keep a swath of torching trees and scattered brush fires from spreading into adjacent meadow grass and unburned forest. We were ordered to post lookouts for falling snags and work with our "faces to the black, backs to the green."

Near noon I was sitting on dozer-rolled meadow sod and talking to Rose Heil who was leaning on her shovel. I liked Rose. An interpretive ranger from Arkansas, she had been a nun for seven years before choosing a different spiritual and social path. Her faith ran deep with its own root system. A husky woman, my height, she'd been a farm girl whose love of earth and sky, born of Wisconsin prairie, had blossomed into a blush wrapping itself around all God's creation. Although religious, she didn't sling her theology around, backing you into a corner — as some Bible-pounders do — for a little testament. Rose had a quiet, inner faith, and the strength of backbone to take a stand. Nor was she shy about working hard, using her farm-honed muscles to fight wildfires and, later, joining a National Park Service crew repairing the damage bulldozers caused during Yellowstone's historic million-acre blaze.

As Rose and I talked, she leaning on her shovel, me resting on sod, a large aspen suddenly swayed in the wind and fell toward us.

"Run!" Rose yelled.

I'd been watching the aspen—standing alone in the ash of burnt grass and brush—as it swayed, and was astonished when it swung in mid-sway toward us, its angle perfect, a cleaver coming as Rose yelled and scrambled. We leapt to our right. Rose tripped, fell, and I tripped over her. I rolled in the dust of the fire line as the tree crashed to the ground: *Whhh. . .ump!* I knelt and glanced at where Rose and I were talking. The handle of Rose's shovel was sticking upright in the aspen's branches.

Rose and I laughed, marvelling, as nervous people do when they've felt the close shave of a potentially fatal accident. We heard noises and looked to our right. A squad of fellow firefighters was walking toward us. Mason, as nonchalant as ever, was with them. His helicopter hadn't come.

## OPEN SPACES

We told them what happened.

Mason stepped back.

"Listen, Vickery," he said deadpan, "that's two close calls for the day. First the fire jumping your head, now the tree. The third time and your luck's out. Don't sit by me in the truck on the way back to base camp."

&#10826; &#10826; &#10826;

The fire, whipped by 40 mile-per-hour winds, exploded across its northern flank the next day, sweeping down into the Akokala drainage. An immense smoke cloud, tinged sooty-orange below and white on top, billowed into the sky. All bulldozers, feller-bunching machinery, and firefighters were called off the line. The fire, as it did in the beginning, began to pulsate: intense heat built in hotspots and exploded outward, throwing debris hundreds of yards downwind; then, flames sucked air inward, superheated themselves and exploded outward again. Officials had thought the fire approached containment. We had even begun to think of the pleasures of going home. Now, with the wind and rampant wildfire, there was no end in sight.

But rains came. . .a sprinkling on the canvas tent the morning of September 16th, and then pouring rain during breakfast followed by steady drizzle. It was the same weather system dousing Yellowstone's fires to the south. Charred logs leaked spumes of smoke as the forest soaked. Black-tailed deer, gathering in clearings of damp ash, took their thirst to the Flathead River.

Word reached us we were being demobilized. Sent home. Thanks to the rain, the fire was contained at 37,000 acres. Suppression cost: $4.1 million.

As our convoy of National Guard trucks whined through smoky fog past the Polebridge ranger station, I looked at the charred bridge collapsed in the river, its steel girders twisted by the fire's heat. Where four park buildings once stood there was nothing but black-stained cement slabs. The countryside: devastated. Remaining buildings: abandoned. A telephone rang incessantly in the empty ranger cabin which, incredibly, was unscathed.

214

Were we soldiers of fire, I wondered, going home? Where were the bands and jubilant women, the flags unfurled? We had defended timber values in Flathead National Forest and esthetic values in Glacier National Park. But if this had been war, who—or what—had won?

We reached a makeshift bridge, built hastily for access to the fire, where we crawled out the back of the truck so it could roll across without our added weight. Several firefighters, other rangers all, led the way, single file, their forms fading into the fog. The truck followed, its red brakelights floating like twin disembodied eyes looking into the gray light of fire history.

I smiled at the image as I, too, crossed the bridge, careful not to slip on the frosted planking. The water beneath, oh blessed water, was clear, shallow, swift. I stopped, turned and listened. The phone at the ranger cabin still rang and a lone bird—its home, like myself, forever branded—sang in the distance.

# PART IV
# SIGN

*It is through the power of observation, the gifts of eye and ear, of tongue and nose and finger, that a place first rises up in our mind; afterward it is memory that carries the place, that allows it to grow in depth and complexity.*

*— Barry Lopez*
*"The American Geographies"*
*Orion Nature Quarterly*

# CHAPTER TEN
# THE THOREAU EXCURSION

Flying.

The word, handwritten with blue ink in a small sky blue spiral notebook haunts me with its singularity and truth. If Henry David Thoreau were here today to glance over my shoulder at the one-word extent of my field journal, he would likely be both pleased and perplexed. He'd be pleased with my simplicity, having inadvertently reduced an intriguing excursion to one word on the cutting edge of silence. He would be perplexed with my temporary lack of explication for he could not know my use of "Flying," hastily scribbled in a Manchester, New Hampshire, motel room en route to a canoe trip retracing one of his most formative voyages, was all-encompassing, a literal reference to journeying, and an allusion to taking off and gaining elevation in order to view—from a historical and physical perspective—a special niche of New England and one of its favorite sons.

The favorite son, of course, was Thoreau.

As the author of *Walden, The Maine Woods, Excursions* and, notably, *A Week on the Concord and Merrimack Rivers*, Thoreau made an indelible impression on the American mind. Scratch any school kid from Maine to California, and one is likely to elicit at least a nodding acquaintance with "that guy who lived on a pond." Yet Thoreau was much more than an alleged pondside hermit. During his relatively short life (1817-1862) he developed a seminal appreciation of nature and wilderness preservation that influenced countless naturalists from John Muir, Aldo Leopold and Edward Abbey to Annie Dillard, Anne LaBastille, Edward Hoagland, John Mitchell and Barry Lopez. Thoreau was a champion of solitude and nonconformity. He was a prophet of the simple life (do your accounting, he said, on your thumbnails). He was an ecologist, environmentalist and conservationist (using a sheet of paper's margins, every available inch, for notes) who would have shamed today's recyclers. He was a defender of civil rights (publicly supporting John Brown's raid at the onset of the Civil War because of his disdain for slavery). He was one of America's first scholars of American Indians and likely would have written an appreciative book about them had he lived long enough. And he helped to pioneer North American phenology, the study of climate's influence on animal and plant phenomena: keeping track, for example, of ice-outs, bird migrations, flower blossomings and tree buddings while becoming one of the continent's first observers of forest succession.

At the heart of Thoreau's interests and accomplishments was his habit of taking notes and keeping a daily journal. It is because of this 7,000 page journal, which Thoreau mined for his books, that scholars know of another characteristic that sets Thoreau apart from other New England sons.

He was a rambler and roamer of open spaces.

"All nature is my bride," Thoreau, loverless and wifeless, said. He visited his bride daily.

Thoreau loved to walk. According to his friend, Franklin B. Sanborn, it was Thoreau's custom for many years to "set forth about half-past two, returning at half-past five." Thoreau found walking "poetic" and "sanitive." As soon as his legs began to move, he said, his thoughts began to" flow as if I had given vent to the streams at the lower end and consequently new foundations flowed into it at the upper." He wore clothes—often brown, gray or green—to blend into the landscape. He owned several kinds of boots for different kinds of weather. He sometimes carried a specially made pack with pockets for ruler, magnifying glass, notepaper and pencils. He knew the freedom of walking upriver while wearing nothing but a hat. Sometimes he walked for exercise, other times like a camel "which is said to be the only beast which ruminates while walking."

He elaborated one night in his journal:

"In the street and in society I am almost invariably cheap and dissipated, my life is unspeakably mean. . . But alone in distant woods or fields, in unpretending sprout-lands or pastures tracked by rabbits, even in a bleak and, to most, cheerless day. . .when a villager would be thinking of his inn,

I come to myself, I once more feel grandly related, and that cold and solitude are friends of mine."

It wasn't just walking that mattered. It was being outside in sunshine and fresh air: weaving and bobbing through trees and brush, feeling snow on his face, hearing the rush of wind, the breath of the earth, and looking at distant horizons. Thoreau liked to stretch out. He was wont to lie face-down on Walden's winter ice to look at the life below. He studied tracks, measured snow depths, ice-skated, and played a flute while floating in a boat beneath moonlight. A sensualist, he sniffed the air, ran his fingers through grass, and threw rocks. . .*plop*. . .into rivers and lakes. The man liked elbow room in order to touch the earth. It was more than a hunger; it was need. Thoreau needed the freedom of open spaces like a bird needs air to fly.

Remove the freedom, put up the fences, confine the spaces, and what we would have had in Thoreau's case is a dead mind.

His spirit? Limp wings impaled by barbwire.

This, fortunately, was not to be. Shortly after Thoreau graduated from Harvard University, where he realized one of his life's goals was "to range this widespread garden, and drink in the soft influences and sublime revelations of nature," he expanded his outdoor excursions to relatively remote areas of New England. One of his most significant trips was in 1839 when he and his older brother, John, made a boat, floated down the Concord River in northern Massachusetts and then rowed up New Hampshire's Merrimack River. Near Hooksett they struck out on foot for Mount Washington, the highest peak east of the Mississippi River and north of the Carolinas, climbed it, then floated back down the Merrimack and rowed up the Concord to where they had started: the village of Concord, Thoreau's birthplace and hometown, not far from Walden.

Thoreau, a disciplinarian, kept a meticulous journal. At first he probably didn't know what he was going to do with his notes, but when John nicked his finger while shaving, drawing blood, and died of lockjaw in 1842, Henry, emotionally crushed, decided to knead his journal into a book.

Thoreau wrote *A Week on the Concord and Merrimack Rivers* at Walden Pond. It was his first book. Although written specifically as a memorial to John, it wasn't biographical. Readers discover little about John who fails to live in the text or, for that matter, between the lines. When I asked Thomas Blanding, president of The Thoreau Society, about this, he explained the absence of biographical information was a silence consistent with literary styles of the time. I understood but wasn't convinced. I was disappointed in Thoreau's failure to bring John literally alive. John had been the apple of Concord's social eye. Everyone loved him, especially Henry. When John died, Henry sympathetically suffered symptoms of lockjaw. There was an obvious, strong bond between the brothers. Had Henry explored it more in *A Week*, he would have enlivened the book and inadvertently revealed more about his own heart and social personality.

Who, for example, did Henry love? Did he ever touch a woman? Did John crack jokes, strumming Henry's sense of humor, making him laugh? Did John buy Transcendentalism, nodding his head to Henry's oh-so-serious pronouncements, or did his more affable nature balance Henry out? What secrets beneath the stars did they share along the Merrimack?

*A Week on the Concord and Merrimack Rivers* was probably Henry's least successful book. New York's Walter Harding, likely Thoreau's definitive biographer, calls the book "one of the most complete failures in literary history." In today's publishing arena, *A Week* would have emerged from a vanity press. Thoreau paid to have it printed. Reviews were mostly critical. Four years after the book was printed, Thoreau's publisher, Boston's James Munroe and Company, told Henry they had 706 copies left and they needed the cellar space.

Move 'em out.

"The wares are sent to me at last," Thoreau noted on October 28, 1853, in his journal, "and I have an opportunity to examine my purchase. They are something more substantial than fame, as my back knows, which has borne them up two flights of stairs to a place similar to that to which they trace their origin. . . I have now a library of nearly nine hundred volumes, over seven hundred of which I wrote myself."

Still, despite our chuckle at Thoreau's expense, *A Week* lives on in North American literature for good reasons. It is a convoluted portrayal of Thoreau's scholarly and poetic intellect woven into a narrative of a New England boat journey. Of all Thoreau's books, as scholar Linck Johnson has written, *A Week* is the book in which he "undertook his most sustained exploration of both the colonial history and what might be called the Indian history of New England." Thoreau spent so much time in *A Week* exploring Indian lore that Johnson felt the book was an "elegy" to brother John and a "memorial" to the Indians whose destruction Thoreau also mourned.

*A Week* also gives Thoreau enthusiasts a launching point from which to explore his seemingly inconsistent philosophy of travel. One minute he was a high priest of staying at home, preaching that wide-ranging travel squanders a person's best energies; the next minute Thoreau was sequestered in his garrett reading travel books fresh off the press. There was an unresolved dilemma here, an internal teeter-tottering, that hounded Thoreau most of his adult life. He wasn't sure if he was coming or going, or how widely a rambler should roam.

ža ža ža

It was precisely this quandary rooted, in part, in Thoreau's reading of explorer and fur trader Alexander Henry, that Dr. Robert Madison wanted me to clarify along the Merrimack River in July, 1989. Madison, an English instructor at the U.S. Naval Academy in Annapolis, Maryland, was a scholar of sea literature, particularly the writings of Herman Melville and James Fenimore Cooper, but he was also a fan of Thoreau's. He had initiated a canoe trip celebrating the 150th anniversary of Henry and John's Concord and Merrimack voyage. He wanted me to help on the rivers and be one of the Thoreau Excursion's five evening speakers. To bait my presence, he flew me to Annapolis for "reconnaissance" four months before the Excursion to speak about Thoreau's influence on contemporary writers to a midshipmen Thoreau seminar. Eight o'clock sharp. This was followed by a lecture .on writing and publishing natural history to the Academy's English faculty. Incredibly, as someone more comfortable in wolf and lake country than a lecturer in the heart of America's Naval

Empire, I was whisked from one Madison-inspired sensation to another. He introduced me to other Academy instructors (English teachers were known by their historic specialty, e.g., "He's Eighteenth Century British"); he showed me slides of his climb of Maine's Mount Katahdin (accompanied by Thoreau quotes, for Madison had retraced Thoreau's Katahdin route); and he enticed me on a windy, all-day canoe trip on the Patuxent River where it drains into the Atlantic Ocean's Chesapeake Bay.

❧ ❧ ❧

The Navy would have been wise to yank Madison out of the English department, put him in a uniform, and fly him to distant backyard tarmacs to recruit top guns. He was good at recruiting. Trouble was, he was too much like Thoreau to be amenable to military missions. His business was English; his hobby was canoeing.

Or was it the other way around?

He anticipated 30 or 40 people on the Thoreau Excursion, among them some of Thoreau's foremost biographers. There was Dr. Walter Harding, founder of the Thoreau Society in 1941, author of *The Days of Henry Thoreau* among many other Thoreau books, and the world's point man on anything pertinent to Henry David. There was Dr. Linck Johnson of Colgate University's English department, author of *Thoreau's Complex Weave: The Writing of A Week on the Concord and Merrimack Rivers,* who was scheduled to speak on Thoreau's Indian studies. Tom Blanding, president of the Thoreau Society, would give the excursion's opening biographical lecture. Doug Kimball, director of education for the Massachusetts Audubon Society, was lined-up for a slide show on the natural history of the Concord and Merrimack. Madison's wife, Sharon Ritter, a lawyer and avid solo canoeist, was going, as was J. Parker Huber. Huber had relinquished a Connecticut University professorship to devote his New Age life to wilderness visionaries Thoreau and John Muir. Besides writing *The Wildest Country: A Guide to Thoreau's Maine,* he had retraced many of Thoreau's journeys. His "Following Thoreau and Other Naturalists" was included in *Thoreau Among Others: Essays in Honor of Walter Harding.*

## OPEN SPACES

Here was an illustrious circle of Thoreau aficionados, a loosely-knit but tightening group, a complex weave of their own, scheduled to gather on two rivers shortly after the peak of summer sun. How could I resist Madison's web, so deftly spun, when, like a baited trap, it sprung?

Within four months, and after much Thoreau-Alexander Henry research, I was back. One day I was in the NPS *Gull* patrolling Devils, Bear and Rocky islands in the Apostles off Wisconsin's Bayfield Peninsula, the next I was in Duluth, Minneapolis and Boston. Jets do that, ripping through distance, stitching place and time. I flew north from Boston in a twin engine commuter plane, everyone packed tight, destined for Manchester, New Hampshire. The flight was short as suburbs gave way to the mountains of New Hampshire. Evening. I gazed out the plane's window as we descended. Westward mountains were silhouetted against a purple sunset. Soon I would be canoeing on two rivers fusing en route to the sea, the landscape liquid, history trickling back to the first shot of the American Revolution and, in its wake, to a saunterer named Thoreau.

This was Thoreau Country. Thoreau's identity was as tied up with New Hampshire as Sig Olson's was rooted in the Quetico-Superior. This was the birthplace of United States history. This, too, like the Kam-Dog, badlands, and Wabakimi-Kopka, was a trail of power.

Where there are dreams and adventures, I reminded myself, there is power. Where there is power, there are trails leading into light.

It was dark when my hosts and I reached our Manchester motel room. Mist fell: a warm, humid spray of a soft July night. Cars whisked by on a wet freeway. We unpacked. Nearing midnight, during a pause in conversation, I pulled out my notebook with its blue sky cover to begin a journal of the Thoreau Excursion.

*Flying* I scribbled in the gathering silence.

Then Bob spoke. He was anxious about the rendezvous of trip participants at Concord, New Hampshire's Technical Institute the following noon. For days, and at great personal expense, he had driven to towns along the

224

Merrimack to line up host families to shelter us. Would they all materialize at the right time? Might logistics crumble? And what about Anne LaBastille, celebrated author of *Woodswoman*, who planned to join us? She was bringing her beloved German shepherds. Bob hated dogs.

I put down my pen. Too many concerns like blackbirds flapped against the hours. I'd write later, ala Thoreau, skipping a mere day. But when my eyes closed upon that Manchester midnight, little did I know I'd continue to be swept along in the flow of events; my notebook would be ruined in a rainstorm; and, backed into a literary corner, I would need to milk memory like a starving man.

₰ ₰ ₰

"Do you want to take a canoe out?"

At first I wasn't sure whether the question was aimed at me, but, yes, it was. Parker Huber, his graying blond hair blowing in the breeze, was standing next to Canoe America's canoe trailer with his paddle, straight-bladed and in need of varnish, in his hand.

At the moment when he asked, I had the pre-trip, stranger-in- town jitters, the shyness of a new dog in a pack. A few hours earlier, as hot July sunshine streamed from a cloudless noon sky, I'd helped Bob and Sharon set up a trip registration station on the cement patio of the Technical Institute's student center, at first stuffing trip literature into Grade VI thwart bags then, with Bob on an errand, amusing Sharon by reading passages from J.W. Meader's *The Merrimack River, Its Sources and Tributaries*. The first excursionists arrived. Gathering time. Introductions. Shaking of hands. Background synopses. With social signals reaching a saturation point, it was a relief to see friend Judy Stern, a clothing designer and writer from Minneapolis. In minutes we were walking along the banks of the Merrimack, its calm backwaters plied by fishermen, the air taut with excitement, hooking the best of times. We reached a public access where Canoe America's Jack McKnight and Leigh MacDonald passed out paddles and lifejackets, generally encouraging trip participants to try out a canoe.

## OPEN SPACES

This was a warmup. We weren't going anywhere. The idea was simply to get acquainted with river life prior to the next day's departure. I watched and listened as everyone milled around, chose partners and slid canoes into the river. But I was uncomfortable. McKnight and MacDonald's canoeing instructions were too youth camp simple; I didn't need to be told how to hold a paddle or step in the center of a canoe, gripping gunwales. Only after I realized everyone was bonded by a mutual interest in Thoreau, not by common abilities to canoe, did I become less restless and open to propositions.

"Do you want to take a canoe out?"

It was Huber again, looking every inch a reincarnated John Muir or, as Stern later described him, "so earthy he could almost stand still and be mistaken for a tree without leaves if he were naked." He spoke with a gentle but confident voice, the voice of a man who meditated regularly as, it turned out, he did.

"Sure," I said. "Let's go."

We slid a Mad River tandem canoe into the Merrimack, Parker taking stern, and headed upriver. Sunshine beat on our backs as the anchoring rhythm of canoe-paddle-water returned. Another river under the keel. I looked with longing at the meandering Merrimack in front of us. We could keep going, heading north, working our way toward distant blue hills which would shoulder into mountains and bring us deeper into what passes for wild country in New England. I knew some of that country. In 1977 I had retraced Thoreau's climb of Mount Washington.

"Parker," I said. "Listen."

We floated. . .losing momentum against the current.

"I think I hear a distant drummer."

A smile spread across Parker's face as I made a friend for life.

226

"Maybe," I said, "we should just keep going and let everyone else head south. Put the group behind us. That drum is getting louder by the stroke."

Parker knew, of course, I was joking. We had obligations. We circled an island and paddled, with the current straight into the sun.

≈ ≈ ≈

Perhaps no naturalist in the history of North American literature has had a more meaningful relationship with rivers than Thoreau. Rivers were the arteries of many of his outdoor travels, their feeling and flow coursing through his thoughts. Thoreau's world was liquid, rich with reflection, wave and lap. Just as he wasn't happy and productive without walking regularly, he wasn't fulfilled without an occasional river journey.

"For the first time it occurred to me this afternoon," he noted in his journal on September 5, 1838, less than a year before his Concord-Merrimack trip, "what a piece of wonder a river is—a huge volume of matter ceaselessly rolling through the fields and meadows of this substantial earth, making haste from the high place. . .to its restless reservoir."

By the time he wrote *A Week*, mining his journal, he had expanded his thoughts about the values of rivers:

"By a natural impulse the dwellers on their banks will at length accompany their currents to the lowlands of the globe, or explore at their invitation the interior of continents. They are the natural highways of all nations, not only levelling the ground, and removing obstacles from the path of the traveller, quenching his thirst, and bearing him on their bosoms, but conducting him through the most interesting scenery, the most populous portions of the globe, and where the animal and vegetable kingdoms attain their greatest perfection."

Rivers became the "constant lure" leading to "distant enterprise and adventure."

Rivers, because of their motion, were more liberating than lakes. Journeys on rivers symbolized the examined life's philosophical and spiritual search. Traveling on a river, and traveling in general, was a flowing from. . .toward. It was earnest living. Wasn't life a journey?

≈ ≈ ≈

The sun Parker and I had paddled into was gone when the members of the Thoreau Excursion finally gathered on the banks of the Merrimack at Lambert Park in Hooksett, south of Concord, New Hampshire. Rain poured as we stood along the river where it widened below an old dam. Thick gray clouds rumbled with thunder. Late morning. The river captains, Becky and Brad Sheeler, with Stan Wass, had decided to postpone departure until the rain, lightning and thunder ebbed.

No sense frying someone first day out.

Unlike the Thoreaus, who began in Concord, Massachusetts, floated down the Concord River then rowed up the Merrimack, we would be going in the opposite direction: canoeing down the Merrimack then up the Concord, Henry and John's homeward route. They had made a circle, a round-trip. We were traveling one way.

We stood for several hours beneath tarps lashed between trees as rain dripped down necks. Some of us strolled upriver periodically, stretching a leg, or across the public access's lawn to a small general store. "Nope," the clerk said, as if he'd said it a thousand times. There's no public toilet hereabouts. Ours don't work. You gotta go down the road a half-mile, take a left, go another mile and maybe the gas station'll let you in." Bladder blues.

Our canoes, meanwhile, were lined up along the riverbank, our paddles chosen, a few photography diehards snapping pictures. I was ready to canoe, get the show on the water. But I was also watching Anne LaBastille, with whom I'd corresponded for over two years. She had shown up the previous day shortly after Parker and I aborted our paddle north. We were walking across the parking lot of the Technical Institute when Anne walked up to us.

## Chapter Ten THE THOREAU EXCURSION

"You must be Jim," she said to Parker, reaching out her hand.

I corrected her at once.

≥● ≥● ≥●

I had enjoyed an abiding interest in Anne ever since she published her first book, *Woodswoman,* in 1976. The book was a personal narrative nailed to her heart's desire: the building of a 12x12 foot log cabin, "West of the Wind," on 22 acres in New York's six-million acre Adirondack Park. The book fueled my hunger to live in the woods. There had been Thoreau's *Walden,* of course, Bradford Angier's *Life in the Woods,* and Calvin Rutstrum's *The Wilderness Life,* among other books, but LaBastille's *Woodswoman* was always in the lighter shadows of thought. Over the years I recalled the photos of Anne notching logs, cutting holes for windows, or laughing with a friend over lunch, and I, like many of her hundred thousand readers, had admired her grit, her perseverance in the face of post-divorce depression, her obvious love of New York's Adirondacks, and her desire log-by-difficult-log to live in the woods. She wanted to simplify her life and, Pass the chainsaw, she did.

Her inspiration?

Mr. Thoreau.

"What I live for," she once said, "is to convince people to appreciate nature."

She did it by example, through lecturing, and by continuing to write. While writing for a variety of magazines, from *National Geographic* and *Audubon* to *Backpacker* and *International Wildlife,* she also published her second book, *Women and Wilderness,* in 1980. That same year she published *Assignment: Wildlife* followed, in 1987, by *Beyond Black Bear Lake,* a sequel to *Woodswoman* which sold equally well.

It was through *Beyond Black Bear Lake* that we made contact. While reading the book, intending to review it, I noticed how the writing cabin she built in the woods behind her main cabin was remarkably similar to my own writing cabin on Rainbow Ridge at Hocoka: same size, same shape. Hers of rough logs; mine of lumber. Anne had named her new cabin Thoreau II and references to Thoreau were commonplace. It was easy to suspect Anne—a cult figure, sort of a guru among woodswomen who wanted to get back to the land—viewed herself as the female rendition of Henry David. But wasn't she being a bit presumptuous? Wasn't her life as a woodswoman the mere tip of an iceberg successfully obscured by opaque literary waters? Was her cabin life as fulfilling as she hoped it would be? How had the land rubbed off on her?

I intended to find out.

I wrote to LaBastille in care of her publisher and suggested writing a magazine profile of her, and a through-the-mail acquaintance began. She sent clips, I did more research on my own, and by the time I met her along the Merrimack she was, at five-foot-four and 120 pounds, blond hair silvering, a woman whose mystique was surfacing.

Despite popular praise ("I've never met a more remarkable woman," Les Line, editor of *Audubon*, said), or perhaps partly because of it, she had led a successful professional life. A native of New Jersey—her mother was a concert pianist, her father a manager of Central America's General Motors in the 1920s, later a language professor—she was fluent in Spanish and had earned a doctorate in wildlife ecology from Cornell University. In 1974 she won the World Wildlife Fund's International Gold Medal for Conservationist of the Year. She was a licensed Adirondack guide and a commissioner for New York's Adirondack Park Agency. In 1988 she was given the Jade of Chiefs conservation award from the Outdoor Writers Association of America followed, in 1989, by a Chevron Conservation Award. Later she would be given an honorary doctorate degree from New York's state university system.

Clearly Anne had ridden the award circuit, her cabin life sometimes forced into a back seat. No stranger to boots, backpacks, and canoes, she nevertheless knew the rustling feel of skirt and blouse, the kiss of lipstick, the touch of lace, the sudden blinding of flashbulbs at Washington's Hyatt

Regency Hotel (for the Chevron Award), and the clink of champagne glasses as she looked city folk in the eye. She appeared to be an eclectic woman, gentle but assertive, guarding her privacy but using fame—which she wrestled self-consciously—to accomplish goals. She chose her companions carefully yet knew the ache of love's end.

When we finally spoke along the Merrimack, albeit briefly, my energies scattered, she seemed to have just stepped this side of shyness. Her manner was mild but firm like a rose's breeze-touched blush on a hard stem. Hard enough, anyhow, to persevere.

"I never want to stop working," she told James Kunstler of *Adirondack Life*. "I can't believe in retirement. I just think I'll do what I'm doing until I drop dead."

Her life had taken some interesting turns by July, 1989. She had briefly lived in her deceased mother's home in Coconut Grove, Florida, replete with TV, while teaching wilderness literature at Florida International University, and she had bought an old farm near New York's Lake Champlain, living there in winter. The house had electricity, phone, and fax machine: unplugging the woodswoman image yet improving professional access and a blooming lecture career.

No word processor, she told me. Never will be.

There was another part of LaBastille's life that was also surfacing, soon to be publicized in her fifth book, *Mama Poc*. For 25 years she had studied Guatemala's giant grebes, a flightless bird indigenous to Lake Atitlan. When she first began studying *Podilymbus gigas* there were approximately 200 birds known to exist. The population plummeted over the years due to the introduction of non-native largemouth bass to Lake Atitlan, the effects of Indian reedcutters, growth in shoreline human habitation, and the lake-draining results of an earthquake. Anne, who had studied the grebes for her doctoral thesis, fought to save them by establishing a refuge and raising Guatemalan appreciation of the birds. It was a gallant effort, yet futile.

## OPEN SPACES

The hardest words she ever spoke came on November 11, 1987, when—at the inauguration of the giant grebe exhibit at Guatemala's Museum of Natural History—she formally declared the giant grebe extinct.

It was a blow to Anne's spirit, an ecological knife in the heart, augmented soon thereafter by the death of a close friend. Anne hurt, and when I sent her a flyer about the Thoreau Excursion, thinking she might know someone interested in a trip in memory of her main man, she did. Herself. She sought solace on the water.

ॐ ॐ ॐ

Softness.

The softness of falling rain, hazy air, and the gray-blue of a new river bending left or right in the distance.

When the rain ebbed at Hooksett's Lambert Park we pushed off. It was wind-into-the-face and gray rain hazing the landscape as we hugged the inside of bends and spread out single file. The faster paddlers crept ahead while slower paddlers brought up the rear. Traveling alone in a Mad River *Ladyslipper*, a solo canoe like my own at Hocoka, I paced myself between groups, enjoying, for moments, rare solitude. The Merrimack was wide, its current barely perceptible beneath waves blowing our way. Woods and houses hugged the shoreline. We passed an anchored airplane and could periodically see and hear a highway on the west side of the river.

Near here, by Hooksett, the Thoreaus had beached their boat, the *Musketaquid*, to head overland for Mount Washington.

At lunchtime, with rain wavering between downpour and drizzle, we learned that a canoe in the rear had capsized when a woman lunged for a wind-blown hat. We made light of it and lent the victims dry clothes. Two hours later, with the rain pouring again, the group aborted its planned take-out at Amoskeag bridge in Manchester in favor of Lavasseur's Landing. We had paddled a mere four miles. Forlorn, wet to the bone, and huddled beneath a riverside shelter, we confirmed Thoreau's remark that "the

232

traveler's lot is but a barren and comfortless condition."

No one complained when a heated schoolbus swept us away.

We ended up at Bedford's Presbyterian Church. I was nervous. In an hour, after a spaghetti dinner prepared by church women, I would give the evening talk. When sun began to shine—steam rising off wet pavement—I took my notes to the privacy of a nearby graveyard, went over them, then returned to the dining hall. Excursionists and townfolk were mingling, eating and waiting. Where exactly was I supposed to talk? The church, someone said. LaBastille, wearing a red and black flannel shirt, and looking Northwoods Dynasty fine, sat across from me. Her words were soft, something tender in them falling like supportive snowflakes onto the paper cups and plates. I ate.

Time. . .passing.

Where is my luggage? Bob's pickup.

Where is Bob's pickup? Not here.

My shoes, socks and pants were wet.

Time—Better check the church out—passing.

Thoreau, who in a bitter moment, once said that in churches "human nature stoops the lowest and is most disgraced," would have guffawed at the irony of me speaking about him in a white church on a hilltop overlooking the Merrimack River Valley. Worse, my wooden podium with a microphone, placed in front of the altar, was elevated above the pews. The floor was covered with red carpet. Behind the altar, shiny organ pipes were mounted against a red velvet backdrop on the wall. There was a wooden cross, of course, and it took me about three seconds to realize the Thoreau Excursion was no ordinary trail of power. I also was going to have to drop one of my vague, sexually-oriented anecdotes, a reference to what a married Manchester French-Canadian told me in 1977. I was hitch hiking. He was driving a delivery van, smoking marijuana in a corncob pipe, and flamboyantly telling me he had a girlfriend in every town except the one I was heading for.

"Otherwise," he added, "you'd be set up for da' night."

I tried setting up for the night by moving a metal lectern to floor level, but I was too low, difficult to see, and the hand-held microphone crackled whenever I moved. People filed into church. I glanced at my notes, accepted my wet feet as lending me subject credibility and, after Madison's introduction, walked nonchalantly up to the podium: a river rat on a new bank. I always knew my theological studies would get me somewhere.

Outside, thank God, a July moon was rising and I could sense its pull and shine.

&#254; &#254; &#254;

Thoreau's internal teeter-tottering, his inconsistency about the values of staying at home versus traveling, was, like my situation, borderline comical.

"Cleave to the simplest ever," Thoreau once wrote. "Home— home— home."

Again: "Staying at home is the heavenly way."

Another time: "I am afraid to travel much or to famous places, lest it might completely dissipate my mind. Then I am sure what we observe at home, if we observe anything, is of more importance than what we observe abroad. The far-fetched is of the least value. What we observe in traveling are to some extent the accidents of the body, but what we observe when sitting at home are, in the same proportion, phenomena of the mind itself."

Finally: "I cannot but regard it as a kindness in those who have the steering of me that, by want of pecuniary wealth, I have been nailed down to this my native region so long and so steadily, and made to study and love this spot of earth more and more. What would signify in comparison a thin and diffused love and knowledge of the whole earth instead, got by wandering?"

Yet Thoreau, who preached a geographical provincialism based on the tenet one should become better acquainted with one's birth country and its twenty square miles than any place else, who insisted one should look closely to observe minute changes in the environment, immerse oneself in it, gnaw at it, worry it like a dog working a bone, becoming—by saturation—as natural an offshoot of a place as a flower or tree, a living barometer of regional ecological dynamics and climate, a true representative of a locale, this man, so reflective and eloquent, so identified with a cabin on a pond, was a major league closet traveler.

We are what we read.

Thoreau was reading back-to-back travel books on Asia, Africa, the Caribbean, Ceylon, Greenland, Tierra del Fuego, Peru, Colombia, Syria, Persia, Japan, the high Arctic and—perhaps especially—the exploration of northwestern and western North America. His authors? Drake, Columbus, Balboa, Ponce de Leon, Frobisher, Cartier, Champlain, Hennepin, Bartram, Charlevoix, Cook, Hearne, MacKenzie, Back and, among others, Alexander Henry.

Thoreau was Anne Tyler's accidental tourist in reverse. Sometimes, instead of traveling and wishing he were home, he was home wishing he were traveling. So he traveled vicariously. He knew the pleasure of sitting next to a fire and reading a travel book on a winter night.

In fairness to Thoreau, and as John Aldrich Christie explains in *Thoreau as World Traveller*, travel books were the most popular literary genre of Thoreau's time. Christie traced 38 years of Thoreau's readings. A fifth of Thoreau's recorded borrowings from Harvard Library were travel books. In Thoreau's published work, he refers to at least 83 travel books. His "extract" books, where Thoreau copied thousands of items of interest, refer to 56 travel books, twenty of which weren't referenced in his published work. His Indian notebooks indicate he read 90 travel accounts: forty-two above and beyond those in the extract books or published work. Overall he referred to a minimum of 172 travel books, not counting nine collections scholars know he read, or the travel accounts he read in magazines.

Many of the books he read were 800 to 1,300 pages long. In the 1850s he averaged a dozen travel books a year. In 1852 alone he read a minimum of 8,849 pages of travel literature. Altogether, as Christie says, Thoreau's travel notes refer to every major continent, the seven seas, and islands ranging from Norfolk in the Pacific to the Canaries in the Atlantic.

❧ ❧ ❧

Perhaps of all the travel books Thoreau read, none had a more formative influence than Alexander Henry's *Travels and Adventures in Canada and the Indian Territories Between the Years 1760 and 1776*. Thoreau chanced upon mention of Henry's book while reading Colonel Francis Hall's *Travels in Canada* while a freshman at Harvard, but he didn't read it until 1837-38 when he was 21, a year before the Concord-Merrimack journey. Even more than Henry Brackenridge's *Journal of a Voyage Up the River Missouri* and Russ Cox's *Adventures on the Columbia River*, Henry's book sparked young Thoreau's interest in exploration and travel.

It fueled the lure of open spaces.

As the preface to the book explains, Henry's narrative describes his experiences, encounters, geographical observations, and natural history impressions of the areas he visited. They were many and wild. Born in New Jersey in 1739, Henry was part of General Jeff Amherst's army when it accepted the surrender of Montreal in 1760. A year later, in a birchbark freight canoe, he headed up the Great Lakes to Michilimackinac (near today's Mackinac City, Michigan), then the center of western trade with Indians. He eventually explored and traded in the Sault St. Marie country, spent a year or two overseeing copper mining on the Lake Superior shore of Michigan, then expanded trade along Superior's southwest shore clear to the Apostle Islands where he helped establish Bayfield, Wisconsin. In 1775, likely because his exclusive trading permit was revoked, he canoed northwest through the boundary waters of Minnesota to the Beaver (Amisk) Lake area of Saskatchewan. One winter, despite bitterly cold weather and inadequate food (surviving on chocolate diluted in water), he snowshoed south to the Great Plains where he met with Indians to talk fur.

Henry's rambling efforts paid off. He was able to retire in 1781 to a general mercantile business in cushy Montreal. He died in 1824. Thoreau was seven years old.

When tracker Thoreau caught up with Henry's book, he was intrigued by its wealth of information about Indians: hair styles, religious beliefs, buffalo hunting, rituals, wartime cannibalism, and Indian treatment of the French and English. There was a difference. Indians and French got along well together. Their cultures merged as they married; there were babies in the meadows; they became the Metis: a half-breed ethnic group centering in southern Manitoba. The English were hated by Indians, particularly by Ojibway who fought with the French against the victorious English in the French and Indian War. The Ojibway never forgot who spilled their blood. Revenge lingered through generations, passed like milk from a mother's breast into hearts of warrior sons.

Those same sons led to one of the most dramatic tales in Henry's *Travels and Adventures*. It occurred in 1763 when Henry, 24, was stationed at Fort Michilimackinac. Henry was a perceptive man. When he arrived at the fort he heard scuttlebutt the local Ojibway might attack. He tried to alarm others but no one took him seriously.

A year later (and as Thoreau mentions in *A Week*), an Ojibway named Wawatam dreamt he would adopt an Englishman as his brother. Wawatam approached Alexander Henry, told him of his dream, and asked him if he could be adopted. Why not, Henry figured. Can't hurt. Soon Wawatam told Henry he had been disturbed frequently "with the noise of evil birds." He also said there were many Indians near the fort who hadn't shown themselves. Wawatam suggested Henry leave the fort. Henry said no. Wawatam and his wife cried, wished him well and then departed.

Game time.

The Indians announced they were going to play baggatiway on the King's birthday. Called lacrosse by the French, it was played with hooked bats, a ball, and two posts at opposite ends of a field. The Indians invited the fort's officers and guards to watch. Henry decided to skip the game, instead staying in his garret to finish letters he hoped to send with a canoe heading for Montreal the next day.

It was a wise move.

At a prearranged time, the Indians—playing outside the stockade—lofted the ball over the walls, grabbed weapons hidden in the clothes of their women, and rushed inside. The fort's guards thought the Indians were just chasing the ball. Henry heard shouts and screams, stopped writing and went to the window. Over 50 Englishmen were being massacred.

"The dead were scalped and mangled," Henry explained. "The dying were writhing and shrieking, under the unsatiated knife and tomahawk: and, from the bodies of some, ripped open, their butchers were drinking their blood, scooped up in the hollow of joined hands, and quaffed amid shouts of rage and victory. I was shaken, not only with horror, but with fear. The sufferings which I witnessed, I seemed on the point of experiencing."

Henry, begging for help from an unresponsive French neighbor, was brought to an attic by a friendly Ojibway woman. He hid in a pile of birchbark containers used to store maple syrup. He heard Indians enter the house downstairs and then their footsteps as they came up to the attic.

"The door was unlocked," he said, "and opening. . .four Indians entered the room, all armed with tomahawks, and all besmeared with blood, upon every part of their bodies.

"The state of my mind will be imagined."

The Indians didn't see him. They left but came back the next day. The Frenchman, fearing his own safety, turned Henry in.

"I now resigned myself to the fate with which I was menaced: and regarding every attempt at concealment as vain, I arose from the bed, and presented myself full in view, to the Indians who were entering the room. They were all in a state of intoxication, and entirely naked, except about the middle. One of them named Wenniway, whom I had previously known, and who was upward of six feet in height, had his entire face and body covered with charcoal and grease, only that a white spot, of two inches in diameter, encircled either eye. This man, walking up to me, seized me, with one hand, by the collar of the coat, while in the other he held a large carving knife, as if to plunge it into my breast: his eyes, meanwhile, were fixed steadfastly on mine. At length, after some seconds, of the most anxious suspense, he dropped his arm, saying 'I won't kill you'."

Wenniway explained he had scalped many Englishmen but had once lost a brother, Musinigon, and Henry should be named after him.

Sure, no problem, Henry probably said.

Wawatam, it turns out, sent Wenniway to protect Henry.

His danger, however, wasn't over. The next day a warrior confronted Henry, stripped him of his clothes (to keep blood off them), and marched him outside toward the woods. When Henry realized it was pointless to walk any farther, one place to die being as bad as another, he turned to face the Indian. The Indian tried to stab him. Henry struggled free and ran back to the fort— Indian in pursuit—where he found refuge.

Henry was eventually smuggled to Wawatam who, with his family, hid him through the following winter. They cut his hair, painted his skin, and dressed him in Indian clothes. Henry hid when strange Indians came around. He hunted with his protectors, fished with them, snowshoed and slept with them. But when warm weather came, he flagged down the first voyageur canoe he could and headed for Sault St. Marie.

He hadn't learned his lesson. The next year he was back trading among Ojibway in the Apostle Islands.

ɜ̀ ɜ̀ ɜ̀

Although Thoreau largely ignored the Michilimackinac massacre in *A*

*Week,* concentrating instead on the friendship between Alexander Henry and Wawatam, he had nothing but praise for Henry's book.

It was a "classic among books of American travel," he said, and it read "like the argument to a great poem on the primitive state of the country and its inhabitants, and the reader imagines what in each case, with the invocation of the muse, might be sung. . ." It was full of scenery, "rough sketching of men and incidents enough to inspire poets for many years," and rich names: "Lake Winnipeg, Hudson's Bay, Ottaway, and portages innumerable. . .an immense and shaggy but sincere country, summer and winter, adorned with chains of lakes and rivers, covered with snows, with hemlocks and fir trees."

Henry was a "voyageur," Thoreau added in *A Week,* "Like ourselves," meaning he and John on the Concord-Merrimack. He wasn't pretentious. His writing style was clear, and he had "truth and moderation worthy of the father of history."

Thoreau also liked the way Henry traveled: by canoe in a simple, primitive, original manner. It conformed to his own young but growing belief that travel should be close to the terrain, by foot or boat, requiring little money and luggage. Scant food. A cup. Spoon. Old clothes. That simple. The old clothes, Thoreau felt, allowed a traveler to avoid appearing important or ostentatious like a tourist, instead giving the impression the traveler was at home. Better yet, a traveler should blend into the social matrix by earning one's way on a trip, taking odd jobs. Rubbing of elbows with people was important: hearing stories, noticing attitudes, touching the pulse of prejudices, isolating values, inflections, hints and nuances. People, the reasoning went, at least in Thoreau's less mobile, less electronically binding, time, were indigenous to landscapes which colored thoughts, dreams, emotions, enmities, hopes and, by exposure, those of a traveler.

It went without saying such contact might lead to the bizarre.

ᶾᵃ ᶾᵃ ᶾᵃ

"Do you want to call for help?"

I was sitting with my host family in Nashua, New Hampshire, at the end of the Excursion's second day of canoeing. We had started downstream from the railroad bridge at Goff's Falls in the morning, slalomed in and out of riffles beneath sun for an hour, then bottlenecked at a rapids created by the remains of a canal lock. The river captains stopped everyone, signaled them to shore, and went ahead to scout the whitewater: class II or III. It wouldn't be in the best interest of the Excursion to lose a Thoreau biographer or enthusiast and generate national headlines: Thoreau Lover Drowns Retracing Thoreau River Route, 150th Anniversary. We eventually shuttled canoes alongside the rapids, ate a shoreline lunch of pita bread, hummis and sprouts, then paddled until midafternoon when gathering overcast brought thunder and rain. After six slow but pleasant miles we stopped at the mouth of Souhegan River near the Jones Chemical Company.

The air—or was it the water?—stunk. I noticed a brown scum along the waterline of canoes. Raw sewage? Chemical waste? We practiced paddling strokes and, when a storm squall hit, thrashing trees, breaking branches, we hastened off the Merrimack to meet our Nashua hosts.

Each night, rather than camp, we stayed with the host families Madison recruited. They took us in singly, in pairs or in larger groups. Social mingling: Thoreau's way. Hosts dined us, visited onto midnight—describing demographics, local politics, the economy—then bedded us down, fed us breakfast and brought us back to the river in the morning, our canoes waiting.

Pretty posh for a Kam-Dog graduate.

My hosts in Nashua were a middle-aged heavyset artist and her husband, a physicist. As midnight neared, we sat in the livingroom, sipped wine, and swapped stories. The best was one the physicist couldn't account for by physical law. As he lay alone in bed one night, the bed began vibrating beneath him. He reached out and touched the sides of the bed. They were still. He also heard a sound, like the snapping of fingers, go around the bed. It was a compelling tale, truly mysterious, a kiss of the twilight zone.

## OPEN SPACES

I must have looked uncomfortable.

"Do you want to call for help?" he'd asked, joking.

Madison hadn't mentioned this. Ghost stories weren't on the agenda. I began to review incidents leading up to the hour, to the tale, paranoia snaking alive, and I marvelled at how different I felt compared to the afternoon's serene moments as I watched canoes slice silently down the river, my own canoe parting water in a gentle hiss of current cut by bow.

My hostess, an abstractionist, wasn't surprised by her husband's confession. She believed him. Besides, she explained, she once dreamt in the same bed of a friend the night the friend died.

My guest bed didn't vibrate that night, though I thought it might, nor did I hear snapping fingers circling blankets and pillows. The stories simply dissolved, melting into morning, as excursionists gathered at Greely Park north of Nashua. Everyone appeared in a good mood. The sun shone. Winds were calm. Even the murky Merrimack had taken on blue sky reflections among shards of reflected sunlight flashing on water.

My favorite color: blue. A favorite light: flashing.

The river was calling.

I stood on shore and watched couples—the novices getting better—load canoes, depart and paddle downstream. There was a clarity to the moment, a polished, clean glass of awareness, yet also a finality. I hugged my hostess, my window into a riverside world, farewell, knowing I'd probably never see her again, and slipped into my canoe. My bentshaft paddle, its wood warm, felt like a familiar tool, as if it had helped build a buoyant life, in the footsteps of Thoreau, in which all things had come together for good.

I reached toward the middle of the Merrimack and sculled sideways away from shore.

Our goal for the day was to paddle downstream past the mouth of the Nashua River and across New Hampshire's southern state line to Lowell, Massachusetts. As I drifted I peeled mud—dried, caked, coming off in clods—from the bottom of my shoes, and remembered another reason why Thoreau admired Alexander Henry. Henry didn't travel like the proverbial objective scientist: detached, insulated from subjective experience. He knew the discomfort of dirt, callous, hunger and danger. Thoreau always liked voyageurs who were rugged, uncomplaining in the face of bugs, wind and cold temperatures, and who could, if need be, crawl up mud riverbanks into woods and survive.

ຂ຺ ຂ຺ ຂ຺

As Thoreau aged, dallying with such journal entries as "Today you may write a chapter on the advantages of traveling, and tomorrow you may write another chapter on the advantages of not traveling," his interest in North American exploration, the great probings into the continent's open spaces, expanded and ripened.

His reading went on unabated.

He was familiar with practically every major arctic expedition: Parry's two voyages in 1819-20, Sir George Back's overland expedition from 1833-35, and Sir John Franklin's journeys of 1819-22. When Franklin disappeared on his last expedition, Thoreau read five books about the search for Franklin. He also read E.K. Kane's two-volume *Arctic Exploration* (1856) and Isaac Hayes's *Arctic Boat Journey* (1860) among other arctic narratives.

Thoreau's interest in the American West ran particularly deep. He owned and read Lewis and Clark's journals of their 1803-06 expedition. He owned Major Pike's account of his voyage up the Mississippi River en route to the Northwest. There was Major Stephen Long's chronicle of his 1823 expedition to Minnesota's St. Peter River (now Minnesota River, which Thoreau steamed up in 1862 shortly before his death), and Henry Schoolcraft's narrative of his 1832 exploration of Minnesota when he discovered Lake Itasca, headwaters of the Mississippi. Altogether, Thoreau read at least 40 books focusing on the American West including accounts of trappers, hunters, fur traders and unofficial documents. Many were read between 1850 and 1860 as soon as they were in print.

If Thoreau positioned himself in New England, much of his intellect and part of his heart obviously leaned westward. He knew as well as anyone America was expanding. The western impulse affected him personally, touched him bodily.

"I must walk toward Oregon," he wrote in *Walking*, "and not toward Europe. And that way the nation is moving, and I may say mankind progress from east to west."

He shared his era's enthusiasm for the paradisiacal dream of America being the new world. It was bred into him at Harvard and was a constant concern. As civilization leapfrogged east to west, he said, each generation was superior to the preceding. Go east and you retrace the "steps of the race" finding history. Go west and you found the future. He was critical of the human plundering of redwood trees in the West, and of man's grovelling for gold in California, but—as he wrote friend Cholmondeley in 1856— the "great west and north west went stretching on infinitely far and grand and wild, qualifying all our thoughts. . .that's the only America I know."

He was stretching the truth, as he sometimes did, but he was acutely aware of how America's geographical limits bulged with each expedition. Although fascinated by America's evolving continental awareness, and its incessant discovery of natural resources, he was most intrigued by the effect discovery would have on the American mind. It would open it, he hoped. Mankind's imaginative quest was at stake. The continent was raw material for the collective consciousness. It bore promise of great poetry and fable.

"I trust that we shall be more imaginative," he enthused, "that our thoughts will be clearer, fresher, and more ethereal, as our sky—our understanding more comprehensive and broader, like our plains,—our intellect generally on a grander scale, like our thunder and lightning, our rivers and mountains and forests,—and our hearts shall even correspond in breadth and depth and grandeur to our inland seas."

By exploring the westward reaches of North America, Americans and Canadians were discovering nothing less than themselves. They were testing the limits of the human spirit. As horizons receded, who could say how land, mind, and history might fuse and flower?

Thoreau's walking paralleled the general movement of the human race. He invariably walked west or southwest. Eastward, he said, he went by force. Westward he went freely. West was the best direction for living heroically and the direction of America's wildest country: its largest forests, highest mountains, and longest, most intricate, river systems, all country for which he increasingly hungered. Few fences. Few cities. Few restrictions on freedom. It was a wonderful country, yet for Thoreau the West was also a symbol.

He put it this way in *Walking* and, on a number of occasions, at the podium:

"The West of which I speak is but another name for the Wild; and what I have been preparing to say is that in Wildness is the preservation of the World. Every tree sends its fibres forth in search of the Wild. The cities import it at any price. Men plough and sail for it. From the forest and wilderness come the tonics and barks which brace mankind."

His point, however, was that wildness, innate to human nature, was slowly being weaned from people by irrupting social intercourse, industries, and a vast network of socio-economic structures. Instincts, senses, and the feelings of organic oneness with nature were being dissipated. In their place was a mindset that made Thoreau leery. Although designed to meet physical and consumer needs, it tended to separate people from what is at the heart of the balance between humans and nature: the reality—felt, known and respected—of interconnectedness.

He could see it coming and, for America, feared its possible consequences.

He used the fable of Romulus and Remus being suckled by a wolf to describe what he meant. Children of empires who were not suckled by wolves, by wildness, grew weak, submissive, undaring and fell prey to "children of the Northern forests who were." Nations were like this. Cut a nation off from its wild roots and it lost strength, moral if not physical.

❧ ❧ ❧

"Your fellow-traveler," Thoreau once signed a letter, and it has been suggested that if he would have had more money he might have traveled more widely, perhaps to exotic lands. Instead he remained in North America where he made 55 trips away from the Concord-Boston area. The furthest south was New Jersey. The furthest north: Maine (several canoe trips) and Quebec. The furthest west: southern Minnesota. To the east he faced the Atlantic Ocean which he gazed across many times while hiking the shores of Cape Cod.

But he never crossed the sea.

Compared to such relatively provincial authors, Christie remarked, as Bryant, Whittier or fellow Concord residents Emerson, Alcott, Hawthorne and Channing, Thoreau's travels were microscopic. Compared to Irving, Cooper or Melville, it's hard to argue Thoreau left home.

One nevertheless senses from Thoreau's extensive reading that he strove for an osmosis of the literary fruit of continental and global travelers: the men and women in the field. Even as he believed a person should focus on one's home or birthcountry, cultivating an intimate relationship with it, he also believed it should be done with as full a knowledge as possible of the wider, geographical world.

Import the world, the evidence seems to say, and get on the open river when you can.

Although traveling led to an "honest experience of life" and fresh appreciations of home, its highest value was personal growth. A traveler should be enlarged, if not transformed, by what a journey "made him" as well as by what it told him or her. The best journeys involved a commitment of self—a giving, immersion, and surrender to what Thoreau described in *Walden* as "the perpetual instilling and drenching of the reality that surrounds us."

Perhaps the question, when it came to Thoreau, was not whether it's better to stay home or travel but how we can best facilitate personal evolution and rise above narrow thought and experience. We do this by reading, as Thoreau's secret life so strongly claims, but also by journeying, getting out, as Thoreau began to do in 1839 on the Concord and Merrimack, rowing and sailing toward a universality of vision. Travel enlarges perspective. It teaches skill at comparison and broadens parameters of understanding. It enables people to clarify, define and love the homes and lands they come from. It fosters appreciation of geographical roots: their waters, mountains, plains, skies, climates, plants and animals, each in its turn becoming more distinct in the illumination of other places.

Variety hones specificity. It enlarges empathy.

Inevitably, Thoreau's goal before and after reading Alexander Henry, before and after his Concord-Merrimack trip, and even as he teeter-tottered about travel was to comprehend life's greater mosaic. The quest, like river travel, reflected philosophical and spiritual parallels. Thoreau knew to see well it sometimes helps to step away, off to the side, or back. Such peripatetic movement—granting fresh views of an amazing world—enabled him to step forward a better man.

This was his challenge and it was, to his last breath, a fine balancing act: a juggling of space and time for maximum view.

&#10070; &#10070; &#10070;

I, too, sought maximum view by the excursion's last day. By expedition standards, the Thoreau Excursion was a lark, a mere thirty-four mile journey in four days in midsummer weather. Thanks to Madison's shoreline logistics, the rest of us were free to paddle, intermingle, drift at will or, in my case, pursue a personal agenda.

My true destination wasn't Concord. It was Walden Pond.

Not only had Walden been a constant inspiration, as place, book, and metaphor, but in 1977—when I tracked down some of Thoreau's original manuscripts at Harvard, retraced his route up Mount Washington, and visited his grave in Concord's Sleepy Hollow Cemetery (someone had left fresh flowers)—I had walked around Walden on a rain-freshened day. It was a rich stroll around a naturalist's Mecca for a young Minnesotan, as meaningful a saunter to the Holy Land as they come. Now, a dozen years later, youth gone, midlife looming, I was going to return, somehow, some way, to Thoreau's favorite water to pay due homage.

We left Lowell, author Jack Kerouac's hometown, on the water not on the road, at midmorning. We launched our canoes upstream of the North Billerica Dam and paddled south up the Concord River. More summer sunshine, calm winds. The Concord, originally called the Musketaquid (Grass-ground River), same name as Thoreau's boat, was the wildest part of the journey. A mix of riverside homes and willows gave way to the Great Meadows National Wildlife Refuge with its silver maples, sunning turtles, great blue herons and stretches of river-edge grass. We canoed spread out or clustered together like surface minnows, occasionally pausing to look at white water lilies, to talk and laugh with each other or, seeking solitude and space, we broke apart to meander from one side of the slow-moving river to the other. LaBastille, with German shepherds Condor and Chekika (well-behaved, after all: Madison even petting them), paddled with scholar Ron Hoag who no doubt mulled his future book on Thoreau's sense of the sublime. Stern, in her canoe's stern, yucked it up with Linck Johnson who joined us after his talk about Thoreau and American Indians, his wit on the river knew no end. Brad Sheeler had Walter Harding to himself while Steve and Eric Deutsch, brothers like the Thoreaus, darted in and out of the pack, bonding blood.

Still in the *Ladyslipper*, I paddled hard and left the group behind, river narrowing, twisting, current quickening, as we neared Concord. I wanted to be at Concord's North Bridge to take photos as everyone arrived. It was at the North Bridge, in Minute Man National Historic Park, that the "shot heard 'round the world'" was fired: where rebellious colonial militiamen fought British soldiers at the dawn of America's Revolution, and where Thoreau—in a patriotic moment—once sang a memorial hymn.

The Excursion ended its river travel at Concord's Old Calf Pasture a short distance upriver from the North Bridge. As we waited for Canoe America's trailer, I borrowed Becky Sheeler's *Dragonfly*, a solo canoe designed for whitewater competition, for a short jaunt further up the Concord.

"It might feel tippy," Sheeler said of the canoe, but it felt natural; a leaf on the water.

While doing figure-eights among sun-sparkling riffles, testing the canoe's maneuverability, I noticed an inscription on a rock alongside the river. Curious, I paddled close:

On the Hill Nashawtuck

At the Meeting of the Rivers

And Along the Banks

Lived the Indian Owners of

Musketaquid

Before the White Men Came.

The modern petroglyph was right, of course. I was still in Indian country, what they might call stolen land, but I was also pivoting and sideslipping between banks Thoreau knew well, near where he'd been born, lived and died. It was his country, too.

Here Thoreau fished, swam, skated and waded. The grass below me, bent and swaying in the current, was descended from grass that likely tickled his shins. On an autumn day, his thoughts buoyant with introspection, he might have sat on a nearby bank, pencil in one hand, the other pressing a yellow leaf against a notebook page as he sketched. Perhaps his feet dangled in the river, minnows near his toes, who knows? What antic escaped his journal, deleted by time? Boyishly he might have plucked a spear of grass, clamped it between his thumbs and blown hard through it: a loud squeaking, almost quacking sound ripping toward the riverbend, making

Thoreau chuckle and smile to himself. Perhaps he squirmed as he suddenly recalled John and how they'd once sat together, upstream or down, talking girls (Hey, she is cute), and seeing who could blow grass the loudest.

John: Gone into the dark night, sucked up into the infinite vault of stars, entombed by silence: dear brother John.

Stung by John's death, nothing could shield Henry from his painful, ineffable loss: no euphemism (He passed away. . .), no Transcendentalist tenet (His soul: united with Soul), no highfalutin pastor's preaching (He walked in the path of Jesus). Henry knew death could be rationalized, glossed with poetry, and colored with leap-of-faith theology, all easily done by the healthy, but it couldn't be buried. The grief couldn't be talked away.

And so Thoreau, struggling to surface from subterranean sorrow, had taken his wound to the land.

Walden's shores, its sunshine, the slow regenerate swing of seasons, pencil and paper, river notes, and a cabin's evening candle were his wings as he strove toward healing. At Walden, where he wrote *A Week* (Be thou my Muse, my Brother, he epigraphed), he drove death and life into a corner. He nailed down a stillpoint in a mysterious world. And of all the places he had been, and would go, physically or in imagination, it was Walden he knew best: its springs and winds, its waves and shifting sands, its animals and shoreline forest, its great solitudes and silences serenaded, at times, by Henry's flute.

Walden centered him, rooted his vision, quenched his thirsts, and healed his wound.

What I wanted to do at Walden the second time around was set fresh foot there beneath night's full moon, bivouac in the woods next to Thoreau's cabin site, and bring it all inside myself in the landscape he knew best. Never mind the mosquitoes, possible rain, or state regulations against overnight camping. I'd become—if need be—an outlaw.

Hadn't Thoreau said nature is the home of outlaws?

250

It's hard to say whether I went along with Johnson, Stern and Ann Arminger, or they came along with me. Leaving the river, we drove through Concord's tourist-thick streets and then pulled into the large parking lot (three dollars, please) at Walden Pond State Reservation. I was disheartened. When I first saw Walden I came upon it on foot, and while walking its 1.7-mile perimeter on a June day I had seen only a lone fisherman. It must have been the off-season. Now, as my companions and I walked along the 61 acre pond, hundreds of people lounged around: swimming, playing volleyball, reading books, hanging out, even a few women in bikinis soaking rays near Thoreau Cove. I realized, step by step, my hope of spending the night had been a Minnesota pipe dream, a fancy that didn't apply to Boston's backyard playground.

I left my companions near Thoreau's cabin site to walk alone down to the edge of the pond. Walden, beneath a full pearl moon rising in the east's blue sky, was calm. I knelt near water's edge, dipped my fingers in the water, and picked up a stone.

Walter Harding was scheduled to give the Excursion's last talk at Concord's First Parish Church in a few hours.

I found another stone.

Madison and Ritter had invited me to share their room at a bed and breakfast inn.

Finally, a third stone.

I had an early flight to catch in the morning at Boston's Logan Airport.

Drop the outlaw hopes, Jim. Face the facts. Go with the flow.

I stood up, slipped the stones into my pocket, and began the journey home.

## CHAPTER ELEVEN
# RETURN OF THE WOLVES

The wolf, like others I had seen near Hocoka, appeared suddenly, caught in the sweep of vision. I had just put on an old Air Force parka with a wolf fur ruff to go outside and get firewood when I noticed the tawny movement on the lake ice near the cabin.

I felt the usual stirring, the jolt of adrenaline, as I grabbed binoculars and stood outside on the deck. The wolf, beneath a rising full moon, trotted across the bay, glanced to its left and then started running ten feet at a bound. It stopped, reconnoitered, and again broke into a run as it headed for an island. It reached a steep, snow-covered slope of rock rubble: one jump, another, a few steps and it stopped in a grove of red pines. The wolf glanced around, its tongue hanging loosely from exertion. Then it was gone.

Wolf tracks cupped subzero moonlight.

I stepped outside on the deck and howled. I howled again. Both were high guttural cries breaking in pitch as they fell. Unlike other howls on other days, no answer came.

I couldn't be disappointed. One of the reasons I had moved to the perimeter of the Boundary Waters Canoe Area Wilderness in Superior National Forest was to be in wolf country. In the wolf lay the spirit of open spaces. I wanted to see wolves, hear them howl and, by whatever means possible, draw closer to the mystery of *Canis lupus*. And I had. My most dramatic experience was with Bojo, but I continued to see wolves over the years while hiking, canoeing, driving and flying with friends in small airplanes. At Hocoka, wolves became a regular part of my life, sharing space, their presence a constant possibility. Ideologically, they were living confirmation that people had in their hearts, albeit grudgingly, the willingness to promulgate regulations shielding wolves, and to uphold legislation protecting the continent's wildest areas, such as the Boundary Waters, which wolves need to survive.

This was good. It spoke well of respect for our remaining natural lands and the innate rights of other species. It was, at least, a beginning.

Time favored the wolf in Minnesota as I pursued my trails of power. Their population throughout the 1980s grew from the 1,200 of Bojo's days to about 1,650 by 1990, averaging a growth of three percent a year. In 1990, Bill Berg, a wildlife biologist for Minnesota's Department of Natural Resources in Grand Rapids, estimated there were 234 packs in the state. Fifteen percent of the wolves were loners.

In Wisconsin, eleven packs of fifty or sixty wolves ranged the northern part of the state. Four of the packs were in Douglas County, three packs in Sawyer County. The other packs were on the edge: moving through the dark night, watching their flanks.

On the national level, wolves emerged as cult creatures by 1990. There were, and still are, wolf postcards, posters, calendars, stationery, coffee mugs, t-shirts, earrings, pendants, rings and tie clips. The National Federation came out with a "Cry of the North" bisque porcelain sculpture of a white wolf "poised," the full-page ads (even one in *Playboy*) read, "atop an icy precipice of full lead crystal." Cost: $225. Minnesota named its 1989-90 National Basketball Association franchise the Timberwolves; its logo a green-eyed blue and silver wolf head set in the green and royal blue of a basketball's circle. Wolf paintings continued to bring *Canis lupus* into full artistic relief. There are stunning photographs of wolves by Jim Brandenburg, Dave Mech and Lynn Rogers, and books to match. Renée Askins of the Wolf Fund began spearheading the task of trying to reintroduce wolves to Yellowstone National Park. There were countless magazine articles, videos and films about wolves including Kevin Costner's *Dances with Wolves*. Millions of Americans and Canadians toured the Minnesota Science Museum's mobile "Wolves and Humans" exhibit destined, in time, for permanent display in Ely's International Wolf Center. The center has become a clearinghouse for wolf biologists, research, art and symposia, replete with a live wolf pack.

How ironic that we came to culturally encircle the wolf—through scholarship, media and consumer taste—as the wolf once encircled us. We used to kill the wolf, no questions asked, our hearts spitting lead. Now we study the wolf, coddle it, sell it, and give it room.

Wolves take what room they can and, in return, give back some of the wildness we've so skillfully destroyed.

❧ ❧ ❧

When the moonlight was bright, I saw the wolf cross to the island. I decided to track the wolf. I am a tracker. I like to see, hear and follow sign...to read the landscape as if its tracks and sounds are braille. A connection is made, a kind of stitching, between who I am, where I live, and what we might become. A primordial synapse is gapped, anxieties are washed away, and anything's possible.

Wolves had been around for weeks. While lying in the cabin's loft I had listened to them howl as a north wind rasped across a nearby ridge to eddy among firs and aspen. One morning a friend and I found fresh wolf tracks and spots of blood near a deer's bedding area. Another day I found wolf tracks near the outhouse. The wolf had come from deep snow onto my packed snowshoe trail, stopped, then trotted away toward a swamp.

It was twenty below, no wind, when I headed down to the lake and across the cove to look for the wolf. The lake surface glowed with reflected moonlight as my ski bindings squeaked in the cold. I stopped a hundred feet out on the lake and bent over to dig through snow down to ice. Slush. Water had flowed up through a crack to saturate the bottom layer of snowpack.

The snow felt like jelly beneath me as I passed Rainbow Landing where I thought the wolf had reached the lake: no tracks. Another 50 yards brought me to sloping shoreline. Here the wolf had come down. It had left its landlocked stride to break loose into open lake space. I stopped, switched on a small flashlight to peer closely at the tracks, then measured them with bare hand and wrist as I had done to the grizzly track in the Wrangells.

Stars, crisp and cold, flickered on the upper edges of vision.

I glanced at the cabin. All kerosene lamps were out; windows were dark, and smoke curled up from the chimney.

I followed the wolf tracks, paralleling them, my ski tracks undulating across the bay. Here the large wolf tracks, sunk six-to-eight inches in snow, were single-spaced. There the wolf had broken into a run. Here it paused to look around before running again. Near the island it had slowed to a trot, three feet between tracks, before bounding up to the island's pines.

Wood snapped.

Had the wolf bedded down, heard me and now moved? Had a tree cracked in the cold?

I thought of skiing to the left toward the sound, then up into the darkness of the island's pines, but opted to go around the island's point. If I had alarmed the wolf, perhaps I would see it running on the lake on the other side of the island. There I found more tracks where the wolf had come down out of the woods to a narrow rock ledge before jumping onto the lake.

The tracks headed north toward distant islands.

I followed.

Soon I saw where another wolf had left the island to trot out on the lake. Its tracks merged with the others where the wolves had come nose-to-nose, likely sniffing and nuzzling each other. They continued north together, one behind the other, their footnotes of motion fading into moonlight.

They hadn't been alone. Nothing, no one, ever is.

I found more tracks where two other wolves had crossed the island, one leaping eight feet from the top of a rock ledge, scuffing loose snow, moss and lichens on the way down. Again I bent over, switched on the flashlight and removed a mitten to finger a wad of kicked-up snow crust. This was tactile stuff: solid, cast-in-white, Class "A" subzero wolf sign. Apparently a wolf pack had converged on the island. The lone wolf I'd seen beneath the rising moon had maneuvered toward the island at an angle to the other wolves, hence its leftward glance. It was a common hunting strategy.

But where were the wolves now? Did they know I was there? Were their bodies camouflaged among shadows of treetrunks? Was that my heartbeat I heard or the shuffling of wolf paws on snow?

ɞ ɞ ɞ

It didn't surprise me a month later when the wolves returned. They usually did every three or four weeks making territorial rounds.

I was sitting in the cabin watching three groups of deer across the cove. One pair stood face-to-face next to a red pine, the larger deer licking the neck and shoulder of a fawn. They parted, bedded down, and the fawn, almost a yearling, began to chew its cud. The other deer, two groups of three, browsed among birch and alder on a rock point jutting into the bay. It had snowed two feet the previous week, thawed and crusted over. The crust supported deer on the lake but not on the deep drifts in the woods. There they broke through the snow, their movements jerky as legs rasped against ice.

Deer are sometimes cut by crust. Worse, collapsing crust bogs them down while fleeing predators like wolves whose splayed paws keep them from breaking through.

Wolves feast at such times.

Suddenly, as I began writing a letter, I looked up from the page and saw two wolves walk out of the woods onto the lake. Their fur looked blond in the bright sun. Easy they came, their gait strong, effortless, winter sun having worked to their advantage. Their time had come. Where's the meat? They stopped, looked around, and took a few steps. The two deer that had bedded down were not more than 300 feet from the wolves. The deer stood bolt upright facing the lake. Not a twitch.

Trouble. The wolf shift.

I thought of the deer then. Like wolves, they are part of the mammalian breath of the land. I had seen them daily as they walked across the lake from mainland to island, island to mainland, often two deer at a time, as many as seven. Once at dawn I saw four deer walking single file on the lake away from the cabin. With the snow-covered lake beneath them, and snow swirling around them, they looked like they were migrating through snow clouds: a faint motion of legs and bodies in a thickening eddy of white. At other times I saw deer walk in the low yellow light of sunset, their bodies casting long shadows on the snow. Once a doe visited the cabin where she tamely watched me shovel paths, haul water and chop wood, waiting for me to go inside so she could eat sunflower seeds at the birdfeeding stations. Another time I surprised an antlered buck beneath a white pine as a shell-pink sunset flamed overhead.

What had Minnesota writer Helen Hoover called it?

*The gift of deer.*

They were a well-spaced herd separated by forest and ridge. Their tracks were everywhere: through alder swamps, in jackpine stands, across ridges riven with cracks where sumac grows, among willows, in and out of cedar thickets, down into hollows and up over rock knobs. Skiing, snowshoeing, or walking I found where they bedded beneath fir or pine, chewing their cuds, belching up wads of cedar leaves and mashed dogwood buds, drowsy perhaps from the comfort of a filling belly, their eyes half closed beneath sun and stars.

But not now. Not as I watched from the cabin.

The deer had noticed the wolves on the lake. One of the wolves trotted toward Pine Island as the other looked toward the cabin and its nearby ridge rich with deer. But, still, not a twitch. The wolf moved on. I went outside and climbed a ladder to the cabin roof where I watched the wolves skirt the island's west end. One wolf stopped, took a few steps and stopped again. It was restless. Curious, Ken the Navigator would say. The wolf seemed to sense scent. The smell of sustenance rode the wind.

Moments later, on the far side of the island, a wolf ran out of a narrows, heading south, then banked left to run the full length of a small bay. Had it spotted the deer? The wolf slowed as it neared the end of the bay before vanishing into leatherleaf, reeds and shoreline trees.

In minutes I was on skis. I followed the wolf tracks into the bay where I last saw the wolf, but the wolf was gone. For an hour I searched more of the lake's shorelines for shapes, using the unfocused scan of the hunter, a scoping of the landscape with broad gazes, sideways, behind me, in front, looking for irregularities of form. Something next to a far shore looked like a deer standing alert. I shot it glances as I poled myself across the lake, gliding between pushes, my arms and shoulders doing the work as the ski wax was scraped clean by the snow's icy crust.

Pole, push...glide. Pole, push...glide. Sun warmth. Sunlight. Pole, push...glide. Oxygen. Endomphins. Higher. Pole, push...glide.

The shoreline deer hadn't moved. It was a tree trunk. I smiled to myself, fooled by form.

The sun was setting as I skied home through a narrows and worked my way to the shore of the mainland where I found the trail down which the wolves had come. Nosing through shoreline cedars, they had leapt onto the lake and had broken through a snowdrift's crust. The leap: the 50 to 100 pounds of wolf: the break. A few steps and the crust no longer gave. I took off my skis, lay on my stomach and looked closely at the wolf tracks. Some showed claw marks at the tips of toeprints. All were half-filled with shadow.

The sun was doing down. Granite ridges. Trees. Wolf sign. Blue sky. Deer sign. Snow everywhere: a bright and shining whiteness. It came together with a rush, fused into a single sensation, and crystallized.

I stood up, snapped on my skis, and skied closer to the cabin.

Shape.

A doe, holding herself mid-stride, looked down at me from the side of

Rainbow Ridge. I stopped, started back and locked her gaze. She and I in the day's last light were linked by the visage of wolves. It was, in its own way, what I'd always been looking for. It was the latest sign of an ongoing trail that began in the Red River Valley. I was on the right track. I looked until I could look no more, then nudged a ski tip forward.

The deer spooked.

She turned, lunged through deep snow and fell to her chest. A wolf might have made its kill then and there. But the deer, still strong, still pulsing with blood feeding sinew and life, gained her sunlit footing and was gone.

Also From
# NORTHWORD PRESS, INC.

*AUTUMN LEAVES*
Ron Lanner and Bob Baldwin

If you're serious about autumn, you'll fall for *Autumn Leaves*, a comprehensive guide to color for the Midwestern, New England and Mid-Atlantic states. You can become the local expert on leaf color. Contains 132 splendid color photos, detailed information on the natural history of 70 species of trees, fall color hotline phone numbers for 25 states and provinces.

Softbound / 6 x 9 / 192 pages / $19.50

*WHITE WOLF*
Jim Brandenburg

The rare and powerful Arctic wolf is showcased in our most celebrated and beautiful book. Winner of 1989's prestigious Chicago Book Clinic Award for illustrated books, it has been hailed by *Outdoor Photographer* as "a landmark in nature publishing." Eloquently written, elegantly designed, it is the documentary of the author's months photographing and studying the Arctic wolves on Ellesmere Island.

Hardbound / 12-1/2 x 9-1/2 / 160 pages / $40.00
Softbound / 12-1/2 x 9-1/2 / 160 pages / $19.95

*LOON MAGIC*
Tom Klein

The book that launched NorthWord Press, Inc., this flagship edition continues to be the loon lover's bible. It remains, after several updates and five printings, the definitive work on the symbol of northern wilderness, the loon. The latest edition features 40 new photos, most in full-page reproductions.

Hardbound / 12 x 9-1/2 / 176 pages / $50.00
Softbound / 12 x 9-1/2 x 176 pages / $19.95

*THOSE OF THE FOREST*
Wallace Byron Grange and Olaus Murie

Winner of the coveted Burroughs Medal as the best book published in the field of natural history, this is a classic on forest wildlife. A celebration of the natural world, dramatized through the lives of a succession of woodland creatures and beautifully illustrated with pen and ink sketches by renowned naturalist Olaus J. Murie.

Softbound / 6 x 9 / 314 pages / $9.95

*EAGLES OF NORTH AMERICA*
Candace Savage

Symbol of freedom, power and integrity, the eagle is the north country's most valued summer resident. Get to know eagles through this inspiring book. Superbly researched and written text, 90 captivating photos.

Hardbound / 8-1/2 x 11 / 128 pages / $24.95
Softbound / 8-1/2 x 11 / 128 pages / $14.95

*WITH THE WHALES*
Jim Darling and Flip Nicklin

For the first time, a book takes you into the whales' domain — under the sea. Flip Nicklin's rare and exquisite photography and accompanying text by researcher Jim Darling take you through all aspects of the whale's natural history. CoverS all major species. Thoughtful and compelling.

Hardbound / 12-1/2 x 8-1/2 / 160 pages / $39.95

To receive our free color catalog or order any of these books, call toll-free 1-800-336-5666. NorthWord Press, Inc., P.O. Box 1360, Minocqua, WI 54548.

# OPEN SPACES

Author of *Wilderness Visionaries* and Contributing Editor of *Canoe* Magazine, Jim dale Vickery has imbued himself with the experience of wild country. He has canoed and backpacked throughout North America's public domain. Few wilderness naturalists have ventured into as wide a spectrum of the North American outback as has Vickery.

Writing for magazines like *Sierra, Backpacker, Canoe* and *Audubon* and lecturing on wilderness and natural history issues, Vickery has found the pulse of the American interest in wild spaces.

An essayist of national caliber, Vickery animates his writings with his wilderness adventures. He lives near Ely, Minnesota right on the edge of the Boundary Waters Canoe Area Wilderness.